Depiction

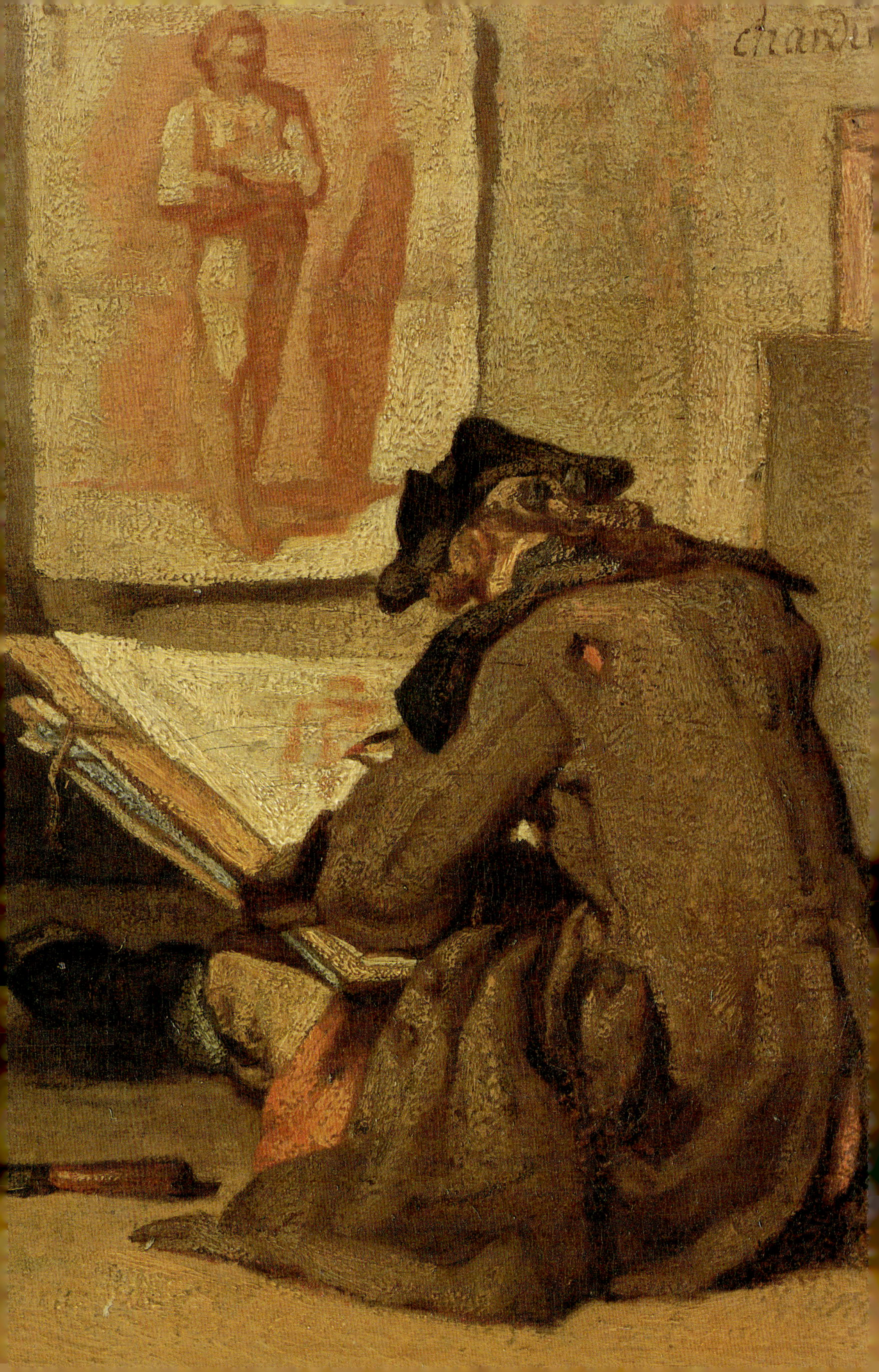

Michael Podro

Depiction

Yale University Press
New Haven & London

For my colleagues in the University of Essex

Designed by Gillian Malpass

Printed in Hong Kong

Library of Congress Cataloging-in-Publication Data

Podro, Michael.
Depiction / Michael Podro.
p. cm.
Includes bibliographical references and index.
ISBN 0-300-06914-6 (cloth : alk. paper)
1. Artists–Psychology. 2. Visual perception. 3. Imagery (Psychology) in art. I. Title.
N71.P64 1998
701'.15–dc21 98-15247
CIP

A catalogue record for this book is available from The British Library

Frontispiece: Chardin, *The Draughtsman* (detail), 1738. Nationalmuseum, Stockholm.

Contents

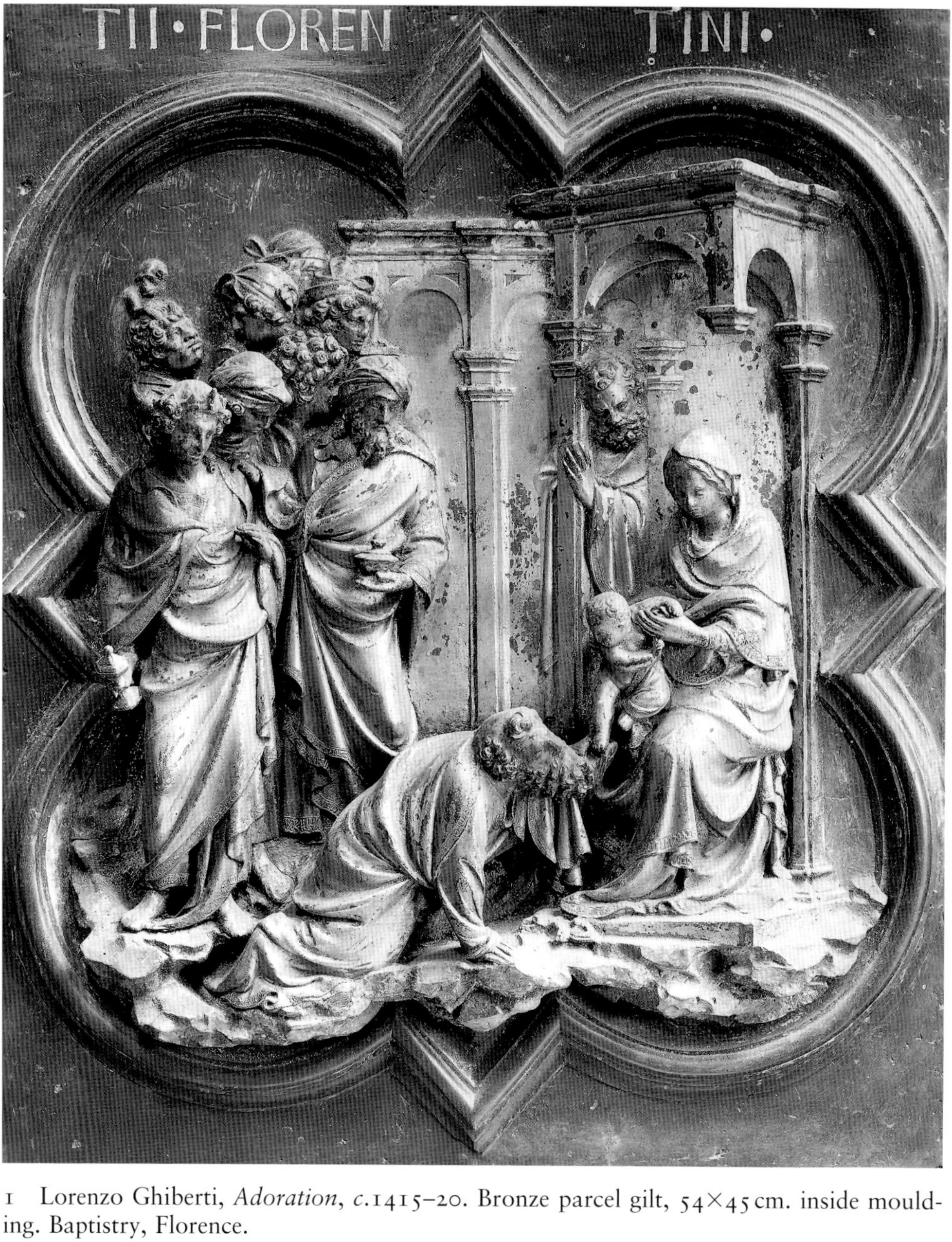

1 Lorenzo Ghiberti, *Adoration*, *c.*1415–20. Bronze parcel gilt, 54×45 cm. inside moulding. Baptistry, Florence.

Preface

PAINTINGS ADDRESS US, and they do so in part through creating uncertainty; our engagement with them involves a continuous adjustment as we scan them for suggestions on how to proceed and for confirmation or disconfirmation of our response. The present book arose from reflections on such adjustment: it was prompted at first by an effort to articulate how the painter's medium, which has its own rhythms and textures, seems both distinct from the represented subject matter and yet at the same time to embody it. What is at issue is not how depictions are made to convey the look of their subject, but rather how recognition – the most basic relation we have to the world – functions in a distinctive way within painting. The artists whose work will concern us did not set out to show the look of the world as something previously known, but rather to extend the thread of recognition in new and complex structures of their own. Our question is with how this could be described. It is not a matter of searching for some system of concepts, rather it is a matter of clarifying certain general notions inextricably connected with perceiving painting – like the notion of depiction itself, of visual imagining, of the plane of the surface, of expressiveness – and seeing how they relate to each other in critical practice.

A large proportion of the works discussed here are in public collections in London, reflecting the fact that the book developed during classes given in those collections; I am grateful to the students who participated in them, as I am to curators who on occasion made material available which was not on view. This prompts a further comment: these are collections to which the public has, or has until recently had free access, allowing spontaneous – often short – visits, more akin to reading and conversation than attending a theatrical performance, something germane to the present book. The hope is still that the curators working to preserve or restore this ideal – which is both practical and symbolic in mutually informing ways – will be successful.

While writing I have benefited from the comments of Dawn Ades, Jorella Andrews, Jonathan Clarkson, Neil Cox, Paul Crowther, Valerie Fraser, Caroline Elam, Robin Greeley, Fiona Hughes, Margaret Iversen, Andrew Harrison, Antonia Phillips, Charles Saumarez-Smith, Jeremy Stone, Paul Taylor, Peter Vergo and Kenneth Wright, and from extended conversations with Svetlana Alpers, Jules Lubbock, John Nash, Charlotte Podro and Alex Potts. To each I am deeply grateful as I am to Laura Church for her patience and advice in dealing with revisions to the text, to Sheila Lee for gathering the illustrations, to Gillian Malpass for designing the book and to John Nicoll for his encouragement over many years.

Earlier versions were read and discussed in detail by Frank Auerbach, Michael Baxandall and Thomas Puttfarken, and much in the present book responds to their criticisms and suggestions.

Introduction

THROUGHOUT THE BOOK I shall use the term depiction to cover representational painting, drawings, prints and relief sculpture where this does not lead to confusion; its extension to free-standing sculpture should not present a serious theoretical problem, although some difficulties would have to be resolved. What holds for the depiction of subject matter holds in some essential ways for painting without a prepictorial subject, the development of twentieth-century abstract painting being inconceivable without the model of complexity provided by earlier depiction. However, I shall not take the transition as unproblematic.

Discussion of paintings could hardly occur at all without calling on analogies between depicting and describing; between the kind of understanding required of painting and of conceptual knowledge; or between seeing things in the ordinary course of events and seeing them in paintings. Philosophical aesthetics attempts to analyse such transitions between one activity of the mind and another, and how one activity or capacity contributes to another, while critical historians have mostly charted the divergence and convergence of specific groups of works and the circumstances in which they were made. The theme of the present book lies in the overlap between them; it examines concepts that have very general application to painting in cases where they are called into question by the character of particular works; our subject is therefore both the concepts and those paintings, reliefs and prints to which they are applied.

The chapters that make up the book were written in the light of each other over the last ten years. (An earlier version of chapter four, on portrayal, appeared in the proceedings of a conference in

Germany, but has been considerably reworked.) The continuity between chapters is one of theme: the first chapter proposes a framework for the chapters that follow. It is concerned with the recognition of subject matter and how it is sustained in a distinctive way in depiction, taking examples from different historical contexts; the central thesis is that the recognition of the subject is extended and elaborated by the way its conditions of representation, the medium and the psychological adjustments the painting invites become absorbed into its content. Subsequent chapters examine specific applications of the thesis. Chapter two is concerned with the surface plane and the relation between two-dimensional projection and three-dimensional form; this is discussed in relation to relief sculpture, and specifically the relief sculpture of Donatello. The third chapter is concerned with the viewer's orientation as we are led to be aware of this by Rembrandt. Our notion of the plane of depiction and of our orientation are closely related and the two chapters should complement each other. The next chapter is about the portrayal of people; it takes up the themes of the previous chapters and introduces into the discussion a further kind of condition – a social framework – which is recruited to the imaginative structure of depiction, examining different roles that may be taken by the artist. Chapters five and six are about Hogarth and Chardin respectively: while Hogarth's art was part of a literary culture, he argued in *The Analysis of Beauty* for the distinctive value of the visual artist; Chardin, by contrast, was seen – and arguably saw himself – as outside the literary culture and so as problematic for it; the issue arises in both cases of the distinctive interest of what is visually rather than verbally articulated. In the case of Hogarth this is bound up with how painting becomes a mode of social behaviour, addressing its subject in a way that depends on the resources of the painter; in the case of Chardin, considered here both in the context of that eighteenth-century criticism and twentieth-century psychoanalytic thought, what is central is the capacity of painting to elicit a sense of intimate reflection on the part of the viewer.

Part One

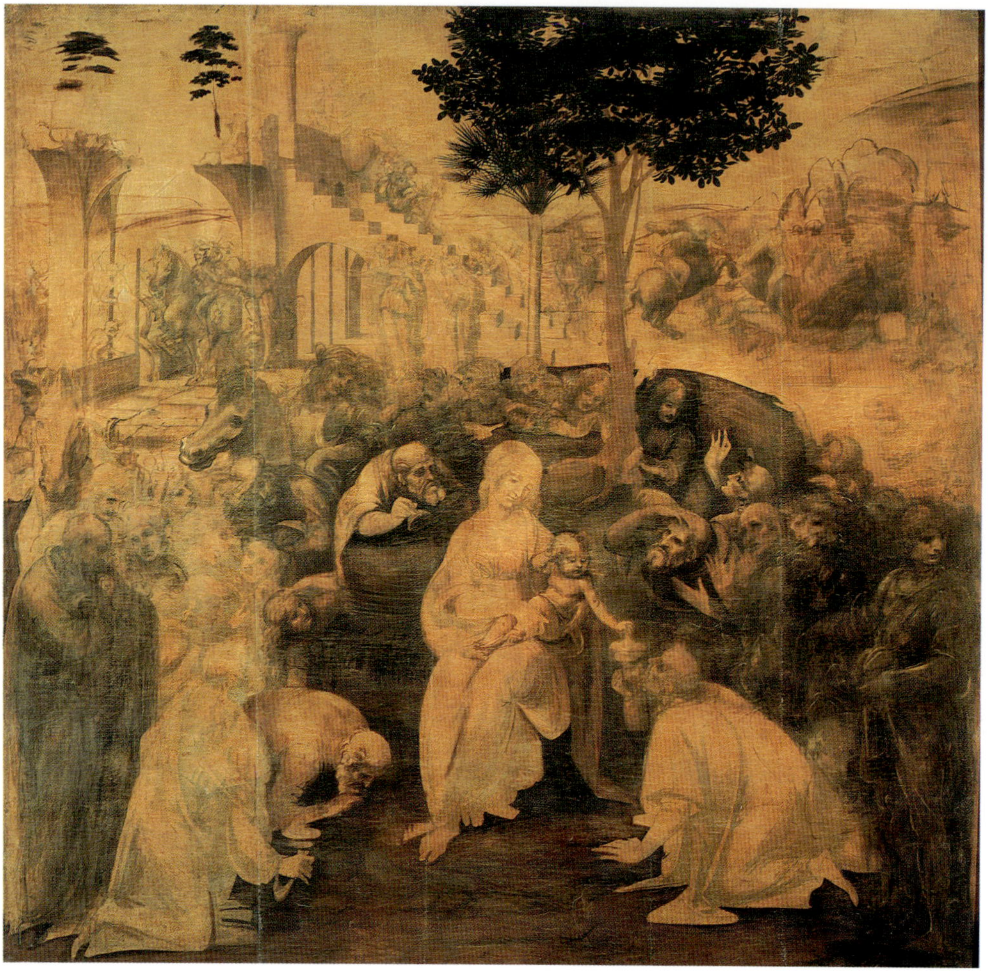

2 Leonardo da Vinci, *Adoration*, 1481. Panel, 246 × 243 cm. Galleria degli Uffizi, Florence.

Chapter One

Sustaining Recognition

I

AT THE CORE OF DEPICTION is the recognition of its subject, and this remains so even when the subject is radically transformed and recognition becomes correspondingly extended; it remains so not because we seek the subject matter *despite* the complications of painting but because recognition and complication are each furthered by the other, each serves the other.[1] Depiction has two main conditions: first our capacity to recognize through difference, and second, the intention to use the object that is materially present – the painting or drawing – to imagine what we recognize within it. To these two conditions we must add two refinements: that we are aware of a difference – although not the exact demarcation of difference – between what is present and what we imagine (the case of their coincidence – using grey canvas to depict grey canvas – being the marginal case); and this imaginative use limits itself to what the painting affords; we do not freely project or associate round it but attend to what projections it corroborates or confirms – confirms through other aspects of the painting itself, or through the traditions of usage, which it brings into play. So much for the broad conditions of depiction. The question that concerns us is how – within those conditions – recognition is sustained.

The answer could hardly be that it is sustained in just the same way as it would be in the ordinary course of events outside painting.[2] While all our looking, pictorial or nonpictorial, is framed by our purposes and these redirect and modify themselves in response to what comes into view, in painting our interest is in imagining. As this imagining is not a matter of having a reverie but perceiving, so the question of how recognition is sustained can be reformulated: how does our imagining use what is there for perception? How can we describe, in general, the mesh between imagining and the use of our prepictorial capacities for recognition?

The writer who has brought recognition in painting closest to recognition in nonpictorial perception and whose position has been at the centre of theoretical argument over the last forty years is Ernst Gombrich, and anyone working in the field is deeply in debt to his thought. He argued that our ordinary nonpictorial recognition of objects relies on mechanisms that we do not control, so that effective depiction involves finding the configurations that activate those mechanisms despite the limiting conditions of painting – for instance, paintings being flat, still and having a very small range of contrast from light to dark compared with the normal illumination of our environment; for Gombrich, to understand how depiction works we must examine how the painter mobilizes the mechanisms of recognition. Painters, so he argued, learn by trial and error to construct forms that yield experiences convergent with – but always distant from – those of the prepictorial subject.

His position has two component theses that need to be, but are not usually distinguished, either by Gombrich or by his critics. The first is that in pictures, when we are aware of the subject we are forced to neglect the painted surface as such; and the second is that we are unable to discern within our experience the border between the surface and the subject; we cannot observe where one turns into the other. The second thesis will be central to the arguments that I shall be pursuing, but the first – maintaining the incompatibilty between attention to surface and subject – has been generally rejected as failing to correspond to our experience; furthermore, holding surface and subject together in awareness has itself been seen as a central interest of painting. In Richard Wollheim's words: 'the artist . . . who exploits twofoldness to build up analogies between medium and the object of representation cannot be thought content to leave the two visual experiences in such a way that one merely floats above the other. He must be concerned to return one experience to the other. Indeed he constantly seeks an ever more intimate *rapport* between the two experiences'.[3] In fact – as Wollheim later refines the point – we should not talk here of two experiences, each of a quite different set of properties, (for this would preclude their becoming related inside our perception of the painting); rather we should assume two different kinds of perceived aspect – of the materiality of the surface and of configurations of the subject – interacting and transforming each other within our experience.

What led Gombrich to hold the reciprocal neglect thesis in the first place was the search for a rational explanation of the mental mechanisms underlying depiction by assimilating them to other models of psychological effect; and the kind of effect he chose was of the triggered reactions isolated by perceptual psychologists; they studied the effects of minimal configurations, for example patterns that reversed themselves or patterns of lines that looked longer or shorter in spite of our knowing them to be the same size, and he thought of pictorial illusion as pivoted on such triggered responses. What marked these phenomena was that the effects were experienced as occurring in our perceiving and not in the object perceived. But even though we think of depiction as eliciting an effect in us, which in some sense we must, it does not follow that it is experienced as discontinuous with what we know is there – the material surface.

There is an infinite range of ways in which the painter's marks elicit recognition and in so doing prompt a sense of illusion, and these are most often remarked upon in what are generally termed painterly effects: where edges may be left unmarked but projected, or forms lost in a play of shadows, or shadows and objects appear equivalently substantial.[4] We are aware that the alterations are occuring within *us* not within *it*, so we are alerted to the functioning of our own perceptual mechanisms as we are in perceptual psychologists' optical effects, where virtual shapes spring into view, or figure and ground reverse themselves.[5] The philosopher Maurice Merleau-Ponty, also in the late 1950s, described perhaps the most famous of such effects when he wrote: 'We see that the hand pointing to us in the *Night Watch* [see below fig. 69, p. 84] is truly there only when we see that its shadow on the captain's body presents it simultaneously in profile . . . Everyone with eyes has at some time or other witnessed this play of shadows, or something like it, . . . it works within us but not by our doing; it hides itself in making the object visible. To see the object, it is necessary *not* to see the play of shadows and the light around it. The visible in the "profane sense" [that is, ordinary nonpictorial perception] forgets its premises'.[6] But psychologists' demonstrations and invitations to project are crucially unlike depiction, which may employ the same mechanisms: for demonstrations are effects that are isolated; we do not expect them to be absorbed into some larger configuration or to be transformed by substructures within its components; and the contrast with depiction holds even if we take demonstrations not of single transformations but of seemingly endless instability. The interest we take in a demonstration, by being just that, is isolated and exhausted by the conceptual point being made. To take up the thought of Merleau-Ponty – and correcting an impression that might be given by isolating his remark on *The Night Watch* – we cannot conceive of our relation to the world as a set of discrete reflexes, and we cannot see our relation to painting that way either.[7] The difference between the psychologist's demonstration and depiction lies in our sense of purpose; on the one hand to exemplify an effect and on the other, in depiction, to engage the imagination. Paintings might be used to make points about perception but that is to see them within a framework quite different from that of the art of painting. How, then, are we to relate the way in which we are subject to perceptual effects and the way our imagination is engaged?

If we take up the thought of earlier literatures of art, whether French seventeenth-century academic theories of pictorial coherence or eighteenth-century theories of multiplicity in unity or the Kantian sense of the play of the mental faculties in unifying a manifold, the answer is that there must be some structure within the painting such that we perceive one aspect given meaning by another, one feature transformed by its relation to another and that these are relations we can find and re-find. If we are to accommodate the sense of an illusion – of that emergence of the subject in the medium – we must do so without losing our sense of such internal structure. Gombrich responded to the problem by arguing that the pursuit of convincing representation had to be reconciled with the pursuit of order or symmetry, postulating that the pursuit of order and representation were two conflicting or at least competing demands, and he conceives of the classic achievements of art as reconciling these demands.[8] But there is a problem about treating convincing representation and the pursuit of pictorial order as reciprocally curtailing, for these demands may sustain each other: symmetries or correspondences are ways in which we see one form on analogy with another and project one aspect onto another; this is integral to how recognition is sustained and developed, for instance, in Ghiberti's panel of the *Adoration* (fig. 1) we attend to the alignment of heads – of the Virgin, Christ child and the kneeling king – and this is part of our realization of what is represented; so is the mirroring and variation of the two figures on the left. Similarly, in Leonardo's *Adoration* (fig. 2), the relation of the two kneeling kings, one before and one behind the Virgin, and the fugue of encircling figures establishes the space in which she is set.

II

As the subject is explored and sustained through the symmetries of its depiction so it is through the procedures of the medium. For example, we recognize a figure in the lines of a drawing and when it is a figure in movement we may recruit the apparent impulse of the line – imagine the impulse of the line – to fill out our sense of the movement, whether in Rembrandt's abrupt stroke which marks Sylvius's gesture (fig. 8) or in studies by Raphael which explore the figure's tension and torsion (fig. 3); in such cases the line relates itself to the figure twice over, once by its shape and once by its apparent impulse. The line connects shape to movement as they can be connected only in drawing. Shape and movement become projected onto each other, so that while making recognition more replete the image takes on a structure that has no equivalent outside depiction. But this is a very incomplete account of the matter.The more complex the coordinates to which the impulse of the drawing adjusts itself, the less identifiable it is with the physical impulse of the mark; for what comes to inform the figure is not so much the impulse but the multiple implications of form that are related through it. Furthermore, as in the sheet of Leonardo studies (fig. 4), the impulse of the line may itself be something we only imagine, and only come to imagine by virtue of the movement of the figure it delineates. What this shows us is that a drawing may signal to us the figure's motility in multiple and interpenetrating ways: by the impulse of the drawn line, by the impulse we imagine the line as having by virtue of the figure it depicts, but also by the controlled complexity of the drawing itself imparting to the figure its sense of inward life – imparting to the figure the poise and concentration of the drawing. It is only at the margins and in reflection that these can be separated from each

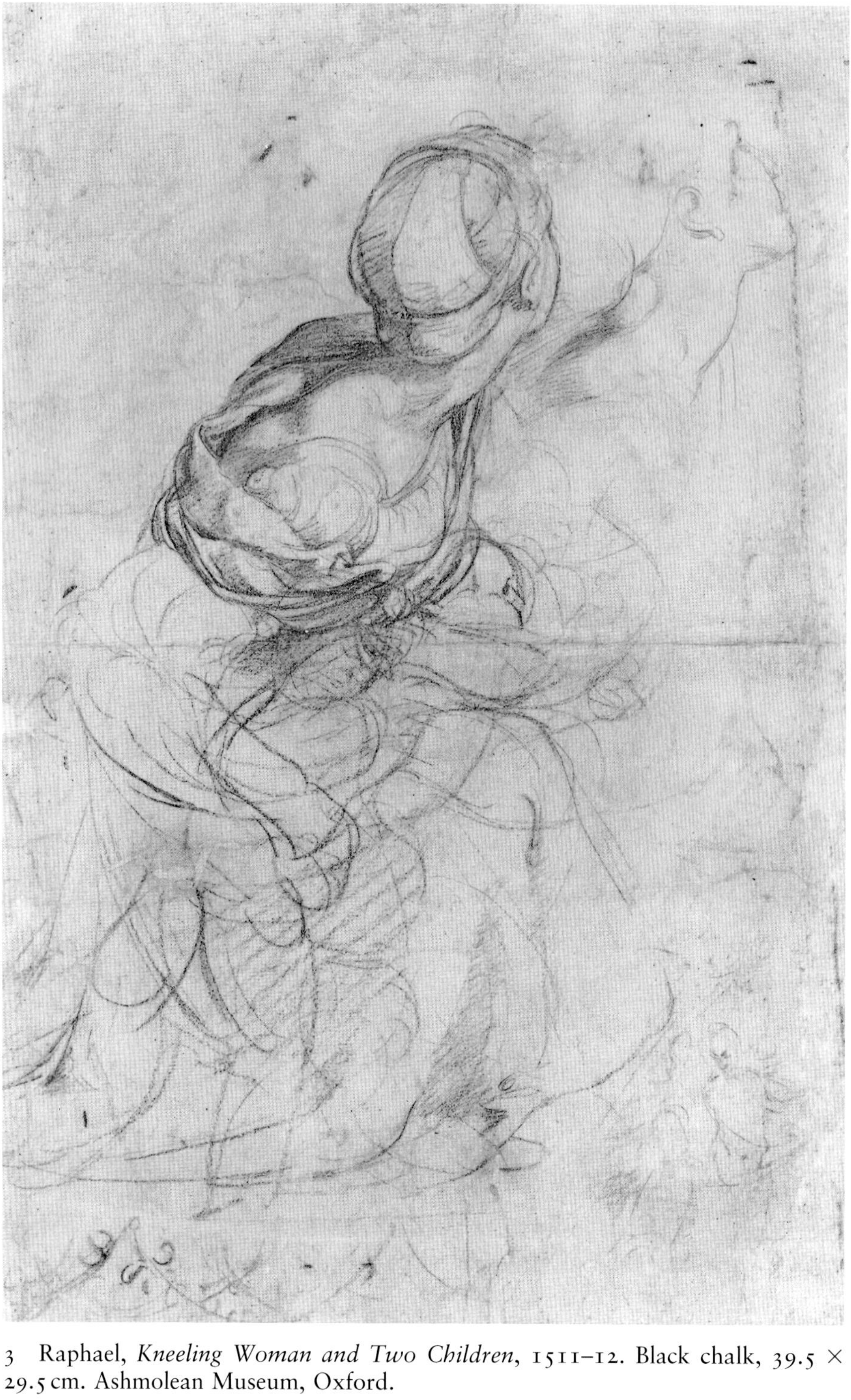

3 Raphael, *Kneeling Woman and Two Children*, 1511–12. Black chalk, 39.5 × 29.5 cm. Ashmolean Museum, Oxford.

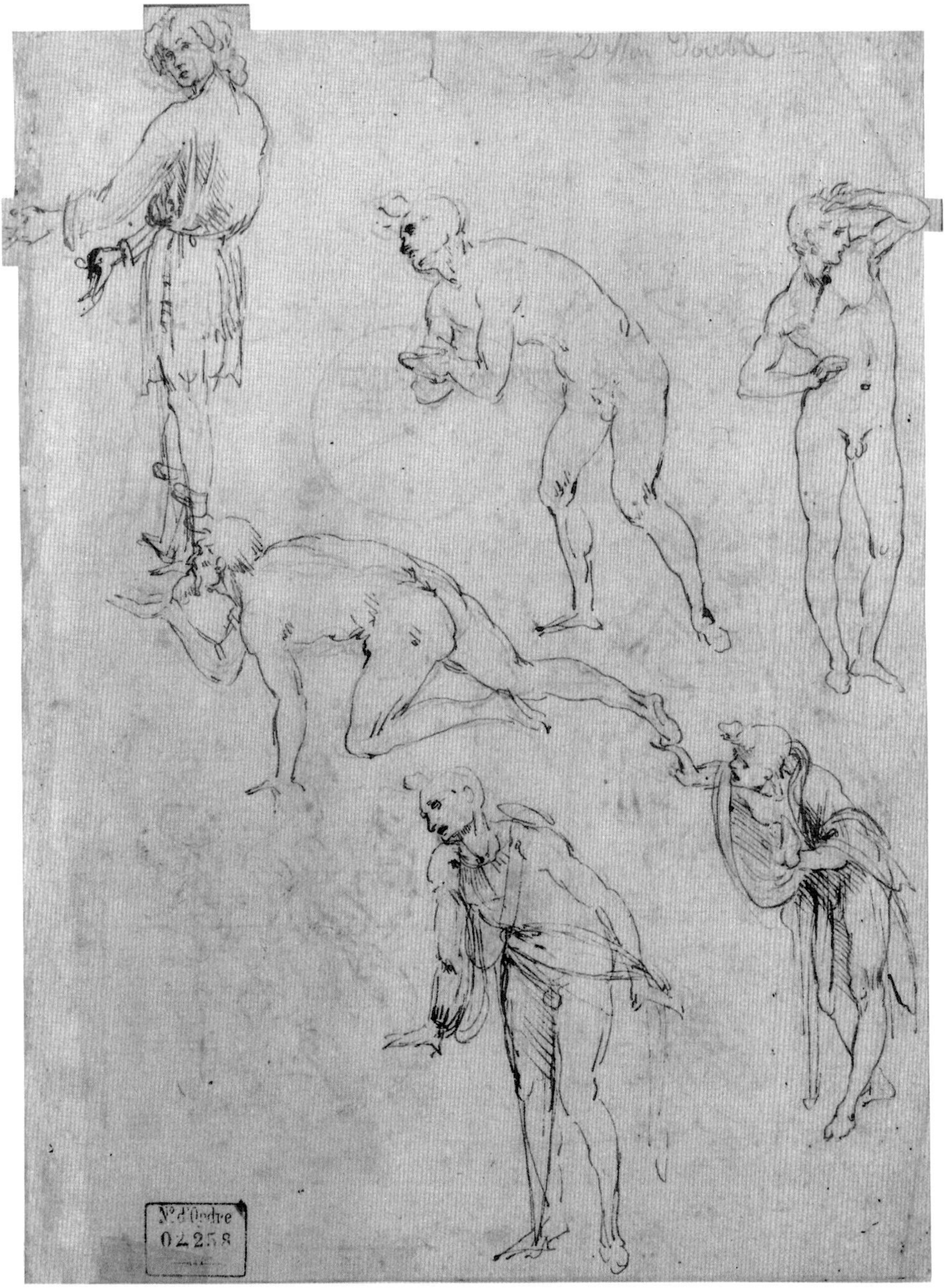

4 Leonardo da Vinci, figure studies for the *Adoration*, *c.*1480. Pen and ink over silverpoint, 27.8 × 20.8 cm. Musée du Louvre, Paris.

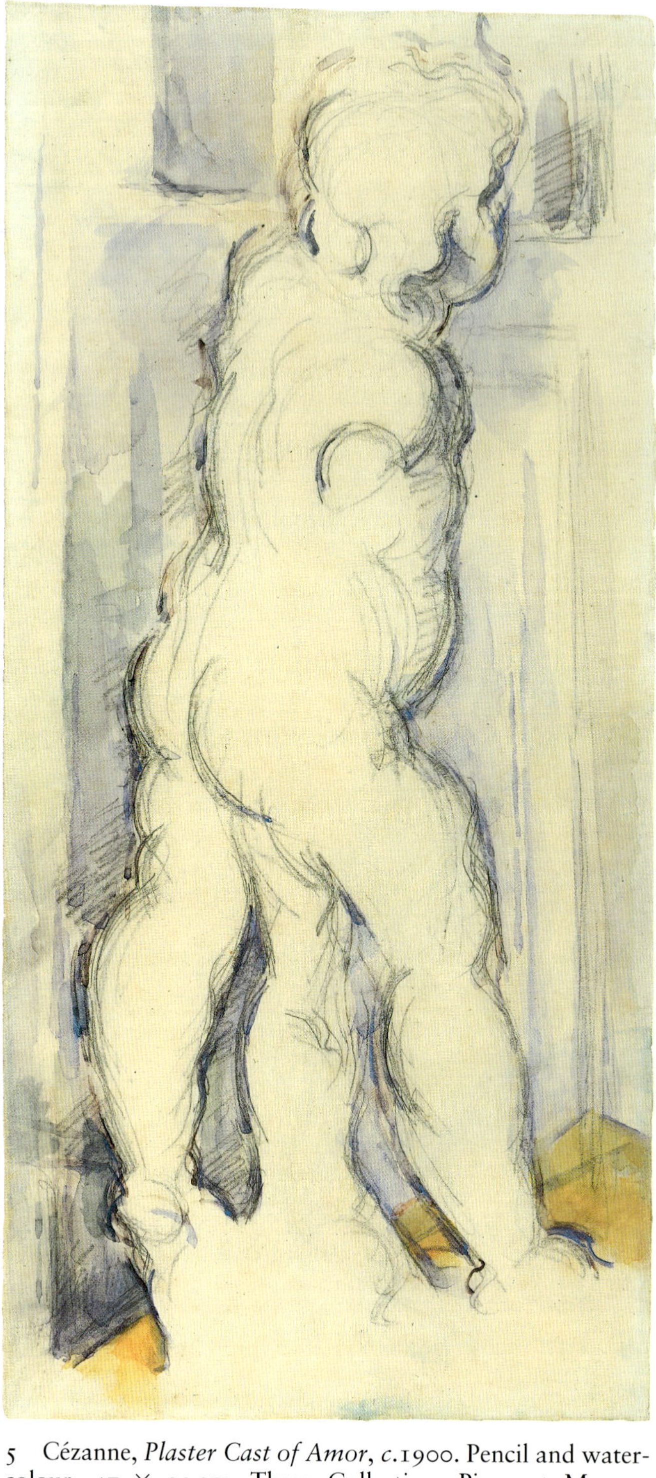

5 Cézanne, *Plaster Cast of Amor*, *c.*1900. Pencil and watercolour, 47 × 22 cm. Thaw Collection, Pierpont Morgan Library, New York.

other. Rehearsing this tradition of drawing, Cézanne in the study of the plaster *Amor* (fig. 5) re-relates the factors – the forms within the turning body are left taxingly implicit, shifts of viewing position – now higher, now lower – are integrated in the overall image, while the complex impulses of the brush round the edge rehearse the sense of movement.

In the recruitment of the paint surface to the subject there is a similar situation to that of drawn line. In Leonardo's studies of drapery on linen (fig. 6) the surface texture of what is depicted and its ground are felt as coincident, and the reflected light from the surface and the depicted illumination of the depicted subject appear as convergent with each other; we do not simply see the drapery depicted in the surface but the texture of the surface focused in the depiction. This, however, is a limiting case. For, just as the energy of drawing was not a matter merely of miming a figure's action, so the relation between the depicted illumination and the light reflected from the surface seldom has the consonance of this drapery study; and, from the sixteenth to the mid-nineteenth century, we find the texture of impasto set against more translucent or scumbled areas and its layers brushed into each other as well as over each other so that depicted light (within the represented subject) and the light reflected from the surface complicate each other, setting up multiple suggestions of continuity through discrete forms and surfaces. For example, in Veronese's *Allegory of Deceit* (fig. 7) the sense of the brush across the heavy weave canvas intimates the physical immanence of the woman's back while the shifts from opaque to translucent paint give a sense of a visual density into which we look.[9]

When we isolate the recruitment of specific aspects of the line or the surface, however, we risk losing hold of a painting's many-sidedness, for instance, in the *Allegory of Deceit* we may remark separately on the qualities of the paint surface, on how the continuity of the line along the woman's arms and across her shoulder informs the whole gesture of her body, on the relation between the imagined low viewpoint in the painting and what we must assume was the low viewpoint of the of the original spectator, but none of these is offered as a discrete conceit, and remarking on them separately risks narrowing and simplifying attention – it interrupts their interdependence and their absorption in our synoptic view, our sense of the subject emerging within the painting. As the painter explores his subject for what it will suggest to him within

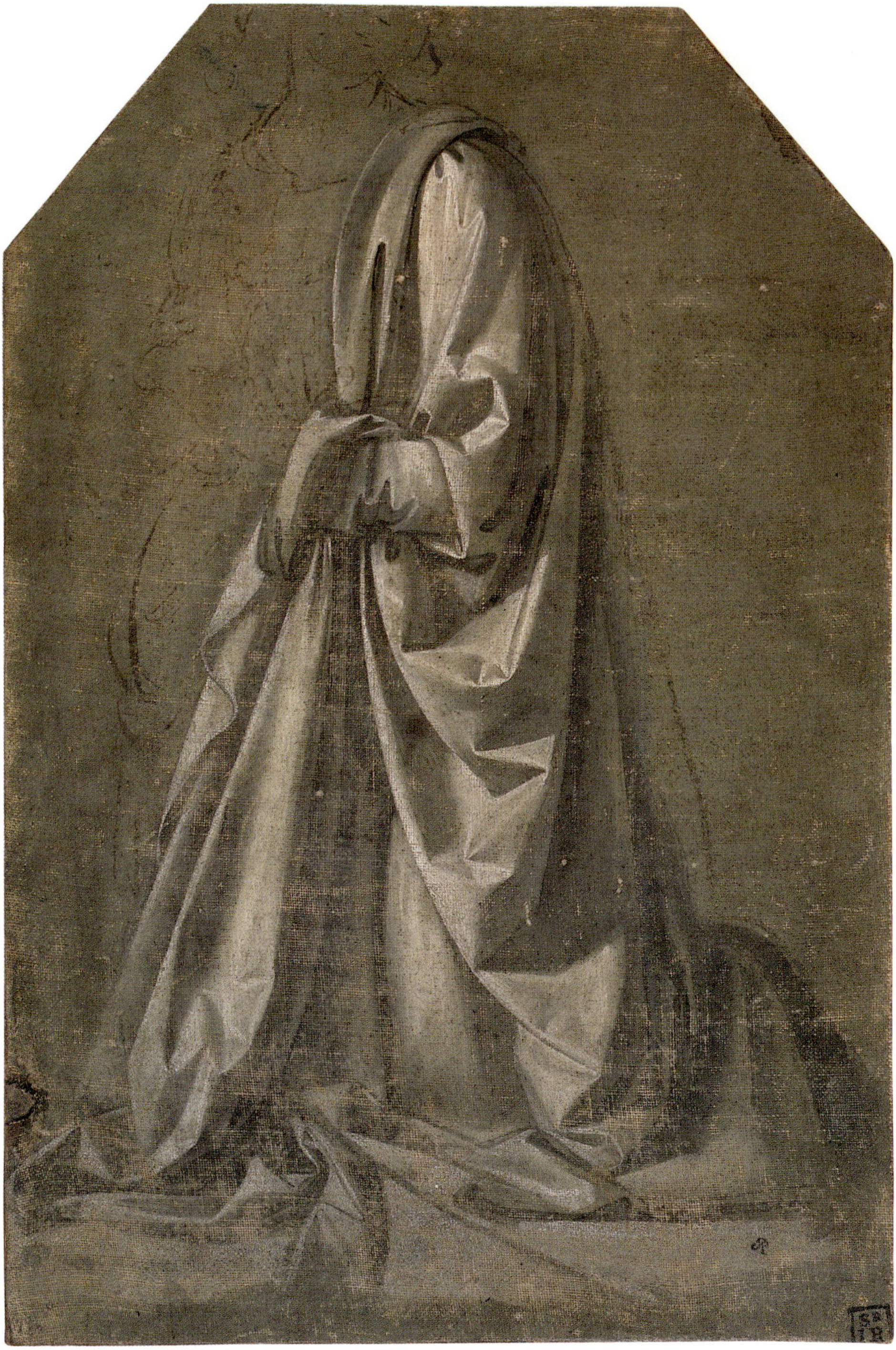

6 Leonardo da Vinci, drapery study, *c.*1474. Brush drawing on linen, 28.3 × 19.3 cm. British Museum, London.

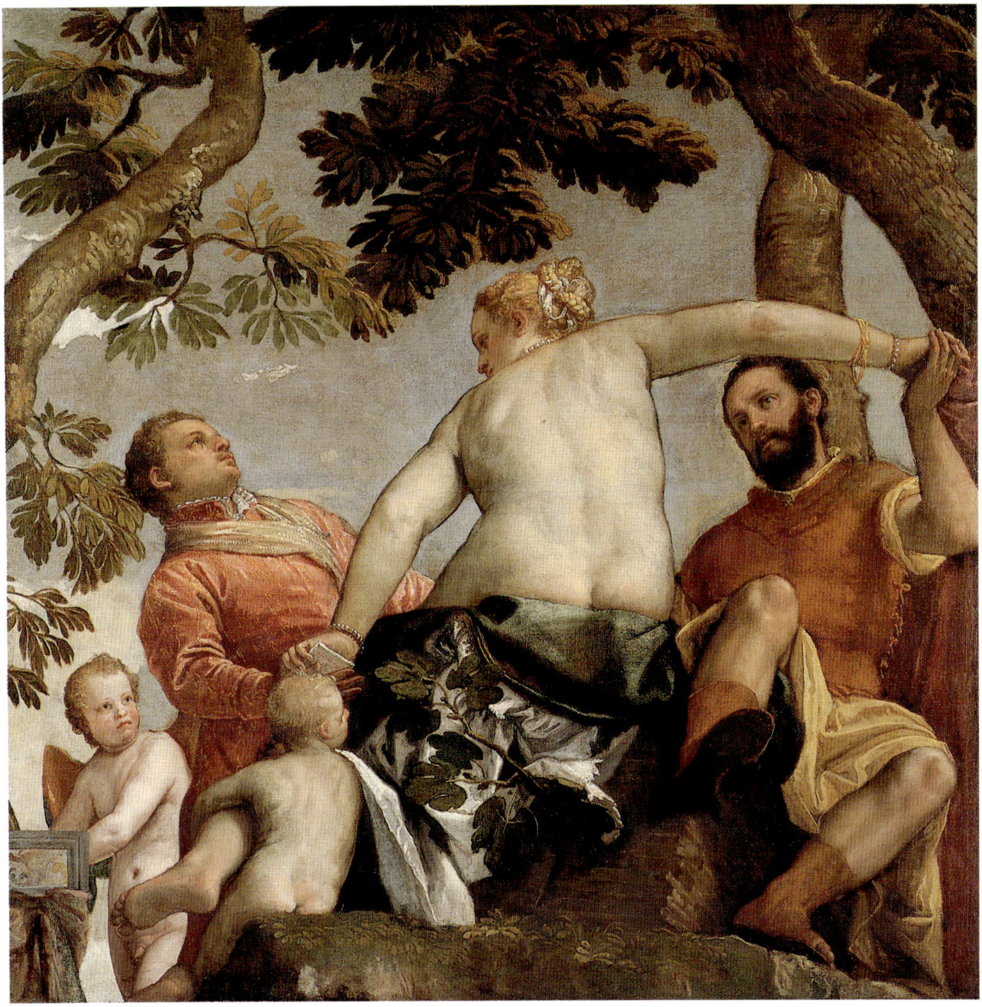

7 Veronese, *Allegory of Deceit*, *c.*1570. Oil on canvas, 189 × 189 cm. National Gallery, London.

the framework of his own mode of painting, so the viewer waits upon the suggestions the painting will offer within the framework of other recognitions; he does not merely respond to discrete questions he already has in mind (is it an oak or an ash, silk or wool?) nor resolve a series of separate questions of what is signified in specific areas or aspects of the canvas. This kind of attention is a matter of letting happen. Admittedly, all our perception involves 'letting happen' – otherwise we should already know what we are going to see – but in depiction (in any art) this letting happen becomes itself something we value in a way that is central to our involvement: once the image emerges, however indeterminately, it would seem to prompt further realization of what is recognized from within itself.

III

While these examples show us how various aspects of the medium's material and procedure may be recruited to make our grasp of the subject more replete, they might also be thought to show something further: that we not only pursue the subject through the medium but at the same time utilize the subject in the cause of the imaginative project of depiction. To simplify grossly, the figure provides an opportunity for exercizing the urgencies of drawing and not only drawing for imagining the figure. We gain a more radical hold on the sense of depiction as having its own sense of purpose through another factor, the way that it retrieves for itself the very distinction between pictorial and nonpictorial seeing; for instance, where the depiction includes a fictive frame or a sill in the foreground, painted as if part of the undepicted environment, leading us to reflect on and re-imagine the transition between the actuality of the medium and the represented subject, what lies – spatially or qualitatively – inside the depiction and what outside. We are invited both to attend to and to imagine away the distinction between real and fictive, the very distinction presupposed in seeing the painting as a representation in the first place. And contrary to what we might have expected, calling into question the real fictive boundary may enhance the vividness of the fiction rather than undermine it. For example, in the drawing and more particularly the etching by Rembrandt of Jan Cornelius Sylvius (figs 8 and 9), the shadow of his hand extends over the represented frame and we are led to wonder how far across the surface the fiction extends, and even, perhaps, where within our experience the shadow turns into mere ink. But reflecting on this does not lessen the force of his imagined presence. It is as if our pursuit of the fiction will turn everything to its advantage, even the adjustment for seeing the fiction – as if the mind not only seeks to enhance the realization of the subject – to sustain its recognition – but to sustain the fictive mode in which it is operating.

This impulse to sustain the fiction is underscored by two further motifs which converge here: first, the real-fictive border, for centuries a metaphor for the boundary between the immanent world and the divine, and by extension between the living and the dead; and second, the recurrent challenge to the visual artist to transcend the merely visual: 'O Rembrandt, paint Cornelius' voice . . . he who would see him must hear him' was a challenge about the image of another preacher, the Mennonite Anslo (see fig. 66, p. 82). The convergence of these motifs mobilizes the structure of depiction as a metaphor of transcending literal vision.[10]

IV

Any account we give of depiction must imply some account of its relations on the one hand to ornament and on the other to those areas of modern painting, particularly abstract painting, in which representation has been called into question. Let us first of all take up its relation to ornament. One way of considering this is to focus on how the real and the fictive relate to each other in the two areas. In depiction the fictive dominates over the the actual, while in ornament it is the other way round. Thus in the case of a Greek black-figure amphora (figs 10 and 11) on the one hand the shield or horse painted on the bowl gives imaginative extension to the actual form, and on the other the actual curvature of bowl vivifies our sense of the horse or shield. It is a question of what recruits and what is recruited whether we attend to it as depiction or ornament. In ornament the fictive transforms the actual, whereas in depiction the actual is selectively called on to enrich and sustain the fiction. The deep affinity lies in this: in neither can we see where the real ends and the imaginary begins, because there is no such boundary inside appearance. In many cases it may be a fine balance between depiction and ornament, for instance in the effect produced by fifteenth-century Italian marquetry where wooden shelves, cupboard doors and musical instruments that are made of regularly shaped pieces of polished wood slotted together are represented by a surface that is itself made up of such contiguous pieces of polished wood (fig. 13). An extension of this effect is the construction in shallow space of a vaulted arch in which we cannot disambiguate the real from the fictive depth (fig. 12).

There is a range of cases in which we find ourselves not so much

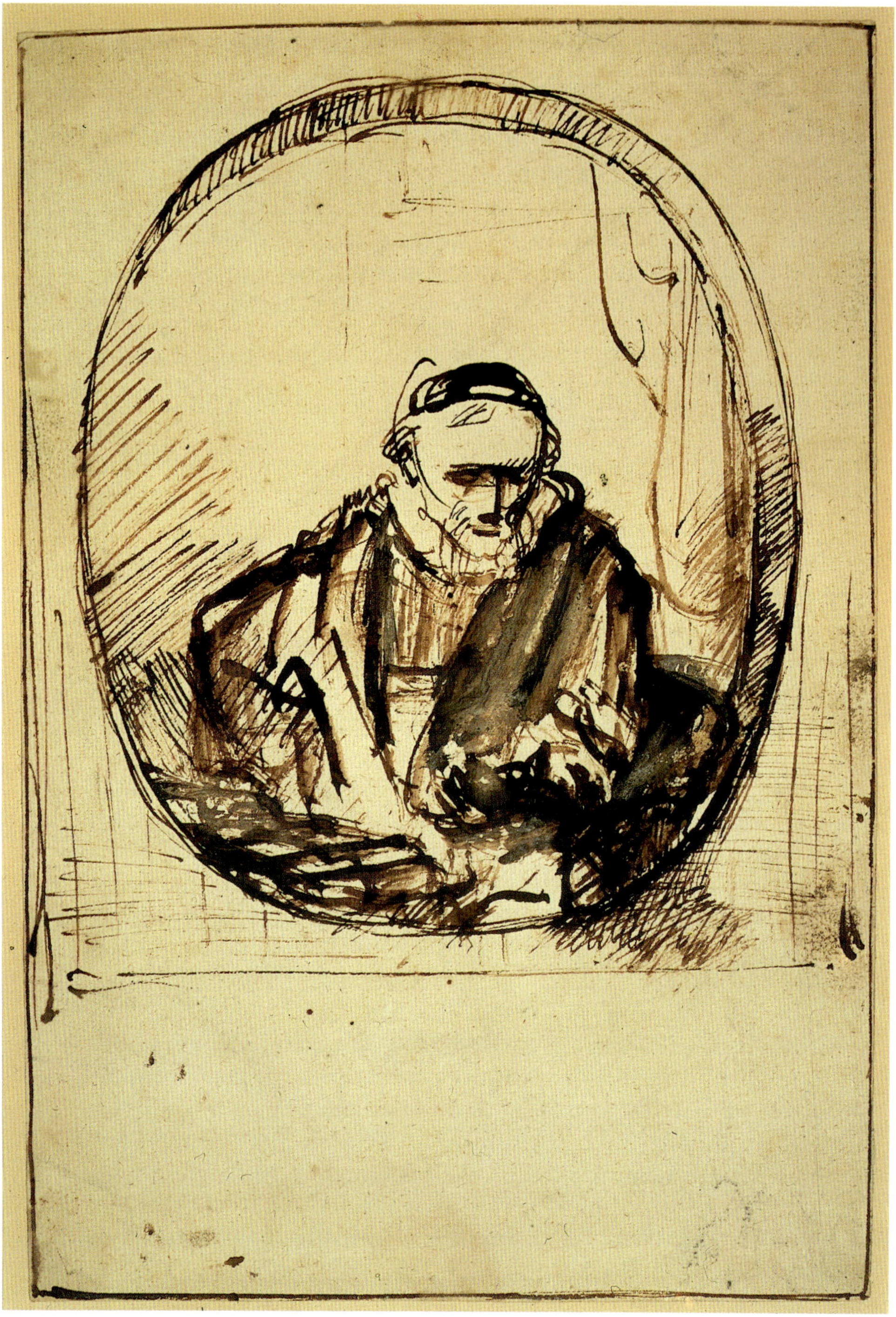

8 Rembrandt, *Jan Cornelius Sylvius*, 1646. Pen and brown ink with white heightening, 28.5×19.5 cm. British Museum, London. (Benesch 763)

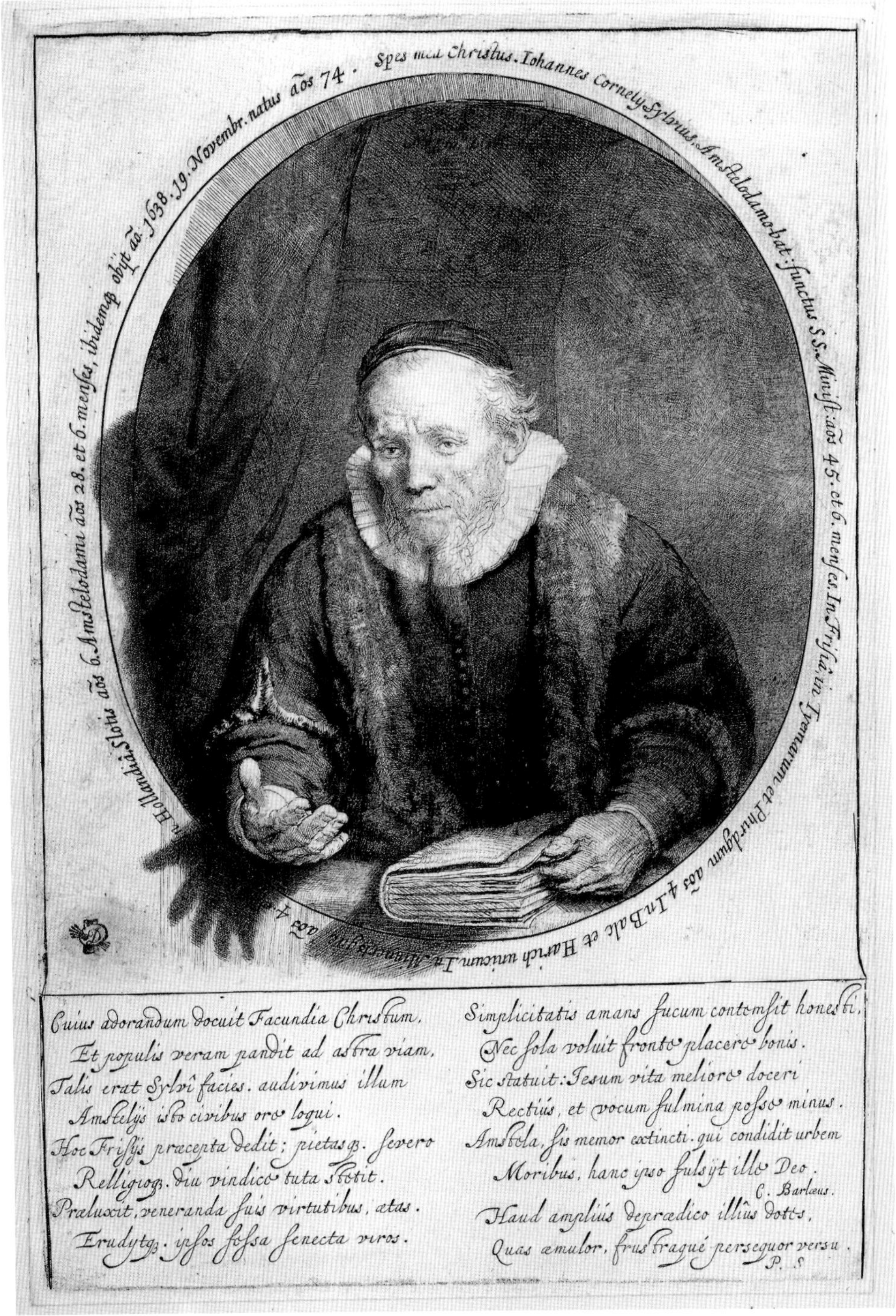

9 Rembrandt, *Jan Cornelius Sylvius. Posthumous Portrait*, 1646. Etching, 27.8 × 18.8 cm. British Museum, London.

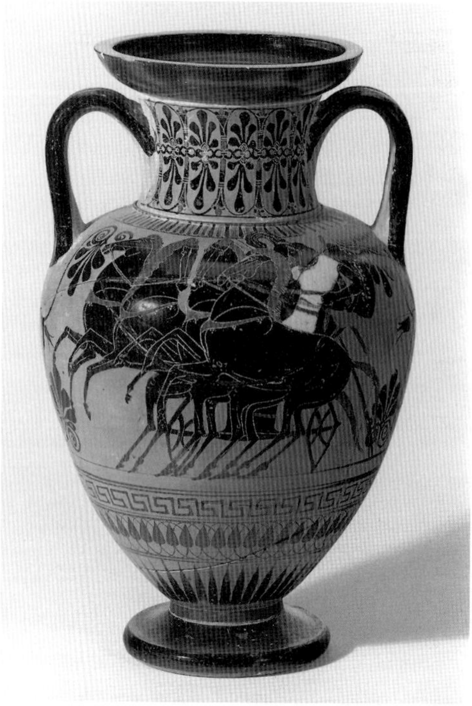

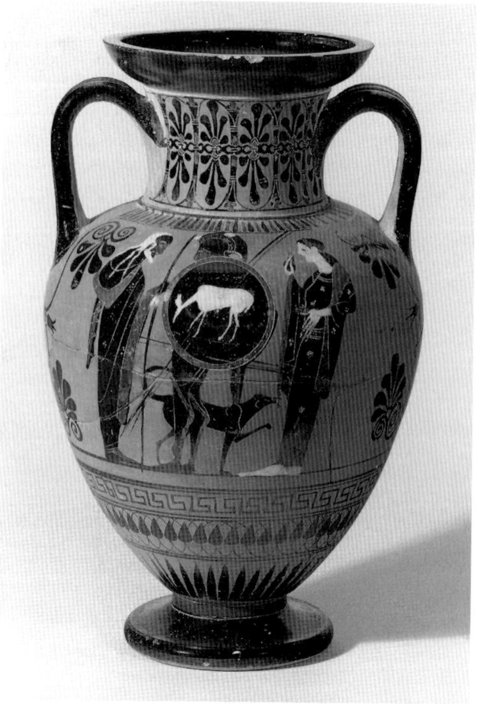

10 and 11 Black-figure neck amphora, *c*.520–510 BC. Fitzwilliam Museum, Cambridge. (GR 31 1864)

in the middle ground between our mental set for depiction and for ornament, but engaged in an imaginatively complex movement back and forth between them. For example, in a Romanesque portico (fig. 14) where a series of columns includes some that appear twisted or knotted or caryatidic; where walls are patterned like interlaced metal grills or where mouldings take on the form of vine tendrils. When we look at these in dissective attention they become fictions (fictively twisted columns, fictive metal grills, fictive scenes), but in synoptic attention, regarding the portico as a whole, they serve to elaborate the structural reality of the building, to ornament it.

* * *

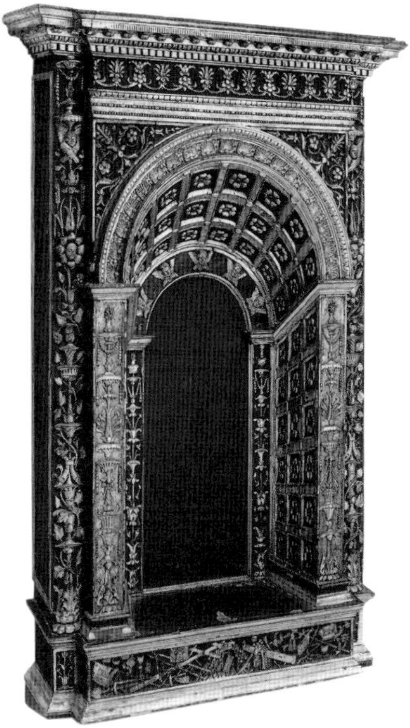

12 Frame, probably the framework of a ciborium, Italian, fifteenth century. Wood, carved, gilt and painted, 147 × 102 cm. Victoria and Albert Museum, London.

13 (*below*) Giuliano da Maiano *et al.*, intarsia cupboards, 1463–8. Old Sacristy, Cathedral, Florence.

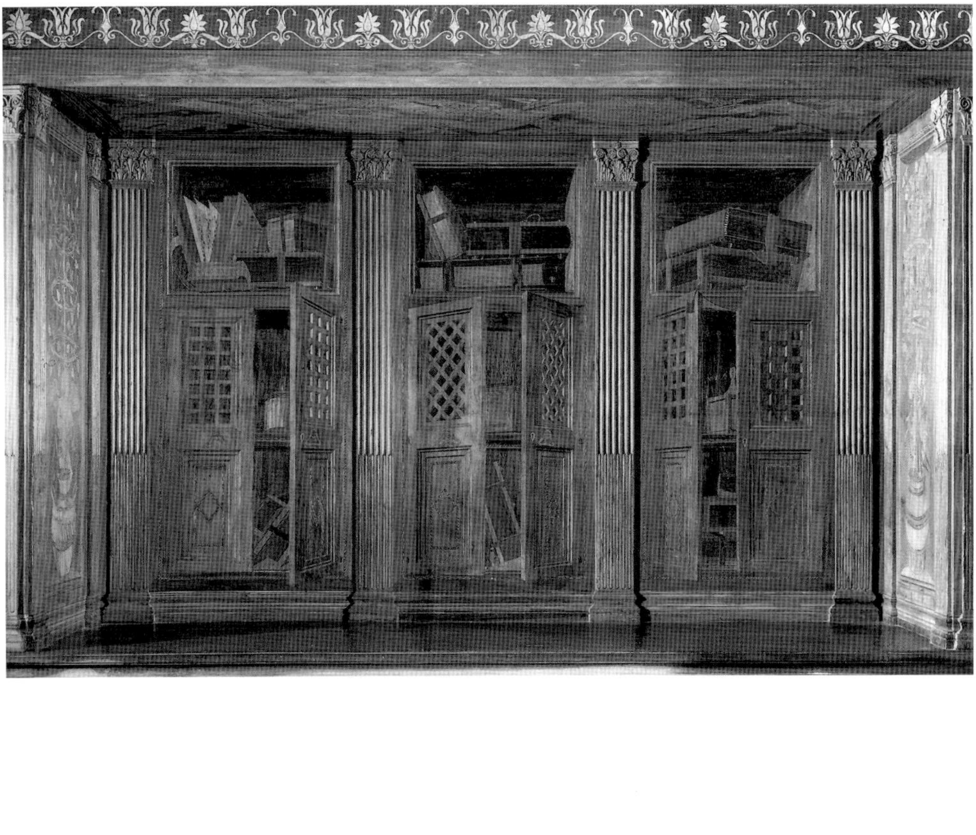

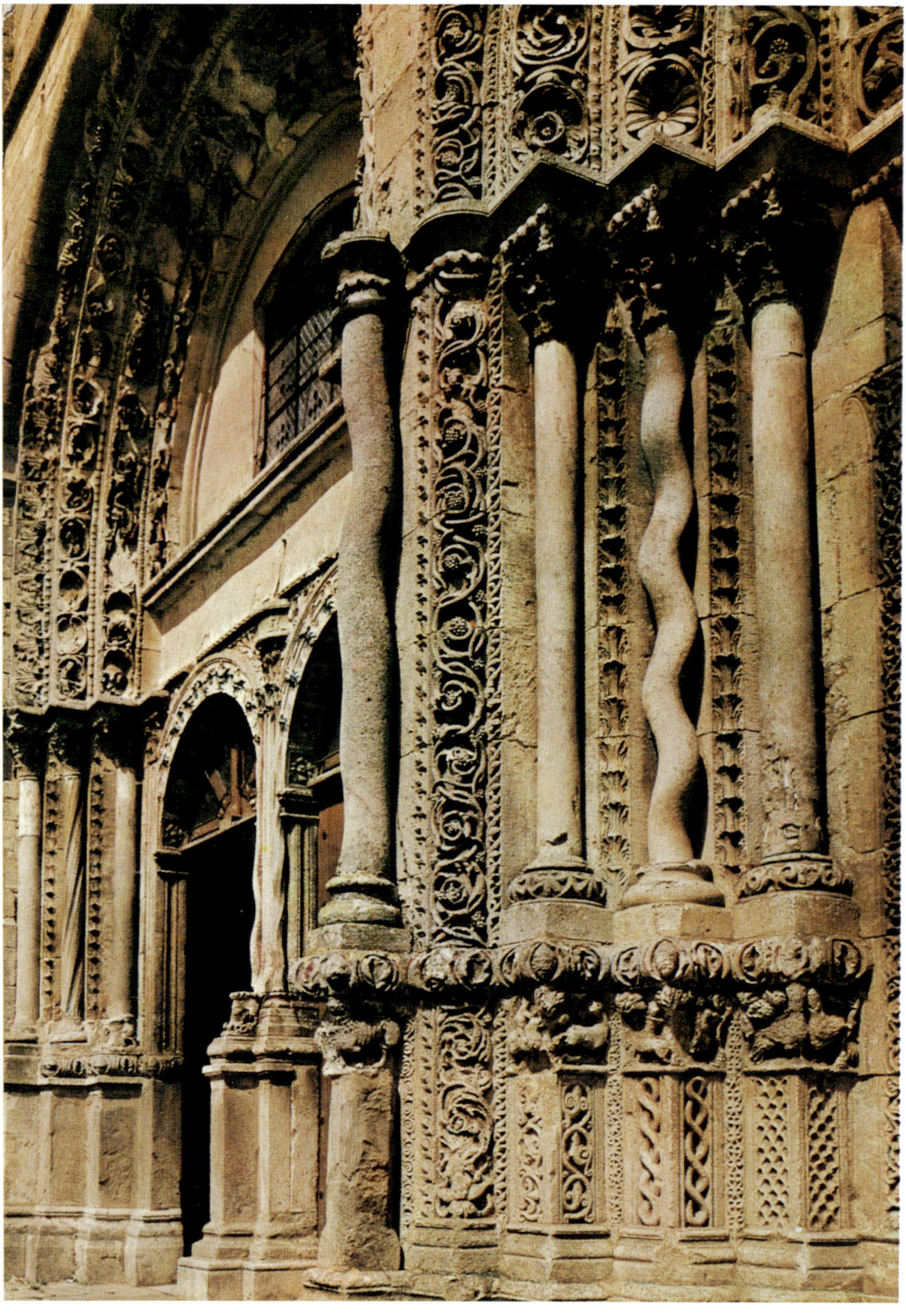

14 Portico of the Church of Saint-Lazare, Avallon, *c.*1150.

V

A second border with depiction as it has been considered so far is with the early twentieth-century painting which called into question the centrality of representation. It did so in favour of factors that it felt were of greater moment for the painter, factors that were already part of the art but lying implicit within it. The concern of my present argument is not to give an account of the diverse and complex development of early twentieth-century art nor to compare its scope with that of earlier periods. It is simply to observe some of these shifts in the conception of painting because they enhance our sense of the tradition out of which they came and because unless we can negotiate the transition conceptually we exaggerate the division and leave criticism on both sides impoverished.

Let us take three cases from the early part of the century. First, Kandinsky's move to abstraction in the second decade was a matter of forming variations on a theme – like the rider or the rowers – which was left implicit (fig. 15).[11] He wrote, in his *Reminiscences* on the experience of failing to see what was represented in Monet's *Haystacks*: 'I found this nonrecognition painful . . . I had a dull feeling that the object was lacking in this picture. And I noticed with surprise and confusion that the picture not only gripped me, but impressed itself radically on my memory . . . And albeit unconsciously, objects were discredited as an essential element within the picture'. The nonrecognition is not an absence of the search for recognition but assumes it; and what the passage and Kandinsky's painting over the crucial years between 1911 and 1914 reveal is how the confusion was also charged with an excitement that he sought to retrieve. He did not, he said, want to make abstract patterns:

> If, even today, we were to begin to dissolve completely the tie that binds us to nature, to direct our energies toward forcible emanicipation and content ourselves exclusively with the combination of pure colour and independent form, we would create works having the appearance of geometrical ornament, which would – to put it crudely – be like a tie or a carpet. Beauty of colour and form (despite the assertion of pure aesthetes or naturalists, whose principle aim is 'beauty') is not a sufficient aim of art. Precisely because of the elementary state of our

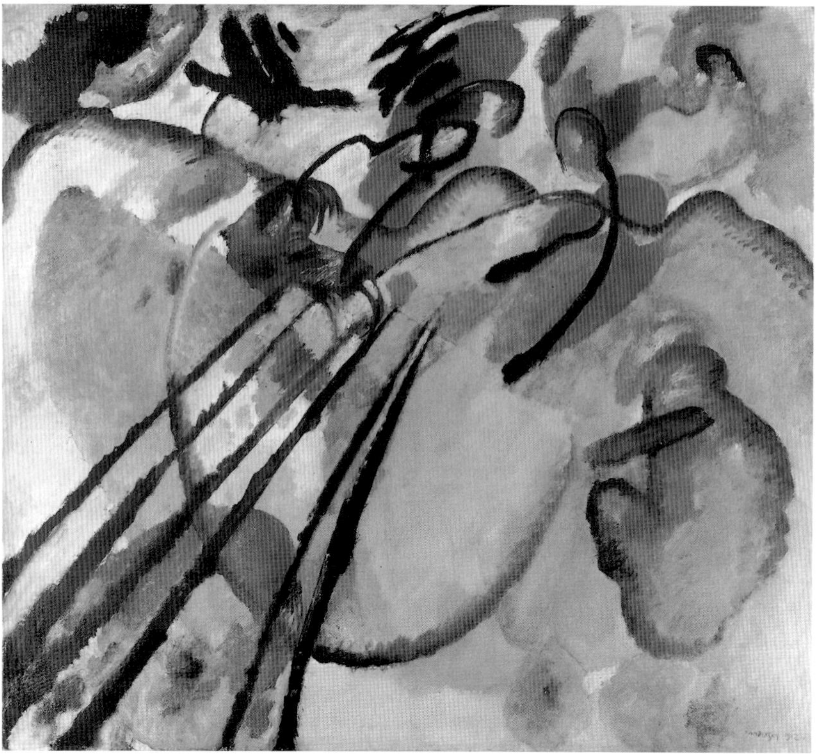

15 Vassily Kandinsky, *Improvisation 26 (The Rowers)*, 1912. Oil on canvas, 97 × 107.5 cm. Städtische Galerie im Lehbachhaus.

> painting today, we are as yet scarcely able to derive inner experience from composition with wholely emancipated form and colour.[12]

It would seem that after about four years the excitement of unresolved recognition ceased to be recoverable, and he sought to centre his painting in the interaction of elements of near geometrical pattern.

The development of Mondrian's art relates to earlier depiction in a rather different way.[13] After giving up the representation of subject matter and after a long process of refinement, setting up patterns against or within which irregularities were given play, he settled on an apparently simple set of the pictorial elements, and these elements were so deployed as to set up variations on themselves (fig. 16); defining lines became separate from their bounding

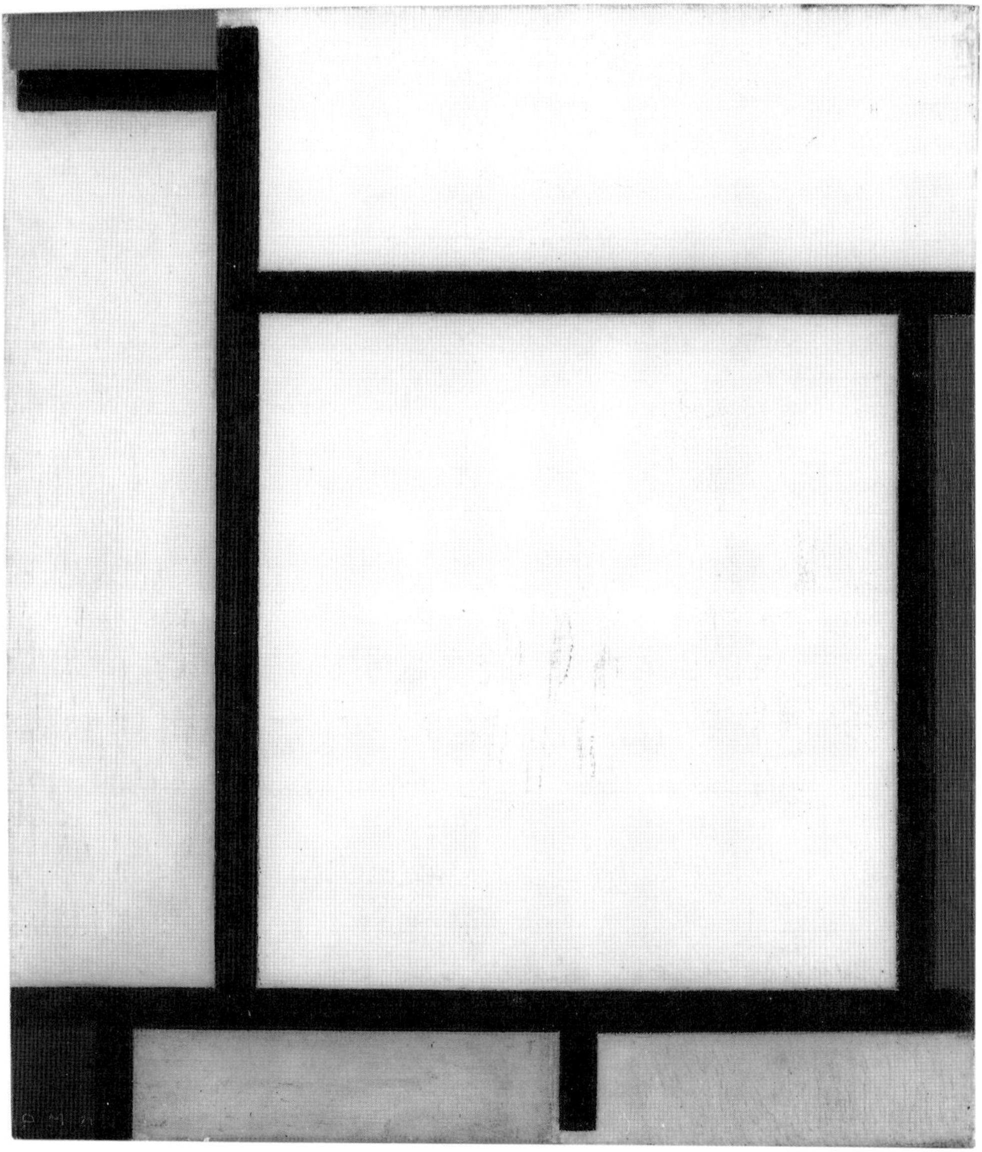

16 Piet Mondrian, *Composition with Red, Blue, Black, Yellow and Grey*, 1921. Oil on canvas, 39.5 × 35 cm. Gemeentemuseum, The Hague.

function, either by ending before they reached an edge or doubling up as striations rather than borders; elsewhere the orientation of the grid and of the surface were differentiated by rotating one 45°

from the other and, in a late work, the intersection of lines became autonomous rectangles; it would be hard to conceive of a practice of this kind – this play of variation – without the cultivation of formal relations in earlier depiction, without familiarity with the consistencies of morphology that run through discrete objects and the re-vision of one feature through another. His own earlier work had shown just such concerns and it was Mondrian's claim for his pure plastic art that it shared the principle of composition with the painting of the past. His commitment to certain limited shapes and parameters of lucidity, which were tested for how much differentiation and sacrifice they could survive, might be thought of as an analogue of the painter's complication of recognition, formal relations replacing subject matter.

The third early twentieth-century artist whose work stands in a rather oblique relation to depiction is Duchamp. Earlier we observed how recognition sustained and developed itself through recruitment of its own material and psychological conditions to make itself more replete, at the same time extending recognition through variation. Repletion and extension are essentially related to each other, two aspects of how recognition keeps itself going. It is recognition in action and it constitutes the structure of the viewers' relation to the painting. But the extension of recognition involves at the same time a delay of resolution and that delay may itself become more or less focal. What Duchamp took from earlier depiction – specifically that of Cubism – was deferral itself: the insertion of confusing screens – literally and metaphorically – between the viewer and the consummation of his interest, a diffusion through multiple references and difficulties.[14] The 'Large Glass', *The Bride Stripped Bare by her Bachelors, Even*, is a work that is both highly contrived but oblique to the traditions of painterly contrivance: images with elaborate literary connections suspended on a screen, inviting us to see them as behind it in an unstructured limbo or sited in actual space behind the glass; in his final work, *Etant donné*, the physical access was controlled by a series of doorways, the ultimate erotic image spied only through a peephole. He set up patterns of avoidance, of withdrawal of the subject from the viewer; he not only delayed the resolution of the image but withheld his work from the public world, laboriously crafting small-scale multiples to form a personal portable museum.

Each of these early twentieth-century figures, however different from each other, seized on painting's complication of recognition while disengaging it from what had been and would continue to be for others its central imaginative potential. Remarking on this is not yet to explicate the historical conditions that brought about these moves or the situations to which they responded, but it throws some light on the complications of depiction by indicating how, for some, it was replaced. Later twentieth-century imaging of previous images can be seen as another such replacement, and yet another would be making visual works the occasion for verbal or conceptual play.

VI

There is an incompatibility between the interest of depiction as it has been characterized so far and what we might call, broadly, semiotic or nominalist accounts.[15] In these accounts imagining and seeing are separated. The separation has had two principal motivations from inside philosophy: first, to account for depiction without using the notion of likeness (a philosophical austerity adopted to avoid problems about the existence of ideas as opposed to things) and second the concern to dissociate statements that are true of the world from those that are true only of our imaginings, dreams, fears and so forth (statements that do not have to be consistent with our statements about how the world is). I shall not take up the first motive as the notion of likeness is internal to the notion of recognition and the project of abandoning it would be a conceptual experiment outside our current frame of discussion. So I shall turn to the second motive. In the cause of objective knowledge that is governed by the demand for consistency, we must segregate the statements about the contents of our imaginings from statements about the world. The claim that we see a house in the landscape by van Goyen, when what is actually there is a patch of coloured paint, so it has been argued by Kendall Walton in a rigorous exploration of the nominalist position, needs to be resolved into statements about what we really see plus statements about what we imagine, with some rules about the conditions under which statements about what we see and what we imagine are related to each other, that is, the truth conditions for statements about what is fictively the case in our imaginings and truths about the non-fictional world.[16]

According to this account of depiction, having our attention drawn to the material characteristics of the painting disrupts our imaginative seeing – it is like disruption of the depicted image caused by a tear in the canvas. For Walton, what we recognize within a picture, its imaginative content, is logically sealed off from our cognition of the material object that is literally in front of us. What such an analysis rightly makes clear is the difference between recognition in the service of depiction and in the service of literal objectivity. But what it excludes is our capacity to experience the hinterland between them, which is where our account locates the core of depiction.[17] Further, Walton's account excludes our capacity to see the subject take on qualities it can have only in depiction. At the very least our interest in how things appear in painting is unlike our nonpictorial experience of them, and the difference is not reducible to the fact that they appear in a painting but *how* they appear in a way that is distinctive of painting.[18]

The concern of this chapter has been to sketch out how depiction utilizes vision in the work of the imagination. Eliciting recognition allows a multiplicity of factors to be recruited including the material character of the surface and our own psychological adjustments. Such imagining is not restricted by the requirement of consistency or conformity with our beliefs about the world; rather it is restricted by how recognitions can sustain and expand themselves to take on an internal architecture of correspondences, allowing the mind to occupy and move about within them, attentive to its elements and gestures and analogizing and connecting them for itself.

Chapter Two

Donatello and the Planes of Relief

THE SURFACE OF A PAINTING has its own material continuity and its own borders, and these are not simply conditions of depiction but can enter into its content, into the interest it has for us. Just as we may be aware of the continuity of a line that intimates a multiplicity of forms, so we may be aware of the continuity of a surface through the array of discrete objects represented on it. Although the marked surface becomes articulated and structured by the recognitions that it elicits, it is not saturated by those recognitions but retains its presence as a surface interacting with the depicted subject. In critical writing over the last century the notion of the plane of the surface has been made central not only to the discussion of painting but to relief sculpture (and even sculpture in general), despite the fact that in a literal sense sculpture has no overall surface coinciding with a plane. Sculpture has such a surface plane only in so far as we imagine one.

Not only has relief sculpture been seen, on analogy with painting, as if it presented its subject in a continuous flat surface, but during the last century the notion of 'relieflikeness' with its imaginary surface plane has, in turn, been made central to the analysis of painting; the result of this was that painting was thought of as having a real surface and also an imaginary surface plane, without the two coinciding. These transferences back and forth between painting and sculpture were made, in the nineteenth and early twentieth centuries, with the aim of articulating depiction's nonliteral cogency, its internal ordering procedure for which the surface plane was thought the crucial factor.[1]

I

Relating the conception of an ideal plane and the actuality of relief has been central to the discussion of Donatello. Relief in bronze and marble had been intensively cultivated in Florence for a century before Donatello emerged as a relief sculptor in about 1415; this was also the decade of the invention of a perspective construction associated with Brunelleschi. The construction was primarily a system for projecting the appearance of a three-dimensional array onto a plane surface, rather than onto another three-dimensional form, so one might think that the sculpture that could most readily assimilate the construction would be very shallow relief, and Donatello, famously, invented a mode of very shallow relief, *rilievo stiacciato*. What he invented, however, did *not* approximate itself to a painted or drawn surface; rather he used the limited depth of carving in a peculiarly complex way, closely related to deeper kinds of relief, including reliefs in limestone, bronze, and stucco, and through these various forms of relief we can trace a consistent preoccupation with reworking the boundaries between the material of his medium and the fictions of his subject matter.[2] In this context the notion of the plane of the surface can take on numerous connotations, and for the sake of clarity it is worth distinguishing them before examining the practice of Donatello and critical responses to it.[3]

The concept of the surface plane belongs first of all to the theory of the perspective construction: the construction might be taken as *regulating* the represention of the object to yield appropriate foreshortening or spatial diminution, so that what we see in the painting or relief does not look anomalous; in this regulative use we may have no strong sense of the plane of the surface at all, for the perspective construction would be conceived as merely instrumental in bringing about a convincing image. But the perspective construction could also enter the idea of representation in a more radical way: the representation itself might be thought of as if it were the cross-section of the visual pyramid. In the first role the perspective construction would be merely instrumental in producing the representation; in the second the painting or relief would be thought of as the *representation of an image*; we would conceive of the picture or relief surface as if representing to us a plane on which the subject was projected, as in the sixteenth-century diagram (fig. 17): the plane of the surface would become

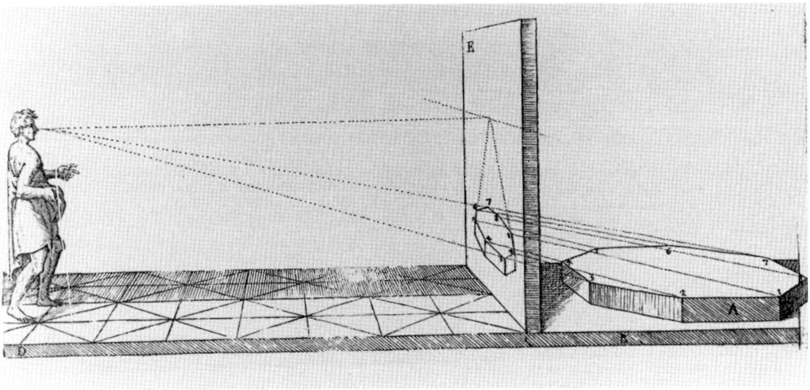

17 Perspective diagram from Vignola, *Le Due Regole della Prospettiva Pratica*, 1583. Bologna.

identified with the plane of projection, and the image in that plane would be an ideal entity lying between the eye and the hypothetical object. We would imagine the shapes in the picture not as representing the subject directly but as representing a projection of the subject. (Clearly, this mode of seeing a picture could be available only to those who had a concept of perspectival projection, however loose.[4])

Secondly, and apart from considerations of the perspective construction, the notion of the surface plane enters the discussion when the represented subject and the plane are thought of as reciprocally adjusted – adjusted so that figures represented are conceived as turning into the plane or as spontaneously forming a good and spatially revealing gestalt within it, as in classical relief.[5] The background to this conception is the need for the subject to present itself lucidly within the shallow space of its medium; the deeper the relief, the more a moving viewer would see uncoordinated aspects of the subject; the shallower the relief, the more the saliences and their shadows would threaten to disrupt its fictive relations. This had been discussed in the eighteenth century by the French artist and critic Dandré-Bardon who had written that if the relief is seen in a raking light it should have less pronounced saliences than if seen with a frontal and more diffuse light which will not precipitate such disruptive shadows; and with regard to the ordering of the figures he praised particularly 'The intelligence in arranging the turn of objects so that we have a sense

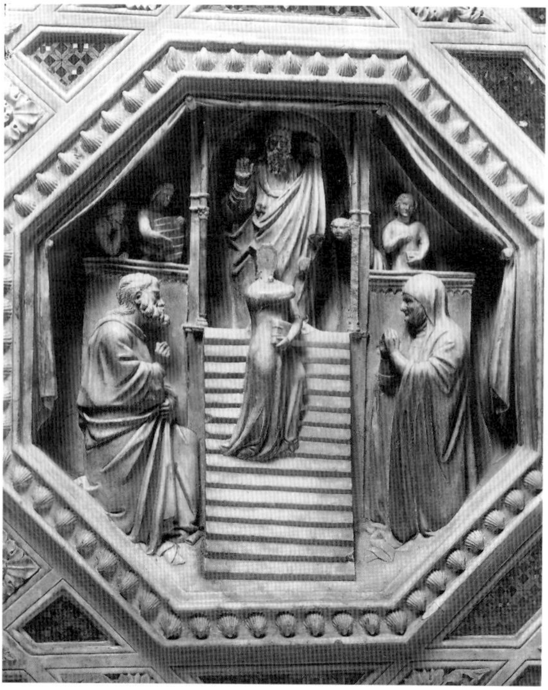

18 Andrea Orcagna, *Presentation of the Virgin in the Temple*, 1360. Marble and coloured inlay, approx. 60 × 60 cm. to outside moulding. Tabernacle, Or San Michele, Florence.

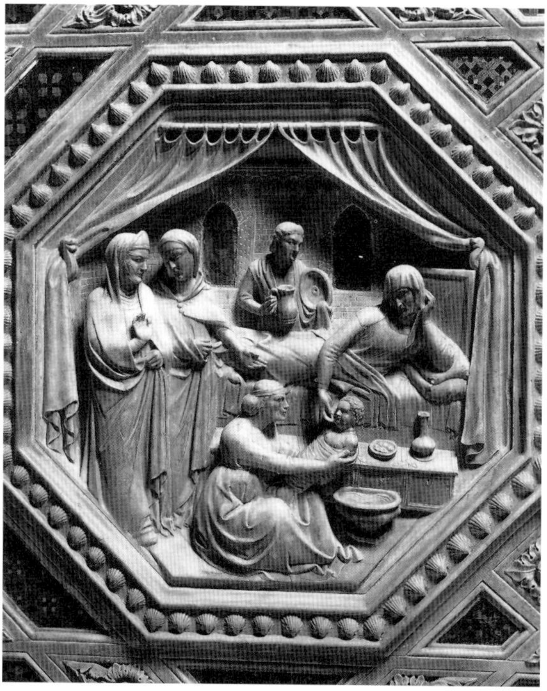

19 Andrea Orcagna, *Birth of the Virgin*, c.1360. Marble and coloured inlay, approx. 60 × 60 cm. to outside moulding. Tabernacle, Or San Michele, Florence.

of their volume.' ('L'intelligence qui a ménagé les tournans des objets, en laisse appercevoir tout la rondeur.') He further remarked that we should never see them as simply stuck onto a ground but with seemingly natural saliences fitting harmoniously with the group of which they form part. All this is said without explicit reference to the plane of relief or perspective.[6] One must surely read Dandré-Bardon here as articulating the practical studio wisdom that reached back to the Renaissance and still underpinned the theory of relief in the late nineteenth century.

There is then, thirdly, the sense of the surface plane as the boundary between the real space of the viewer and the fiction represented upon it. This third sense of the surface plane is invoked, for instance, where the contrast is made between reliefs in which the figures are seen as saliences in front of the supporting back-plate and where figures are seen as lying behind the imagined fourth wall of a stage, an opening that reads as the interface of the real and fictive world, for instance in the reliefs of Orcagna (figs 18 and 19). Each of these notions, not necessarily well distinguished, is utilized by Donatello's commentators.

II

If we go back to the 1880s, we find that the relation between the medium of shallow relief and its subject was conceived in very negative terms: Guido Hauck in 1885 invoked Lessing's distinction between literature and the visual arts and asked how we could distinguish between what was distinctive about the possibility of relief sculpture as opposed to painting, and he answered that it was a matter of whether the illumination of forms came from within as in painting or from without as in sculpture. But he had no positive sense of what relief could achieve beyond maintaining the consistency of visual appearances. He saw Ghiberti's second Baptistry door, for instance, as failing to achieve coherence because the foreground figures seemed to break free from the plane behind, and even worse, to cast shadows upon it (fig. 20). The relief sculptor, he insisted, needed not only to observe the principles of perspectival foreshortening but to control the saliences so as to make the shadows correspond to those that would fall on sculpture in the round; from a photograph, he says, we should not be able to distinguish them. For Hauck, we might say, the plane of the surface was invoked in the service of verisimilitude.

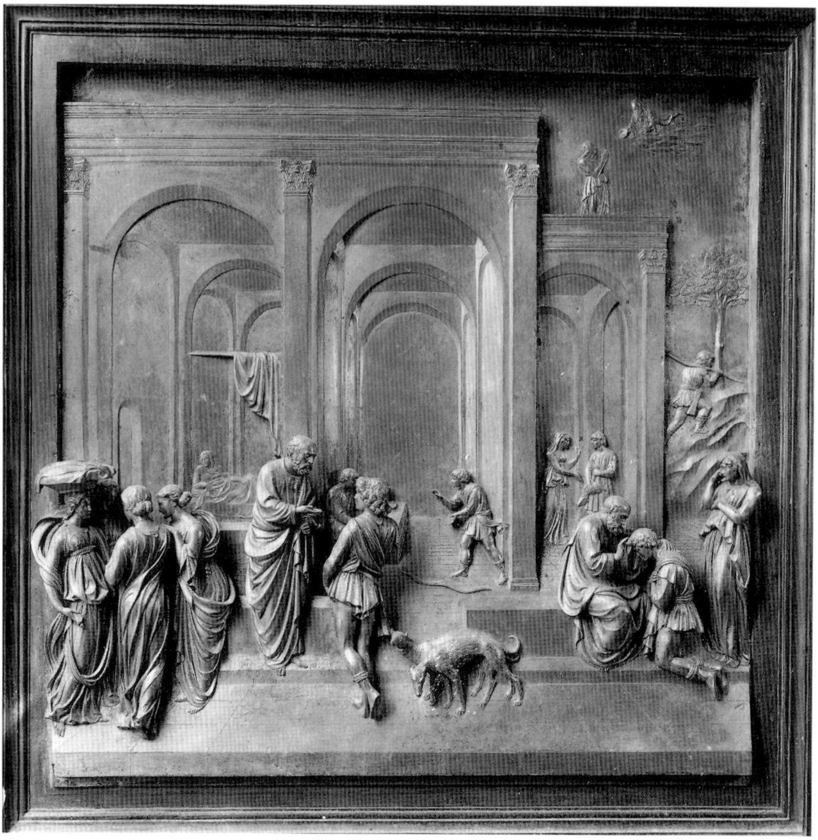

20 Lorenzo Ghiberti, *Jacob and Esau*, *c.*1440. Gilt bronze, 79 × 79 cm. Bronze door, Baptistry, Florence.

Subsequently and under the influence of the sculptor Adolf Hildebrand's *Das Problem der Form in der bildenden Kunst* (1893), the negative concern for avoiding conflict between the actual depth and the depicted depth became the positive demand for consonance, where the viewer was aware of the reciprocal adjustment between configurations in the surface plane and the spatial determinations of the subject; it ceased to be a matter merely of avoiding disruption – of maintaining verisimilitude in foreshortening and shadow – and became a matter of making the work available to a particular mode of attention, a mode that he extended from the possibilities of relief to painting and to sculpture in the round. His ideas were carried into the discussion of

Donatello, albeit tentatively, by Frida Schottmüller in 1904; she saw Donatello as failing to fulfil this ideal with any consistency, and was critical of the relief beneath the statue of St George on the façade of Or San Michele and the *Feast of Herod* in Siena (figs 21 and 28), along with Ghiberti's reliefs, of which she said that the foreground figures float free without any spatial coherence.[7] It was Hans Kauffmann in 1935 who saw Donatello as comprehensively fulfilling the Hildebrandian ideal. He wrote of the St George relief:

> the image is shown in the marble with that complete visibility of all parts . . . the carving opens the plastic form to the frontal plane, the stone being excavated in layers rather than penetrated in depth . . . the same formal order underlies the statue and the relief.[8]

And of the statue itself:

> Despite the spatial gaps which separate the parts from each other and require us to imagine them together [*hindurchzugreifen*], the frontal aspect is enclosed in a closely bound coherence in the plane [*Flächenzusammenhang*]. One form rests against another without intervening spaces, no breaks disrupt the surface . . . All forms are extended in the plane and treated as in a relief, the trunk is more extended than rounded, and the left lower arm as if flattened so that we are hardly aware of planes receding inwards. No parts protrude into depth or outward beyond the coherence of the plane.[9]

In the same spirit he describes the bronze relief of the *Feast of Herod* as opening up, through its use of perspective, a series of levels parallel to the front of the relief, and in the figures of the foreground scene 'the arm leaves no gap in relation to the body and each figure passes by gradation into the next . . . With each new step in depth the relations running from side to side are freshly realized'.[10]

In 1975, forty years after Kauffmann, Artur Rosenauer discussed the Donatello relief in similar terms. 'The combination, the com-position [*Kom-positzion*] of individual elements is only possible on the presupposition of a viewer who, through the act of seeing, makes the combination possible . . . The possibility of gathering together the individual elements from the sculptural ensemble into the plane is Donatello's original achievement'.[11] But what sense of the plane was involved?

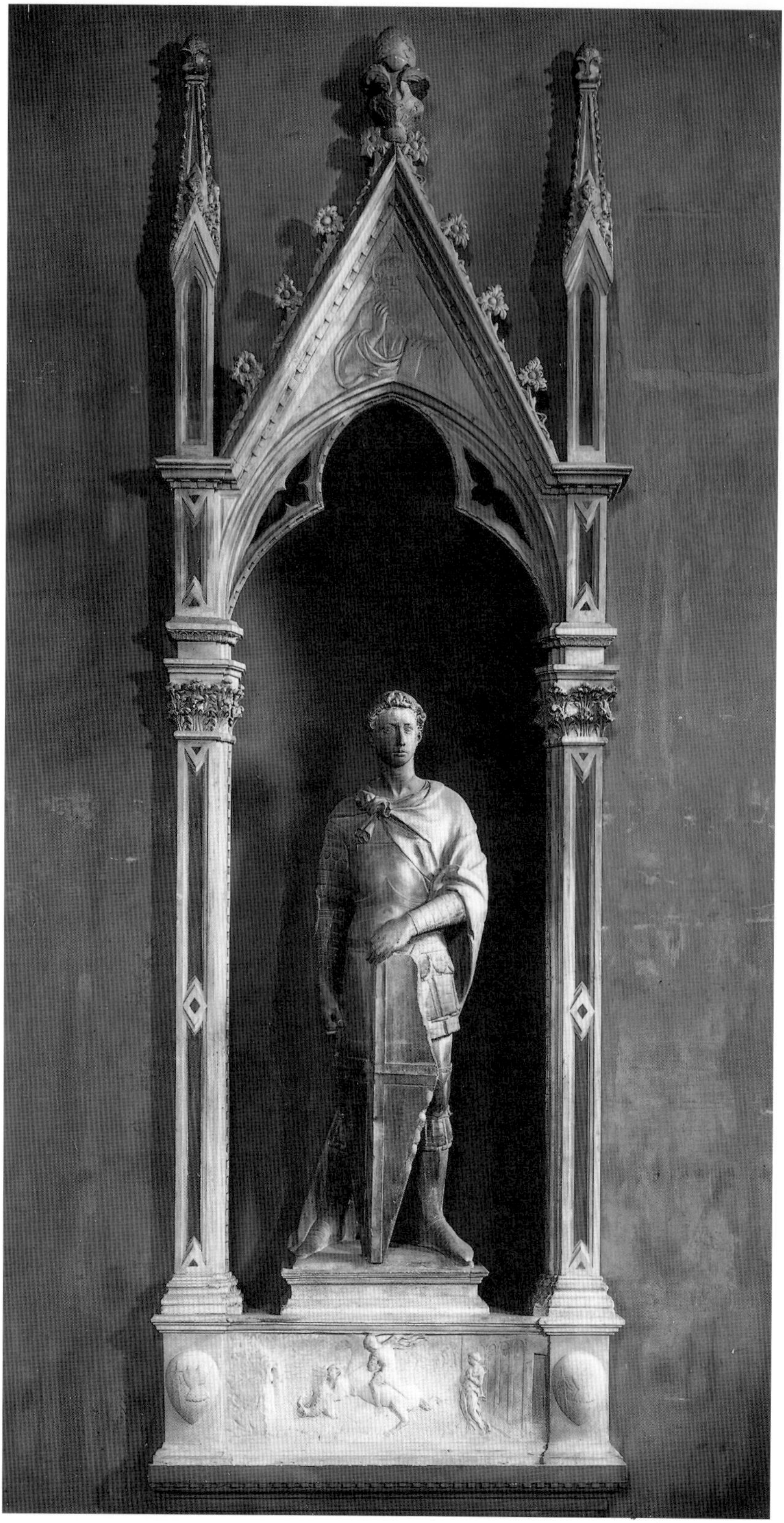

The pursuit of such coherence was recognized as problematic in the case of the *Cavalcanti Annunciation* (figs 22 and 23), central to both of Rosenauer's studies of Donatello. In this relief there is, in Rosenauer's terms, a conflict between two spatial systems, the real and the fictive, and it becomes acute in the juxtaposition of the deeply carved monumental figures and the foreshortened chair set flush with the closed door at the back. Rosenauer, in order to resolve the problem of this hiatus, insists on the dominance of the viewer's orthogonal relation to the scene; this means that the viewer adjusts his attention to see the subject as if in a consistent projection and so see it pictorially. (In his later account he talks of a fertile tension between real and illusory space. In each interpretation Rosenauer finds the unity of a 'view' transcending the hiatus between the foreshortened chair and the rounded figures.[12])

III

The *Cavalcanti Annunciation* was indeed a good test case for the kind of coherence sought by Rosenauer and exponents of the previous tradition of criticism. As we observe the relation of the two figures, the reciprocity of their movements, the way in which the angle of the head of Gabriel tilts back, away from the viewer in contrast to that of the Virgin, we are made acutely aware of the space in which they are set: the actual space is activated for us. (This retrieval of the actual space is comparable with the smaller scale use in the *Annunciation* by Ghiberti.) In imagining the two figures as responding to each other, we *use* the space rather than take it for granted, and there is no imagining that unifies or homogenizes the space of the figures and the effect of the foreshortened chair. To see the work in this way seems strained and reductive, for the readjustments required of the viewer form an ineliminable part of the work.[13]

Such destabilization of relations between the medium and the subject is not just a matter of the very deep carving of the *Cavalcanti Annunciation* but a persistent feature of Donatello's reliefs: for instance, in the *Dead Christ Tended by Angels* (fig. 25) the body of Christ seems constituted by the undulation of the marble, touched by one angel from in front while the other takes the weight of his head from behind: as both angels stand on the frame no consistent spatial resolution presents itself. And beyond that, the material continuity of the marble, from the frame to the

21 Donatello, *St George Tabernacle*. Or San Michele, Museo Nazionale, Florence.

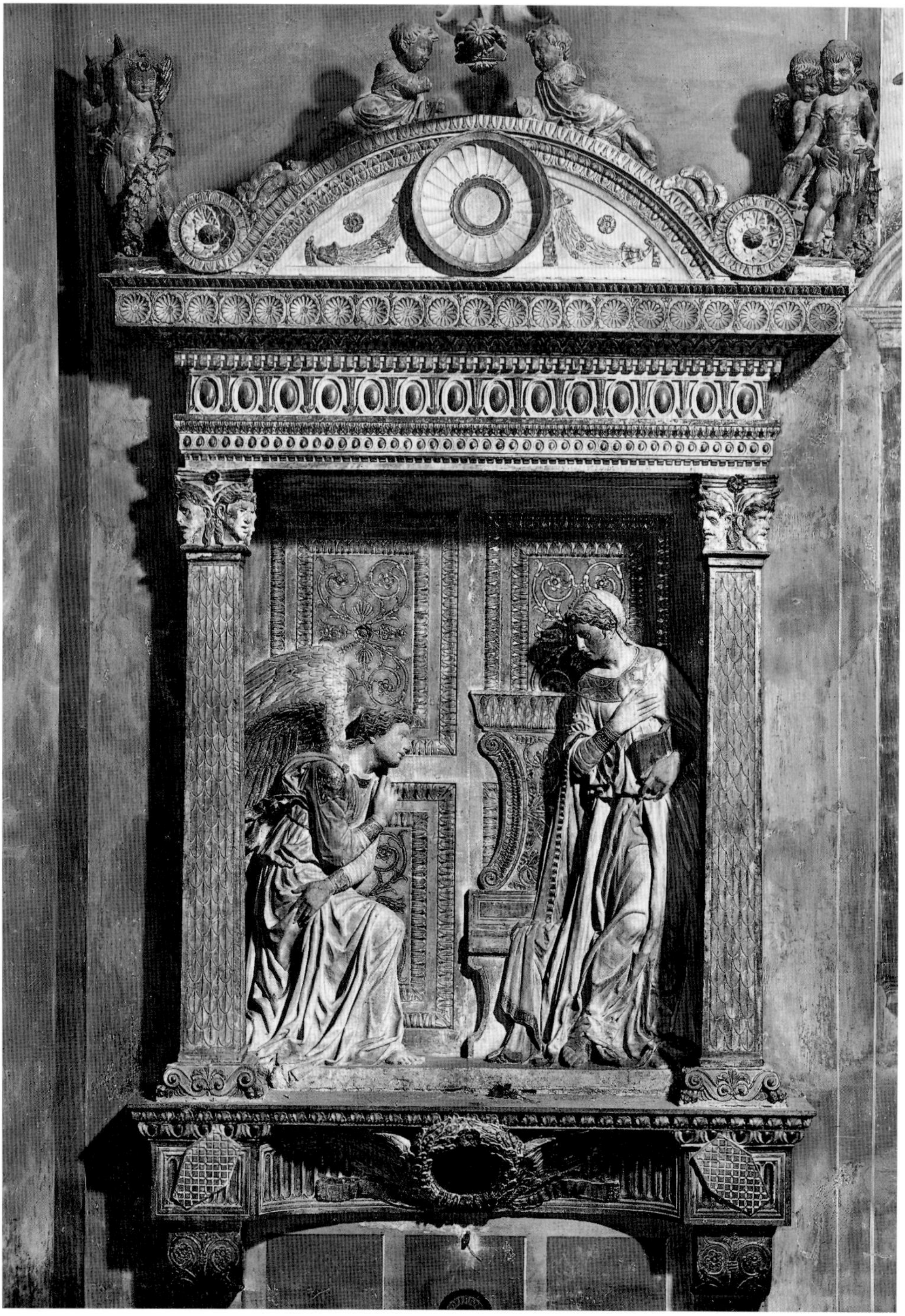

22 (*above*) and 23 (*facing page*) Donatello, *Cavalcanti Annunciation*, *c.*1433. Limestone, gilt and polychromy, 420 × 248 cm. (base). S. Croce, Florence.

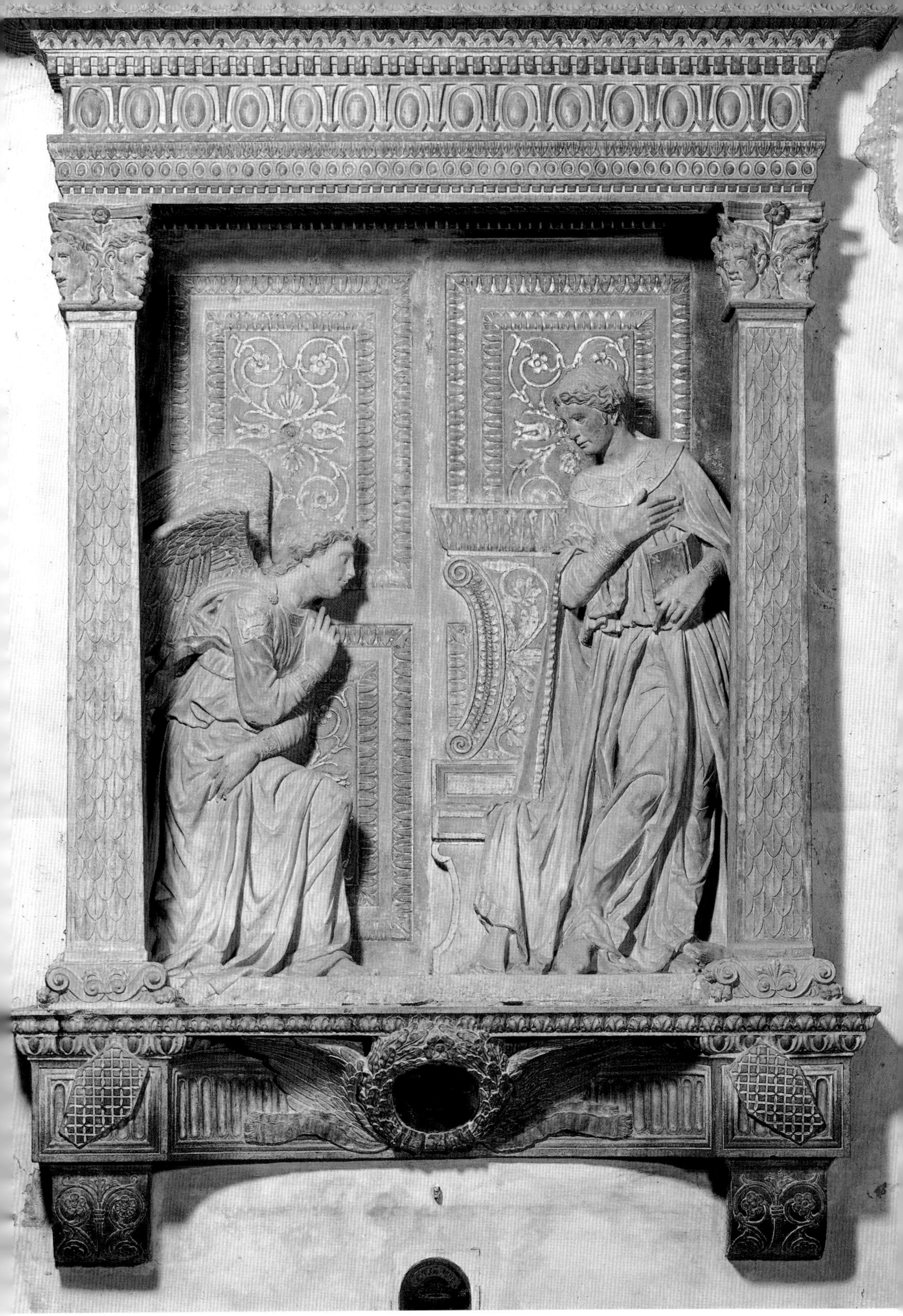

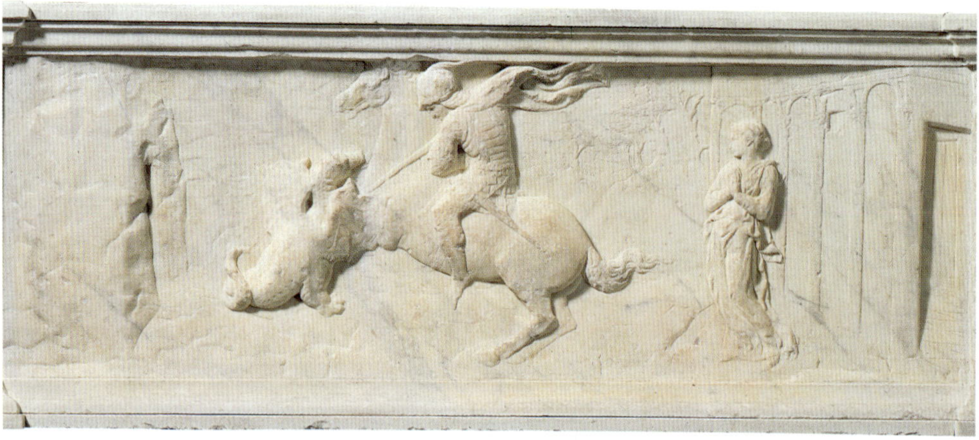

24 Donatello, *St George and the Dragon*, 1417. Marble, 39 × 120 cm. St George niche, Or San Michele, Museo Nazionale, Florence.

25 Donatello, *Dead Christ Tended by Angels*, c.1440. Marble, 80.6 × 114.3 cm. Victoria and Albert Museum, London.

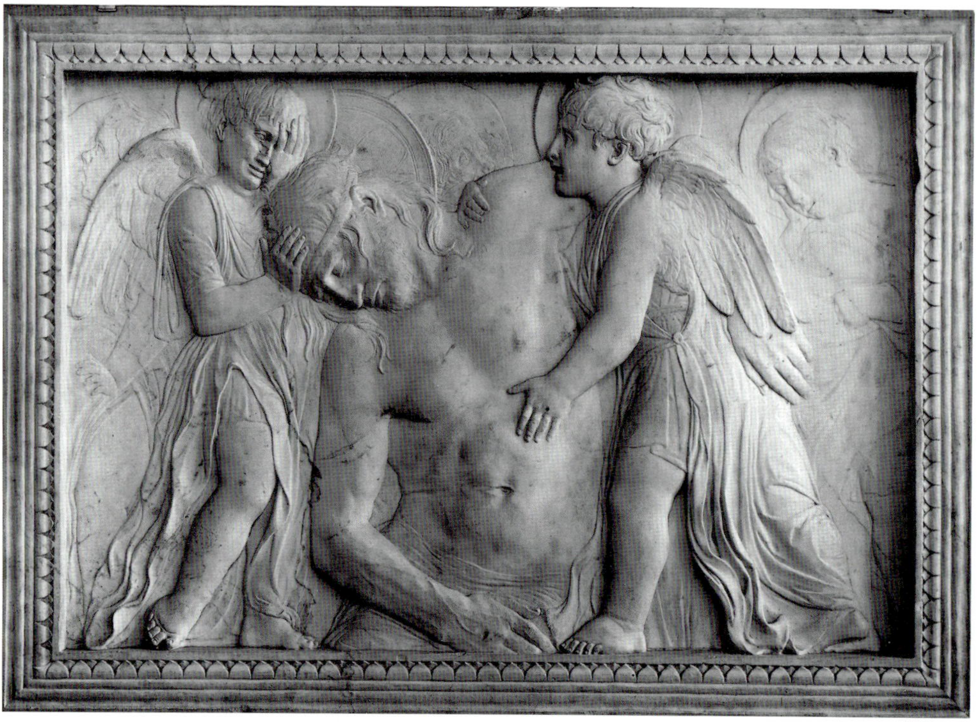

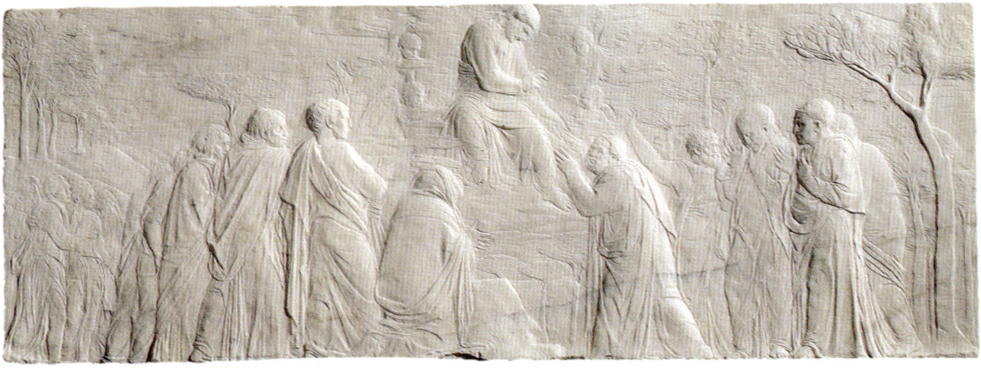

26 Donatello, *Donation of the Keys and Ascension of Christ*, *c.*1435. Marble, 40.6 × 114 cm. Victoria and Albert Museum, London.

figures and one figure to another is in tension with our imagining the discontinuities implied by touching and holding; but in their tension continuity and contiguity give focus to each other.[14]

In the relief from Or San Michele, *St George and the Dragon* (fig. 24), the inconsistencies in the use of the surface are of a different kind. In the centre the horse, rider and dragon form one closely interlocked group: they do not simply stand on the earth beneath their feet but press against the background so that ground and background cannot be disambiguated. (Schottmüller said the ground reared up – which she thought a failure – but surely she was attending to how the relief looked and felt. In contrast, Kauffmann wrote, 'the dominant character is the interweaving of all forms . . . In the continuity of planes one leads into another . . .', ignoring the tension in the use of the ground; while Rosenauer made the overall sense of illusion dominant.) What is missing from these later accounts is some sense of variability and flexibility in the use of relief, the features at one moment embossed against the dominant plane of the surface, then the plane of the surface becoming de-emphasised in the line of trees that threads across the relief intimating extensive space, finally our sense of the surface is reasserted on the right where undercutting excavates an interior space running behind the architectural façade. If we attempt to make the relief consistent or harmonious we lose this elasticity.

The notion of a shifting relation between subject and surface is peculiarly pertinent in the most optic of all the shallow reliefs,

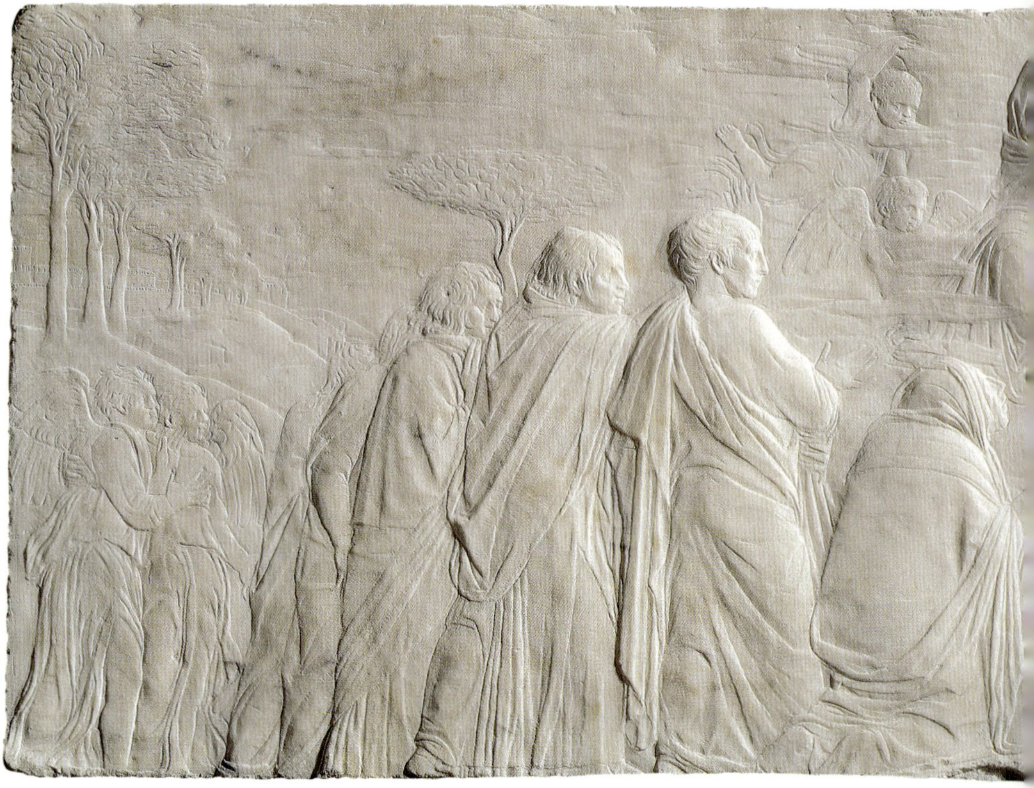

27 Donatello, *Donation of the Keys and Ascension of Christ*, *c.*1435. Marble, 40.6 × 114 cm. Victoria and Albert Museum, London.

the *Donation of the Keys* (figs 26 and 27). Here the ground plane slopes away below the bottom edge of the relief. The generally remarked sense of enveloping atmosphere may lead us to conceive ourselves as looking through the surface to the distance.[15] There are many details that enforce this, like the juxtaposition of distant trees and foreground plants. But there are countervailing factors: we cannot take the surface for granted, for where it swells forward it substantiates the figures that coincide with it and they in turn enhance the sense of the marble's depth; that illusory degree of salience passes uninterrupted into the sense of space beyond the surface – for instance, through the disciple further back who both echoes the foreground figures and is partially occluded by a tree. Our awareness is in constant transition between the near and the far, the surface both substantiating the figures and transparent to

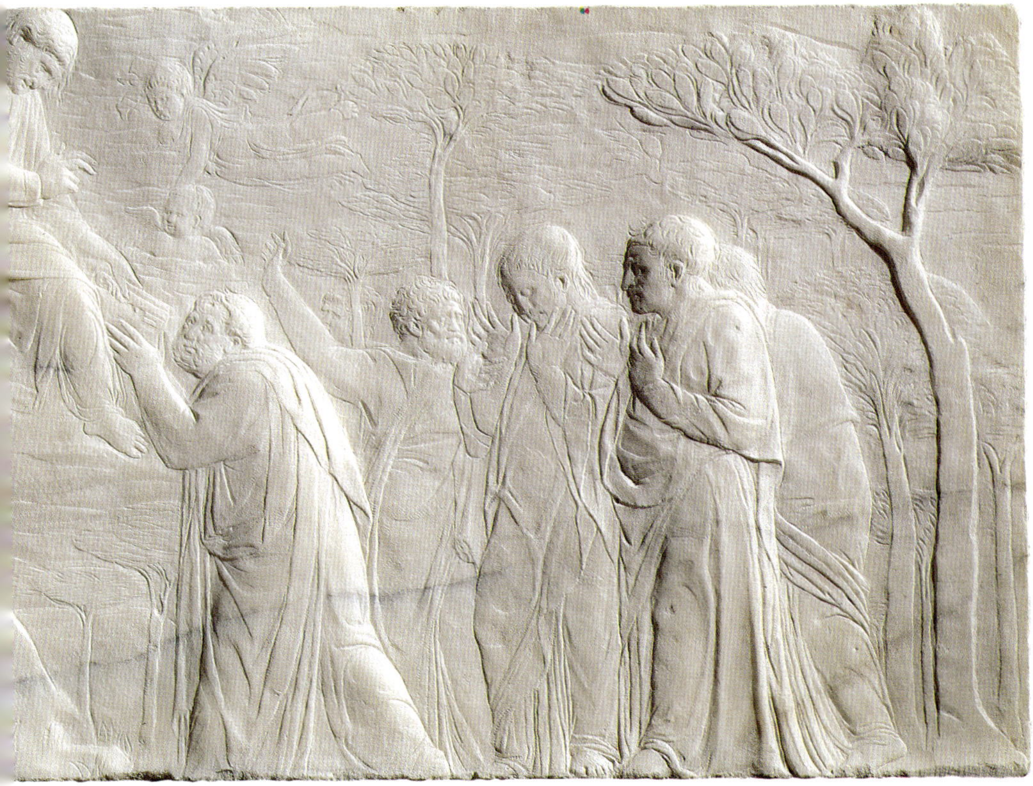

the space behind. There is another detail that should warn us against pursuit of a summating consistency, the complication in the relation of Christ and Peter; for Christ marginally overlaps Peter, and Peter himself does not look up at Christ but away from him and is therefore not quite absorbed consistently into the scene as a whole; his looking out has to be transformed by us into his looking up at Christ.

In the Siena *Feast of Herod* (fig. 28) we are invited to reflect on our perception in a different way – and one that anticipates later moves by Donatello. The events are set within an architectural scaffolding which prompts the sense of intersecting vistas: our vista with its view is only one of many possibilities; musicians in the next intersection have their backs to us and the main scene; and beyond that the episode of St John the Baptist's head being

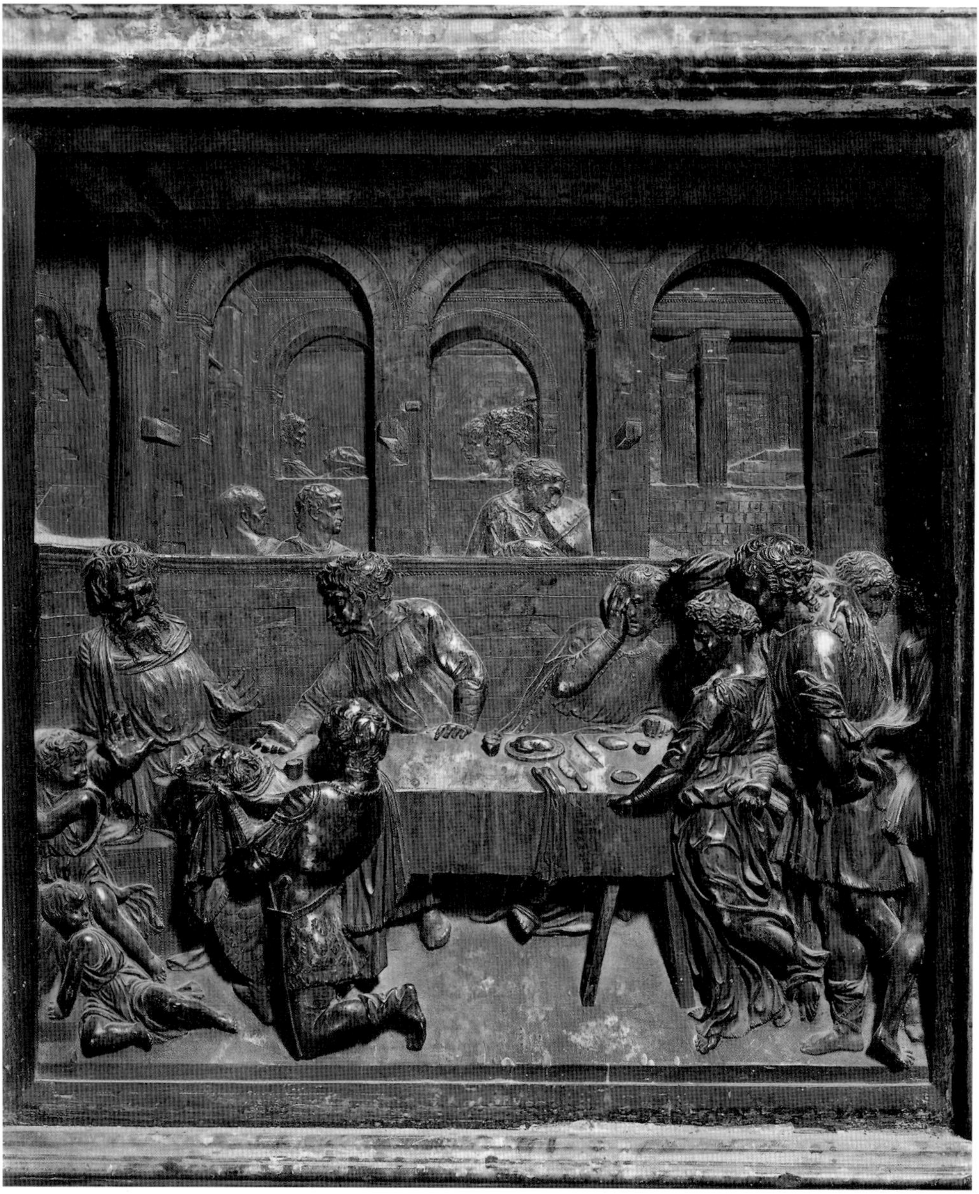

28 Donatello, *Feast of Herod*, 1427. Gilt bronze, 60 × 60 cm. Baptistry font, Siena.

presented – presumably to Herodias – runs at right angles to our line of sight in contrast with the presentation to Herod. What this suggests is the introduction of the *invisible* procedure of the

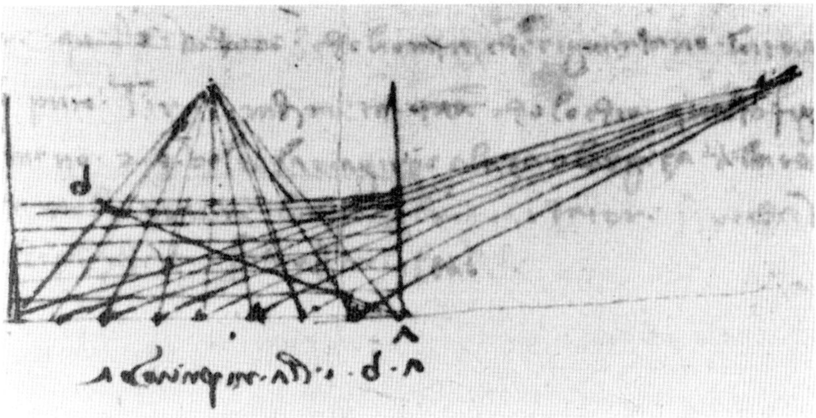

29 Perspective diagram by Leonardo. Manuscript. Bibliothèque de l'Institut de France, no. 2172, p. 41.

perspective construction into the manifest structure of the scene* (fig. 29).[16] The purpose of invoking the procedure is not to suggest that the perspective construction was a necessary condition for showing one episode frontally and the other in profile but rather that our sense of the perspective procedure gives an added energy to imagining the transition between viewing frontally and from the side.

In other early Florentine applications of the construction there are comparable dramatic uses beyond adjusting scale and profile in the cause of consistency. In Masaccio's *Tribute Money* (fig. 31) the action spirals out from Christ being accosted for the tribute money and his instruction to Peter. Having gone off into the the left background, Peter duly catches the fish with the coin and

* Alberti's construction itself involves two superimposed stages and two orientations to the depicted subject: first one draws a rectangle marking the limits of the picture surface through which the subject is conceived as being seen. In the simplest demonstration the subject is a squared pavement and the receding lines start at equal intervals along the rectangle's base line. In the second stage we cease to think of ourselves as looking through the surface but imagine a profile view of the relation between viewer, transparent picture surface and the pavement seen through that surface; we now re-use the equal intervals marked on the base line of the rectangle to represent the transverse lines of the pavement; we can use the same intervals on the base line twice over because we are representing squares. Where the lines from the viewing eye to the points on the base of the rectangle pass through a verticle that represents the surface (for which the side of the original rectangle might be re-used) we have the intervals for registering the transversals on the original surface.

30 Masaccio, *Trinity*, *c.*1427. Fresco, 667 × 317 cm. S. Maria Novella, Florence.

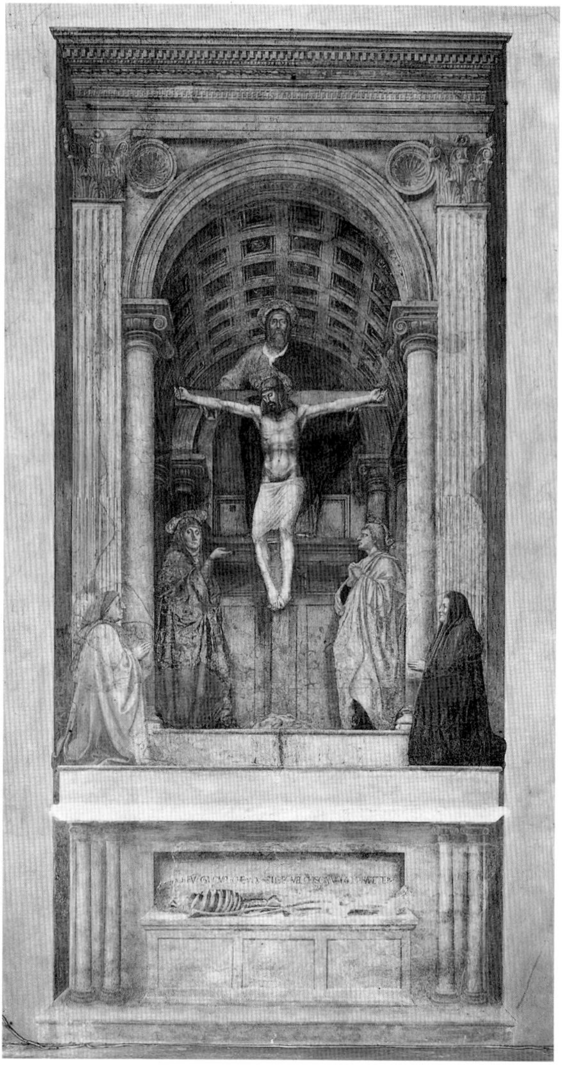

32 (*facing page*) Andrea del Castagno, *The Trinity Appearing to St Jerome*, *c.*1453. Fresco, 300 × 179 cm. Corboli Chapel, SS Annunciata, Florence.

31 (*below*) Masaccio, *Tribute Money*, *c.*1428. Fresco. Brancacci Chapel, S. Maria del Carmine, Florence.

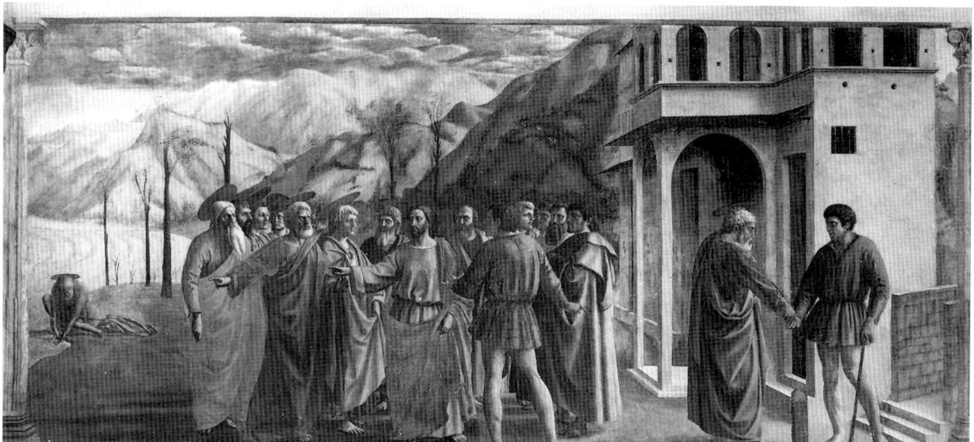

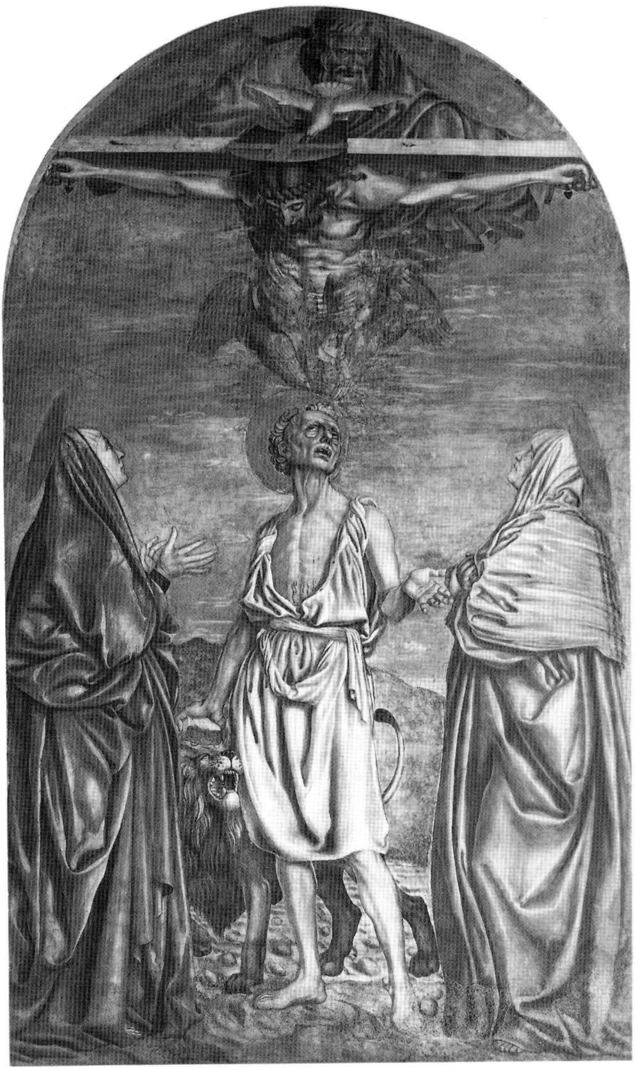

returns on the right where he hands it to the tax gatherer. Time conspires with space as they frame attention to each other's controlled continuity. In Masaccio's *Trinity* (fig. 30) the systematic sense of spatial consistency achieved by the architecture is disrupted by the scale of God the Father; Masaccio has found a new metaphor of transcendence, which is not a matter merely of scale but of an anomalous deviation from expectations set up by the system of receding orthogonals in the vault.

Andrea del Castagno took elasticity in the use of perspective much further in his small altarpiece of the *The Trinity Appearing to St Jerome* (fig. 32) in the Church of the Annunciata in Florence.

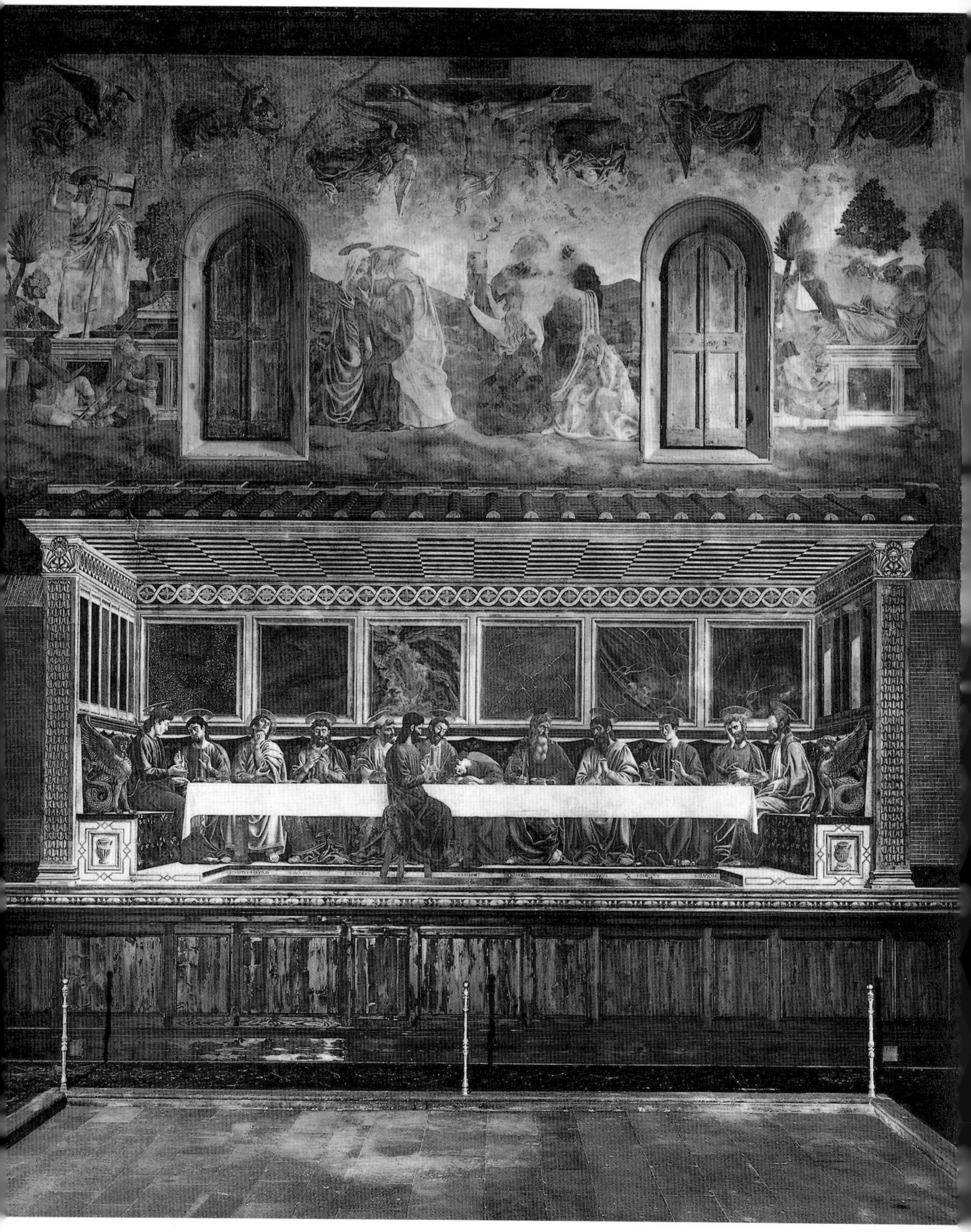

33 Andrea del Castagno, *Last Supper and Scenes of the Passion*, 1447–50. Fresco. S. Apollonia, Florence.

The represented oblique view of the Trinity is to be understood not as Jerome's view but our view of Jerome's view, the embedding of one perspective within another registering divine intervention. In his *Last Supper* (fig. 33) Castagno orchestrates the mystical presence of the event in the refectory by flickering patterns on the floor and ceiling, and by the *trompe-l'oeil* effect of the roof tiles. Here the perspectival co-ordination both enforces the continuity between the real and fictive space and turns it into a magical effect by optical devices which baffle the mind. The perspective construction yielded these kinds of reflective premium in the first fifty years of its application, before it became so internalized and malleable within compositional procedures as to be taken more or less for granted, except in ceiling painting.

IV

Other orientational implications of perspective came into play where Donatello modelled in stucco a series of relief roundels in the vault of the Old Sacristy in San Lorenzo (figs 34–8);[17] there are four apostles and four scenes from the life of St John the Evangelist. In the representation of the miracle of John raising his follower Drusiana from the dead the composition is highly centralized: Drusiana being the one figure in black against the white of the other figures and the terracotta of the architecture. The scene has intensive perspectival determinacy: a series of arches in the middle ground are continued in the side walls of the vast barrel-vaulted space and a flight of steps leads up to the platform on which the miracle is taking place; but, for us as viewers, the perspective is dissociated from our bodily situation. The image faces us only when we discount our position standing on the floor and ignore the context in which we see it. When, in contrast, Donatello represents John's ascent to heaven our orientation looking up and our sense of the verticality of the buildings are drawn into our sense of the subject: our looking up is recuperated by the scene represented as if seen from below. (This is enforced by the light from the small windows below when it catches the foreground platform, enforcing the sense of its real salience while being part of the scene.) But there is yet another contrast between the scenes in the life of St John: the roundel of *St John on Patmos* would seem to imply we are looking down on John as he looks up

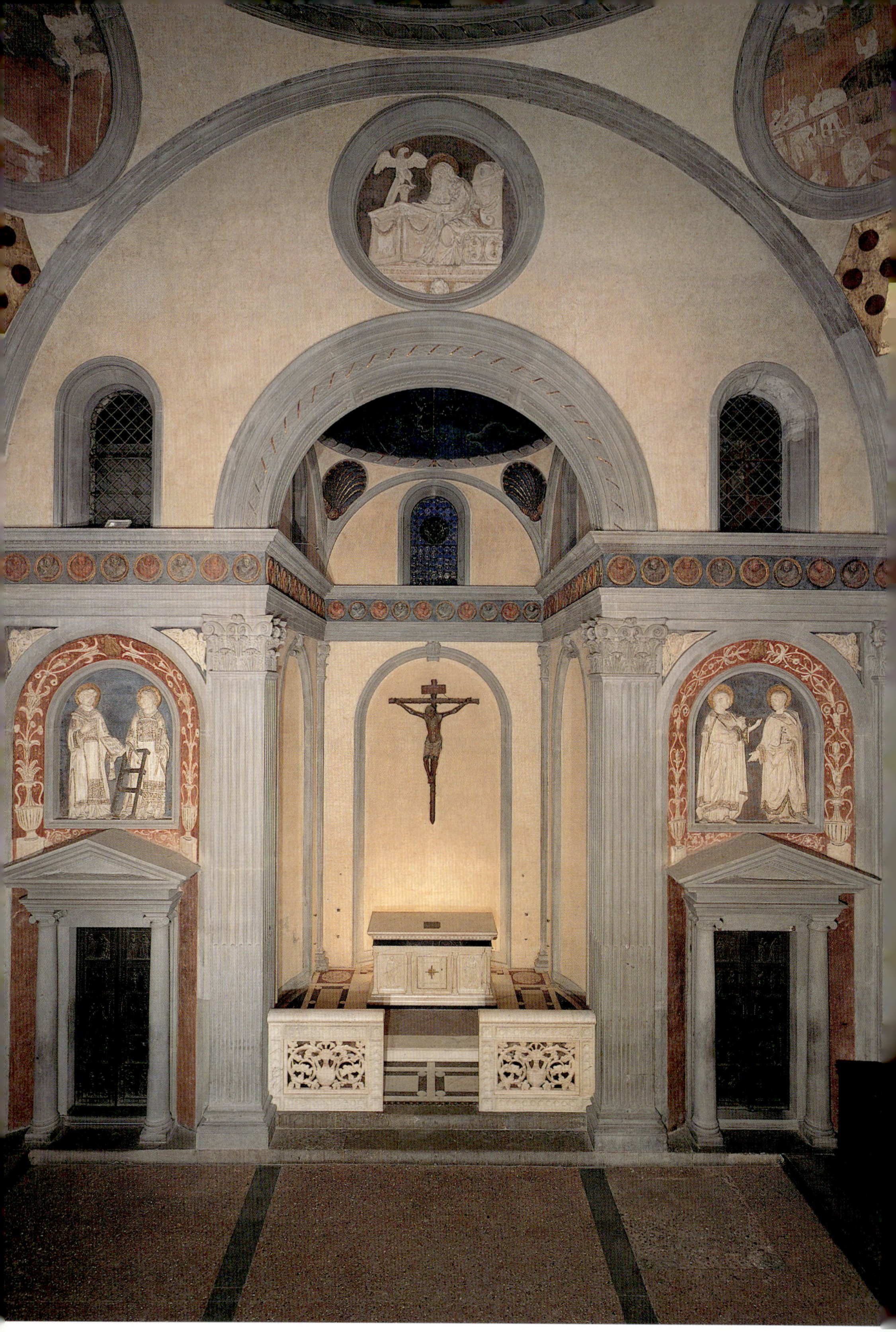

at Christ and the other figures of his vision. Whereas in the representation of the four apostles our orientation is absorbed consistently, each being represented as seen from below, our orientation in the scenes of the life of John is used with peculiar variability around the vault.

V

At the end of his life Donatello was engaged in producing a major bronze monument for Cosimo de' Medici, again in San Lorenzo, now forming two symmetrically placed pulpits in the nave (figs 39–43).[18] Despite extreme uncertainties about the original scheme of which they were part, and the extent of the work by assistants, certain things are clear. Most importantly it was a funerary monument and the sarcophagus form suggests that the Resurrection pulpit was conceived as a tomb altar or wall tomb. We must imagine ourselves as in a space that was, like the Old and New Sacristies, also a mausoleum. The form of the bronze sarcophagus provides a comprehensive image within which individual scenes are held. At one end we look through the foreground columns into the scene of the Maries looking into the empty tomb. We the viewers are placed firmly outside the space of the action. On the Resurrection face of the sarcophagus – with Christ in Limbo, Resurrection and Asension – actuality and fiction are re-related, for the dominant plane is now behind the scene that opens out toward us, suspending the boundary between the viewer's and protagonist's world, an effect enforced by its illusionistic buttresses and the absence of a containing frame.

In the scene of Christ before Pilate and Herod (or Caiaphas) on the Crucifixion pulpit, the instability of these factors, the sense of perspective, the real fictive boundary and adjustment of the viewer's orientation are peculiarly evident: the vaulted spaces offer orientations to left and right but the viewer, in contrast to his relation to the comparable vaulted scene in Padua (fig. 44), is never frontally or symmetrically orientated to them; the resulting sense of going back and forth confirms and is confirmed by the movement of Christ sent back and forth from Pilate to Herod. Not only is the sense of our orientation played upon, so is the real fictive border; the base of the relief is made to function as a barrier below which figures disappear while others look out into our

34 Old Sacristy, San Lorenzo, Florence.

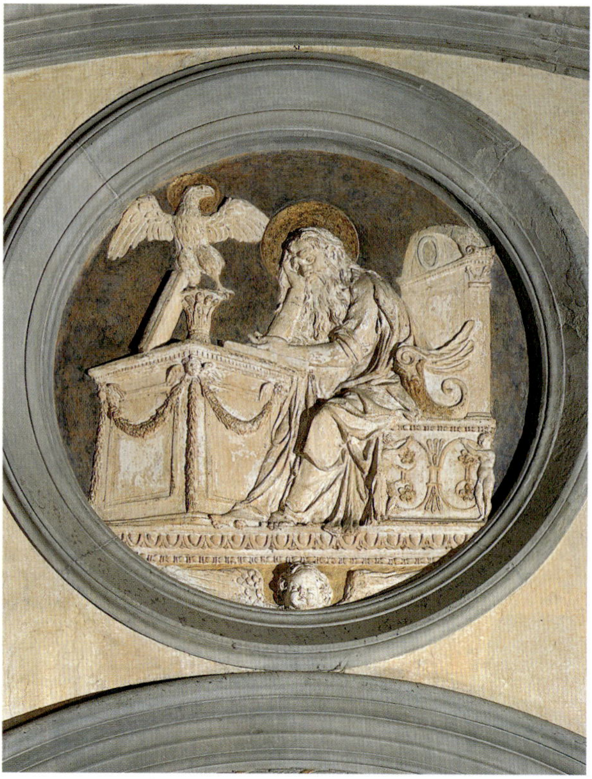

35 Donatello, *St John the Evangelist*, *c*.1435. Stucco with pigmentation, internal diameter 215 cm. San Lorenzo, Florence.

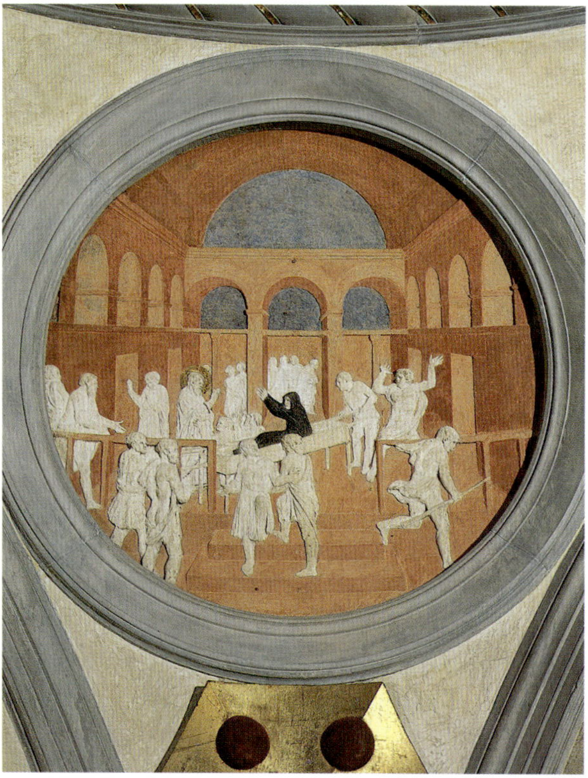

36 Donatello, *Raising of Drusiana*, *c*.1435. Stucco with pigmentation, internal diameter 215 cm. San Lorenzo, Florence.

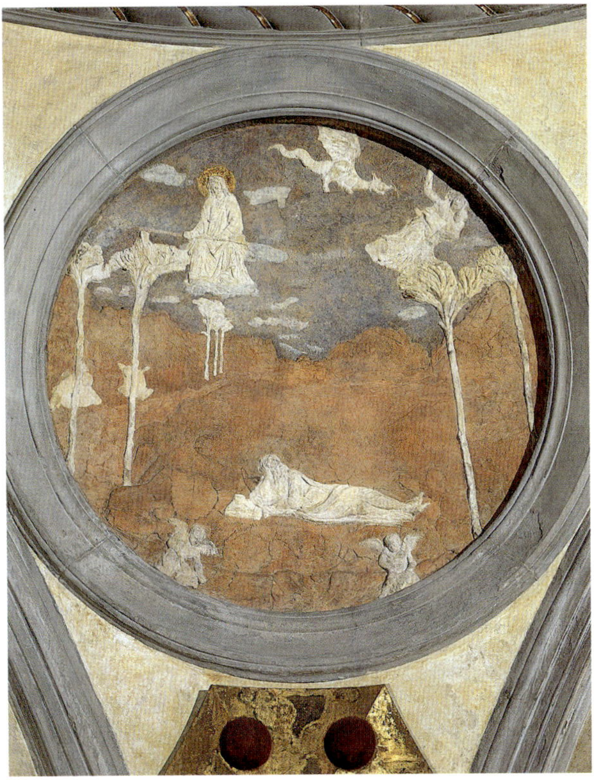

37 Donatello, *St John on Patmos*, *c.*1435. Stucco with pigmentation, internal diameter 215 cm. San Lorenzo, Florence.

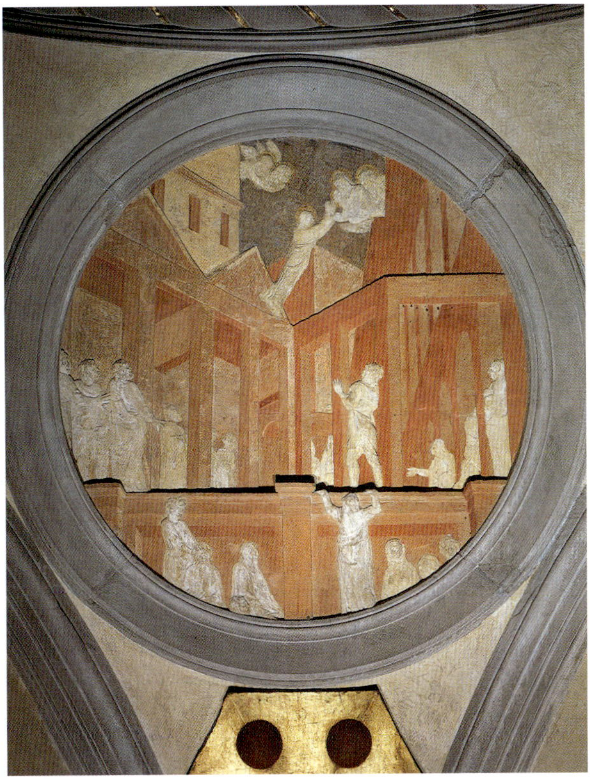

38 Donatello, *Ascension of St John to Heaven*, *c.*1435. Stucco with pigmentation, internal diameter 215 cm. San Lorenzo, Florence.

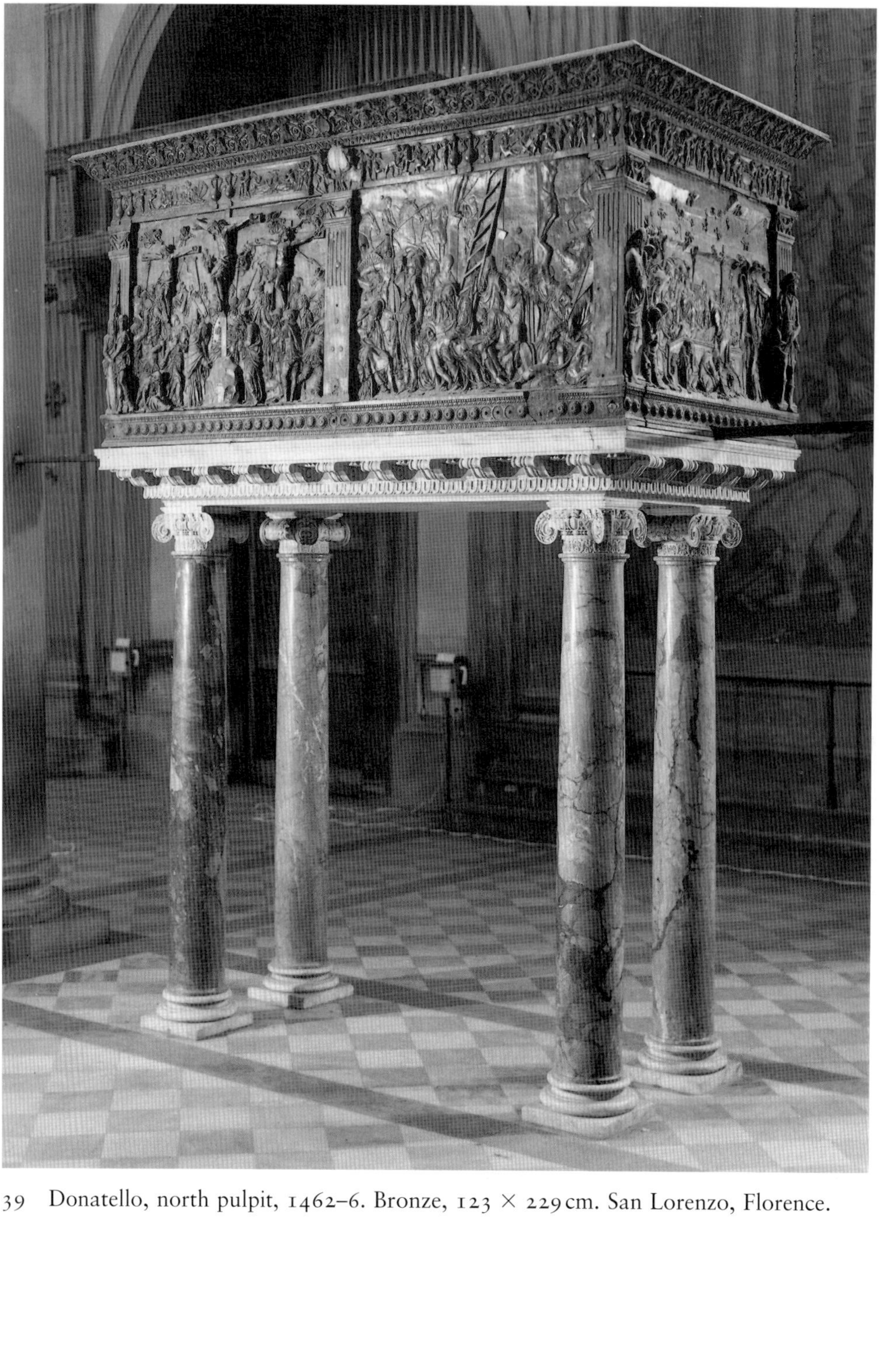

39 Donatello, north pulpit, 1462–6. Bronze, 123 × 229 cm. San Lorenzo, Florence.

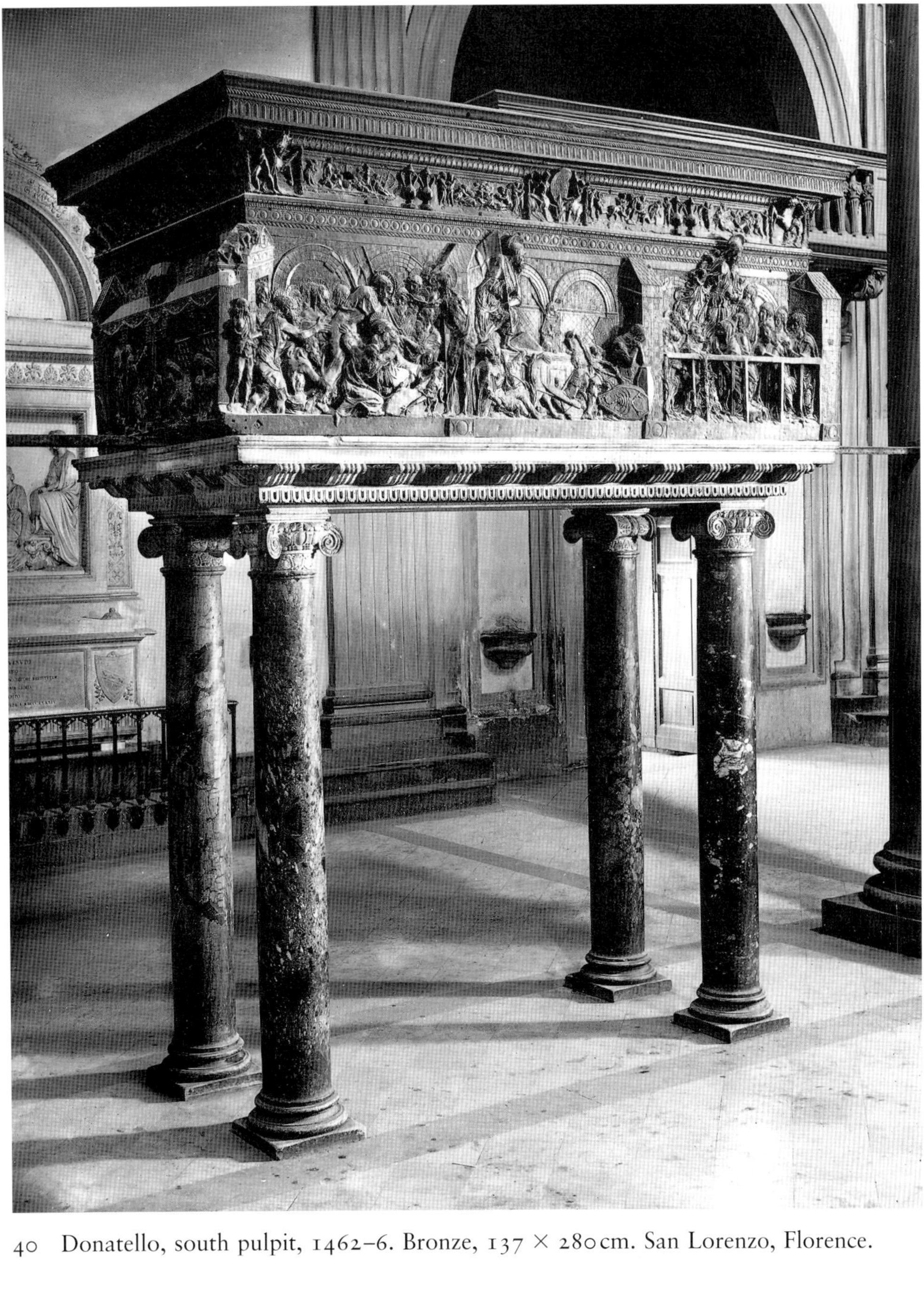

40 Donatello, south pulpit, 1462–6. Bronze, 137 × 280 cm. San Lorenzo, Florence.

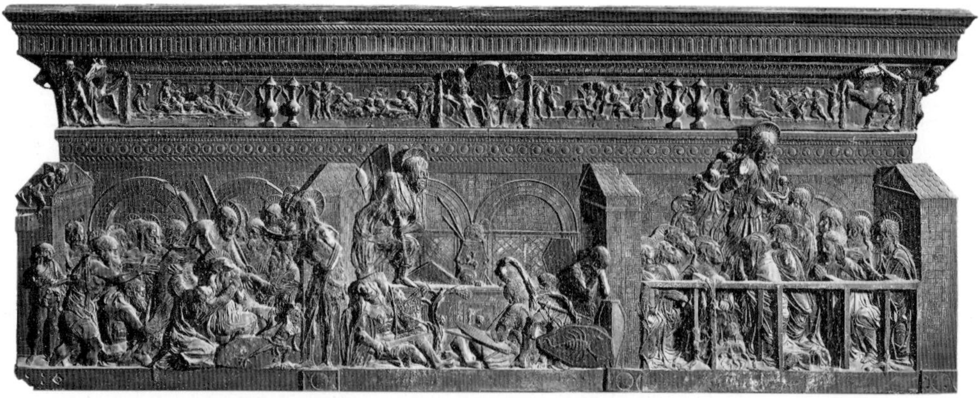

41 Donatello, *Christ in Limbo, Resurrection and Ascension*, 1462–6. Bronze. South pulpit, San Lorenzo, Florence.

42 Donatello, *Maries at the Tomb*. South pulpit, San Lorenzo, Florence.

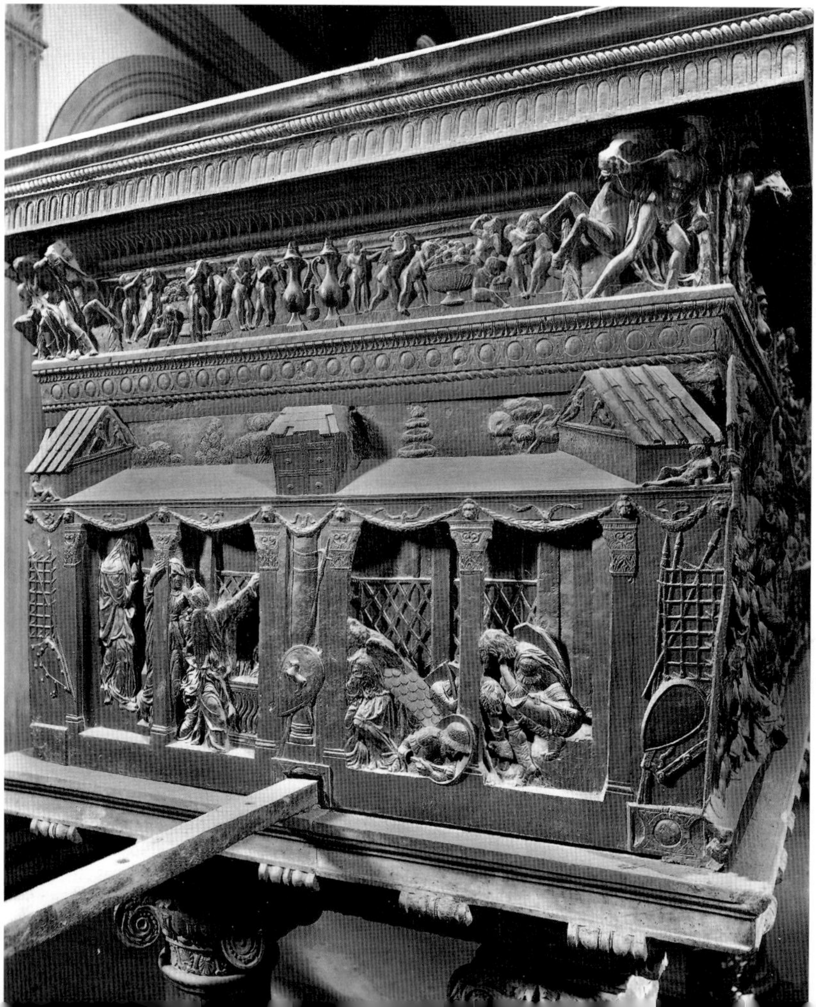

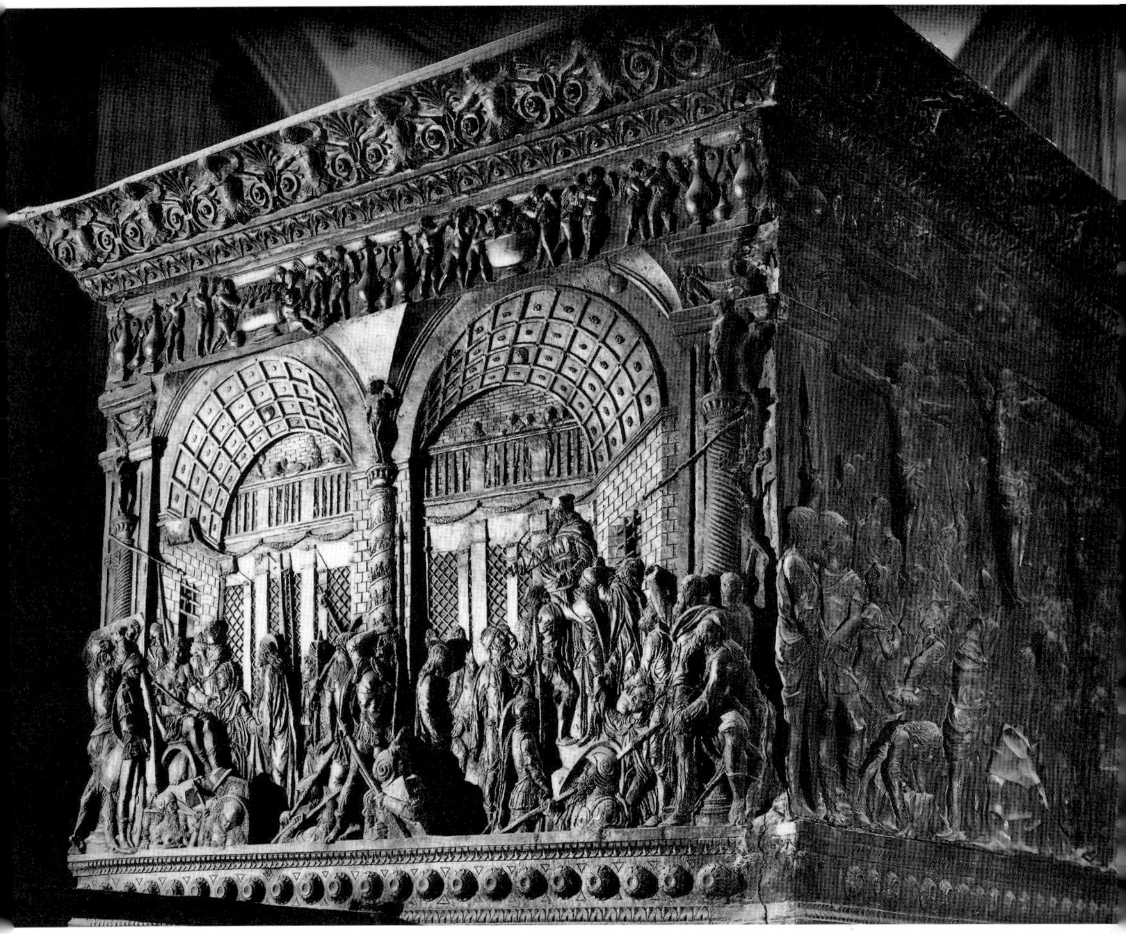

43 Donatello, *Christ before Pilate and Caiaphas (or Herod)*. North pulpit, San Lorenzo, Florence.

space or seem in danger of falling off. The transition between real and fictive space becomes uncertain not just in these devices but throughout the relief, in the treatment of the barrel vaults but most acutely in the treatment of the figure of Christ; in both scenes he is obscured by the undercutting of the figures in front of him so that in focusing on him, even with the slightest movement of the head, the shifting spatial relations take on, within the relief, a uniquely vivid actuality.

Some use of the dominant plane may still be seen in other scenes of the Crucifixion pulpit. Again we observe variations that

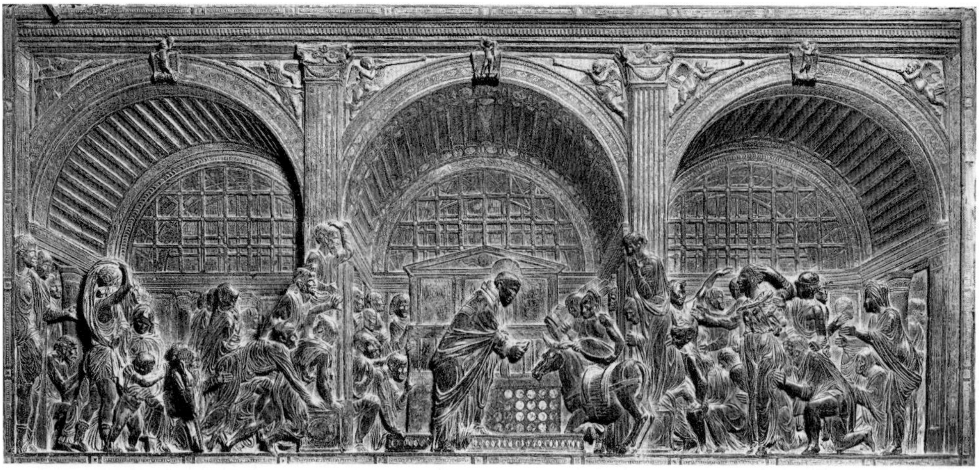

44 Donatello, *Miracle of the Mule*, *c.*1450. Gilt bronze, 57 × 123 cm. High Altar, S. Antonio, Padua.

establish different relations to the viewer: in the Crucifixion the scene is placed symmetrically, facing the viewer and in front of the dominant surface, in the Lamentation it is in profile and fuses with the surface, and in the Deposition the scene falls away behind it. If only the Deposition seems in any serious degree by the hand of Donatello, the overall shift of the use of the dominant plane is a Donatellesque thought. Here, too, what is being varied is how we imagine ourselves to be placed in relation to the scene; closer or more remote, included or excluded.

What runs through our engagement with the reliefs is the demand for flexibility. The coherence of the subject and the continuity of the material have multiple alignments to each other. There is no one mode of attention to the representation which is exhaustive, and this mobility is essential to how we relate to the subject. Whether it is the shift between the figures and the background chair of the *Cavalcanti Annunciation*, or the sense of foreground features being part of the furniture of the real world and also part of the fiction – as in the *Cantoria* (fig. 45) or the late pulpits – or the shift in orientation implied by the vaults in the scenes of Christ before Pilate and Herod, or the transitions between different uses of the marble surface in the *St George and the Dragon* and the *Donation*, we have always to revise and adjust our perceptual set.

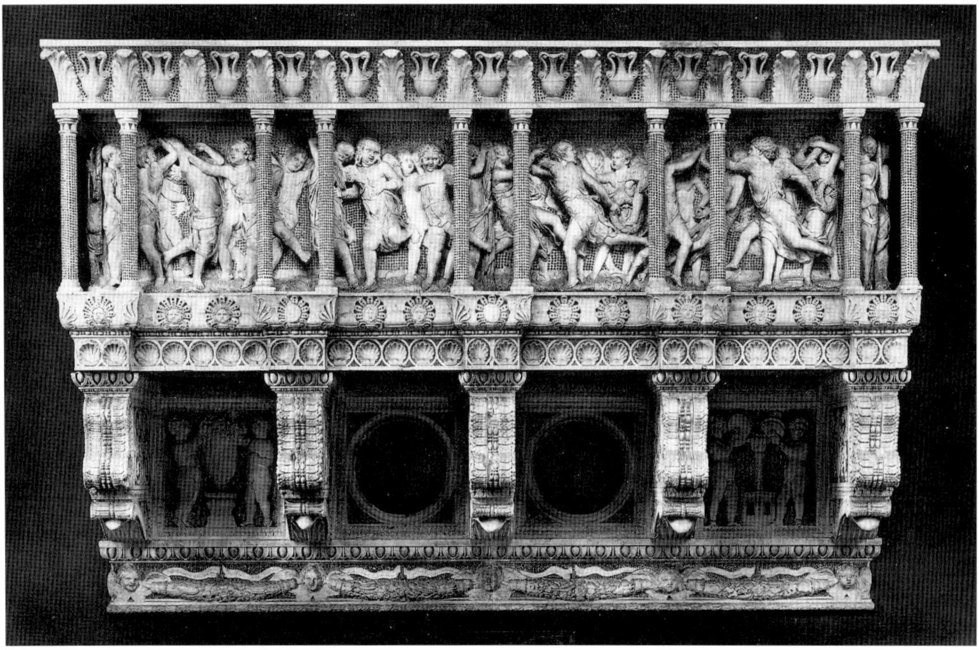

45 Donatello, *Cantoria*, 1439. Marble with gold and coloured mosaic inlay, 348 × 570 cm. Museo dell'Opera del Duomo, Florence.

We might regard Donatello reliefs as exemplary of depiction in its wide sense in that the cohesion of a work is never a single consonance between the material and the subject, leaving us without adjustments to make; there is never a single perceptual set or consummating consistency but always a crucial disequilibrium and the constant sense that the work may appear to us differently.

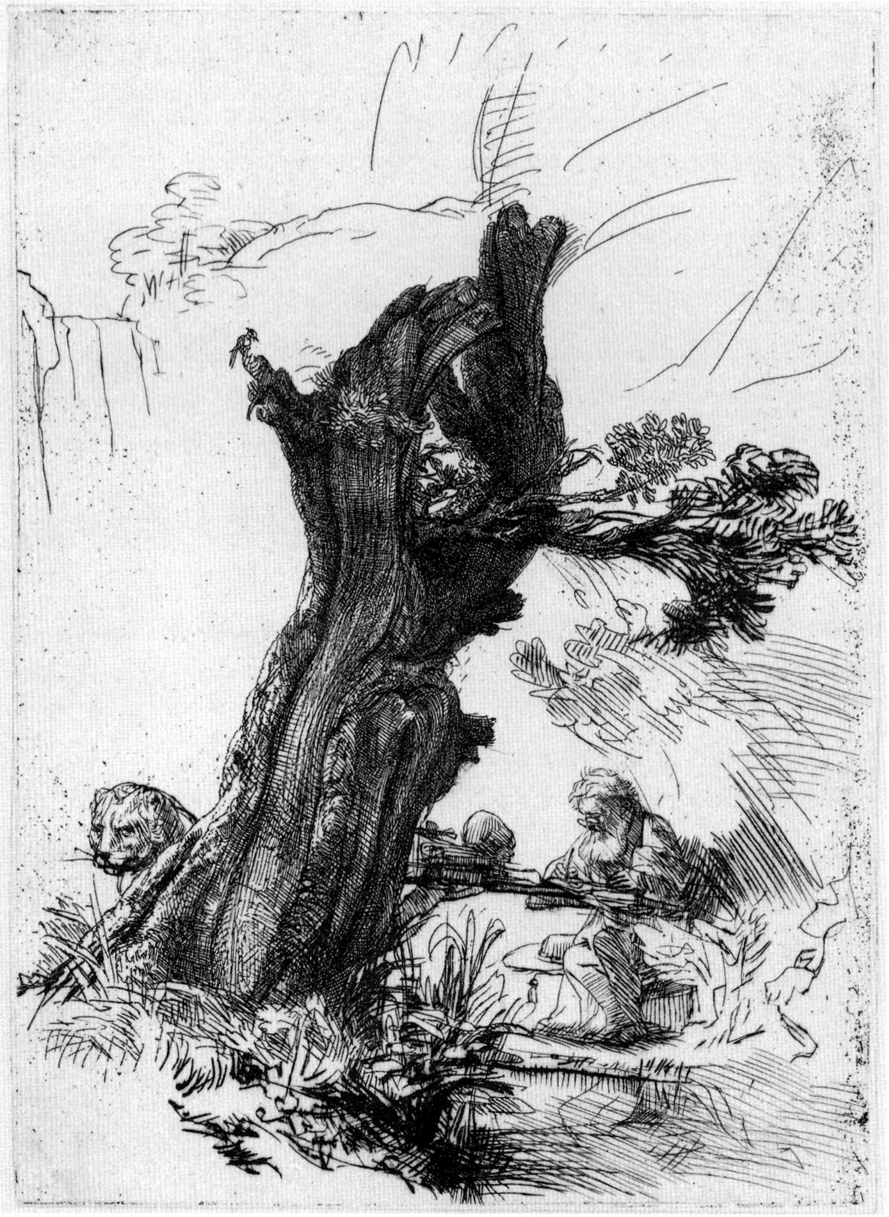

46 Rembrandt, *St Jerome beside a Pollarded Willow*, 1648. Etching, 17.9 × 13.2 cm. British Museum, London.

Chapter Three

Orientation in Rembrandt

I

WE ORIENT OURSELVES TO DEPICTIONS in two ways: to the surface and to the subject. Most of the time the two are left undistinguished. What will concern us in this chapter is where they are differentiated and they interact. This does not include anamorphosis where the image resolves for us only when the painting is seen at an oblique angle and the surface is lost to us, for this would not be a case of our orientation toward the surface and the subject represented on it being related to each other.

As a rule we think of pictures as presenting themselves to be seen perpendicularly to our line of sight; but even without anamorphosis this is not invariable, as we have seen in the case of Donatello's *Ascension of St John* (fig. 38), where depicting the subject as if seen from below and the fact that we look at it from below have a reciprocal aptness, our viewing position accommodated within our sense of the fiction. There is a related effect in Giotto's scene of *St Francis Appearing to the Brethren at Arles* in the Bardi Chapel in Santa Croce, Florence (figs 47 and 48). Looking at the wall from outside the narrow chapel we make the broad and unreflective assumption that the cloister represented is symmetrical and that it is symmetrically represented on the wall surface. But as we attend to it more closely there are arresting visual cadences: the white foreground colonettes coincide with the uprights of the arches behind and those coincidences appear to occur through the accident of an oblique view of the symmetrical cloister – of our own view.[1]

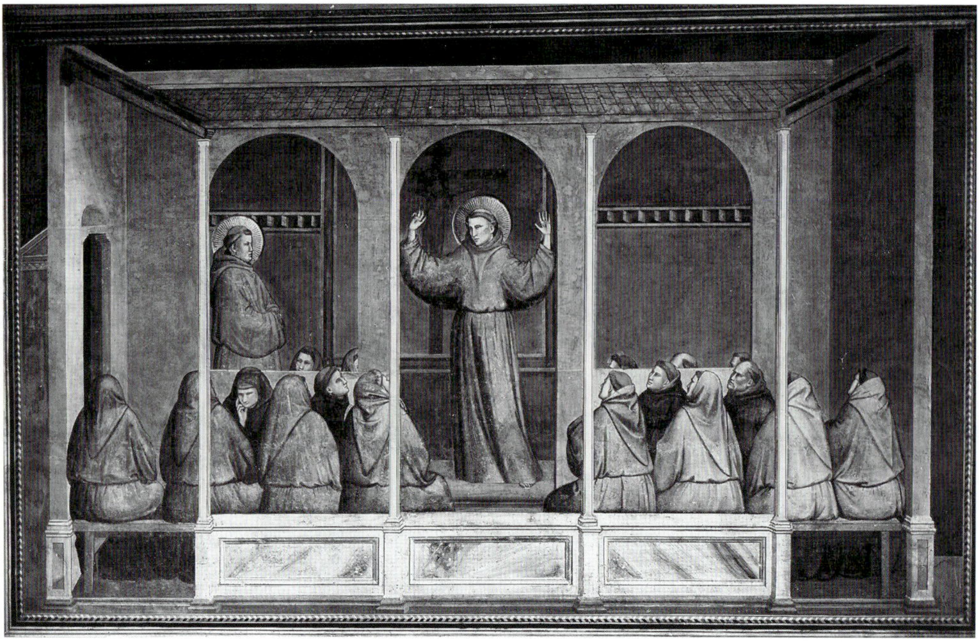

47 Giotto, *St Francis Appearing to the Brethren at Arles*, 1315–20. Bardi Chapel, S. Croce, Florence.

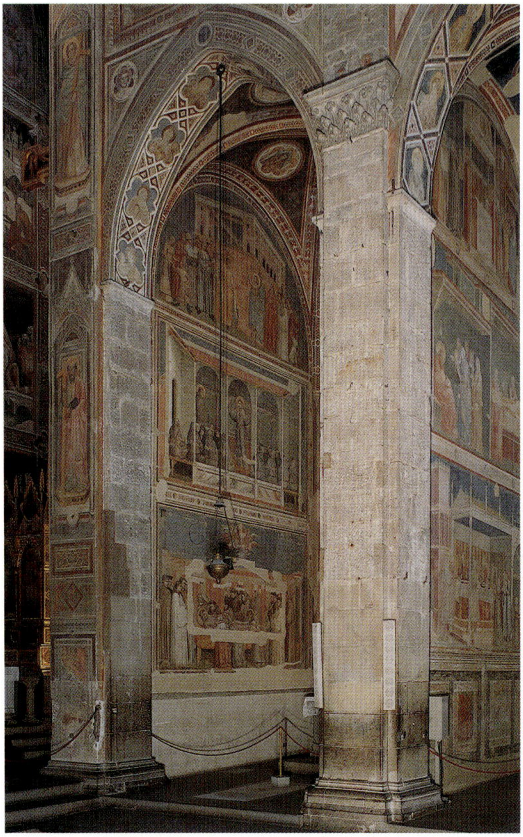

48 View of Bardi Chapel. S. Croce, Florence.

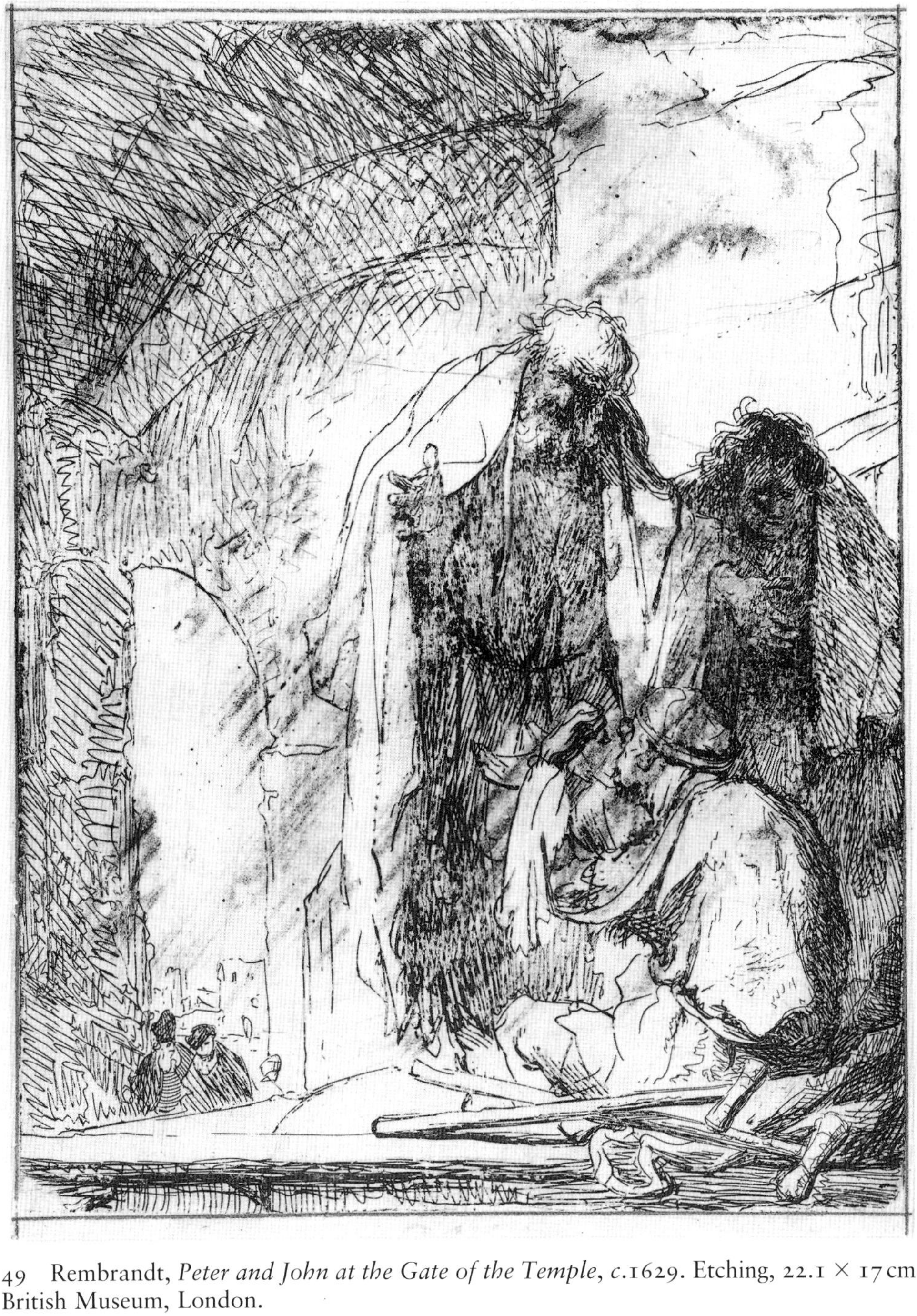

49 Rembrandt, *Peter and John at the Gate of the Temple*, *c.*1629. Etching, 22.1 × 17 cm. British Museum, London.

The play between the orientation to the surface and to the subject might be thought to be dependent on an architectural setting determining the real spatial relation to the viewer. The frescoed wall, the roundel in the vault and the ceiling painting are fixed while we, the viewers, move in relation to them; this makes possible the sense of a *rewarded position*, one in which we feel the fit between our position and the picture, a fit that enables us to include our orientation in imagining the subject. This conception of a rewarded position was analysed by Thomas Puttfarken and as part of his argument he showed how this had implications for the difference between small- and large-scale works. Nevertheless, while we assume that cabinet pictures, prints and drawings face us and we face them perpendicularly, they may still bring our sense of our own orientation into play.

II

There is a recurrent feature across a large number of Rembrandt's prints and paintings, particularly from the late 1620s through to the late 1630s and occasionally beyond: there is a low viewpoint which has the effect of occluding the middle ground and bringing foreground figures up into the picture plane; in this way the figures that lie on the other side of the occluding ridge approach the main foreground group from the oppostite side to the spectator, and we seem invited to conceive a symmetry between them and us, to see their position on the other side of the dominant plane as the counterpart to ours. In the early print of *Peter and John at the Gate of the Temple* (fig. 49), the arched opening reverses the arched back of the apostle while the position of the figures coming up from behind suggest a correspondence with that of the viewer in front. There is a similar effect in a late version of the subject (fig. 50); the foreground scene that is facing us backs onto a further scene facing away. We can trace an analogous symmetry in the next grand-scale etching, the *Raising of Lazarus* (fig. 52); the etched frame that Rembrandt inserted emphasized the border and correspondence between the viewer's space and the depicted space; the frame, furthermore, takes up the sweep of Christ's gesture which is mirrored in the rising viewer in the background. This kind of thought is widely echoed in Rembrandt's imagery (fig. 51). In the *Draughtsman and Model* (figs 53 and 54) this becomes highly explicit. In each case the suggestion is of the viewer's position being mirrored on the other side of the dominant plane of the surface.

This might be thought to reflect the very process of etching in which the image drawn on the plate reverses itself when printed; the capacity to keep in mind its rotation is intrinsic to reworking the image between states.[2] But this effect recurs in both painting and etching; for example, in the *Girl with Dead Peacocks* (fig. 55) we observe the monstrous shapes that she sees, and try to imagine how they would appear in the eyes of the child. In the very early painting of *Balaam* (fig. 58) there is a related effect. Where Lastman (fig. 56) followed the text (Num. xii, 27–35), making the angel invisible to Balaam but barring the way, Rembrandt has placed the angel beside and behind Balaam and his donkey. The effect is that the viewer looks into Balaam's eyes, mirroring his stare. The event, represented by Lastman as it would be seen by a third party outside the encounter, has here been split open to insert the viewer, subjecting him to the staring bewilderment. (This way of visualizing the episode had been devised several centuries earlier in a twelfth-century capital at Saulieu of the scene (fig. 57), using the possibilities offered by the transition between the sides of the capital. Rembrandt could hardly have known this and devised his solution without the sculptor's advantage.[3])

III

We may see the compositional device of intimating the viewer's counterpart within the image as a special case of a more general way in which Rembrandt's compositions form themselves round their subject, suggesting that the spectator's view is one of several possibilities; the effect is that the subject is not felt to be absorbed or summated in the way it is represented, in the particular view. We can observe the effect in the so-called *Anastasius* (fig. 59), a school copy, where the arch that frames our view is repeated both behind and at the sides.[4] The viewpoints that are potential in the *Anastasius* may be occupied as – most vividly – in his *Judas* (fig. 60). The compositional mode may be seen as closely corresponding to a sense of drawing in which the continuity of the pen's movement is imagined as passing round the figure. (It is hardly accidental that the great originator of such drawing was Leonardo

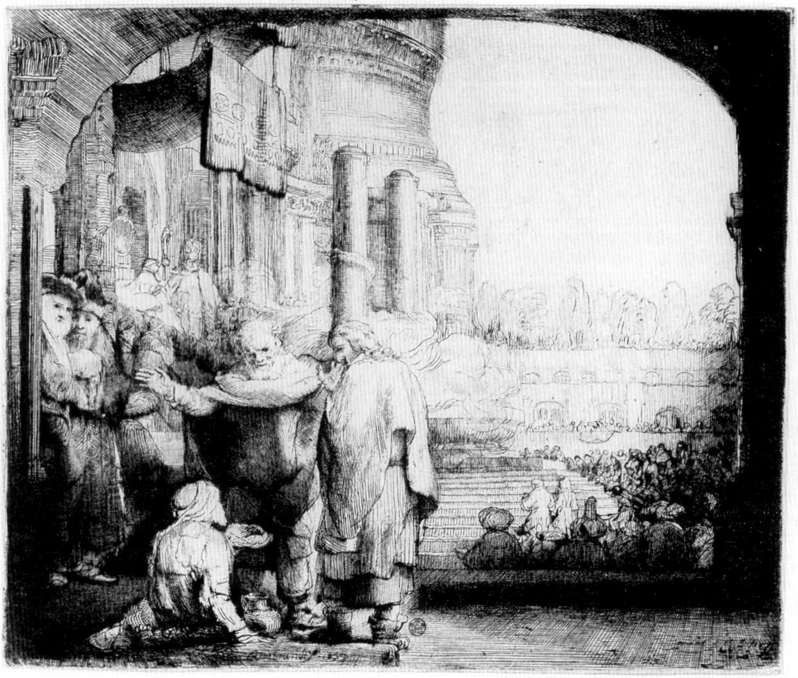

50 Rembrandt, *Peter and John at the Gate of the Temple*, 1659. Etching, 17.9 × 21.6 cm. British Museum, London.

51 Rembrandt, *Christ Preaching*, *c.*1652. Etching, 15.5 × 20.7 cm. British Museum, London.

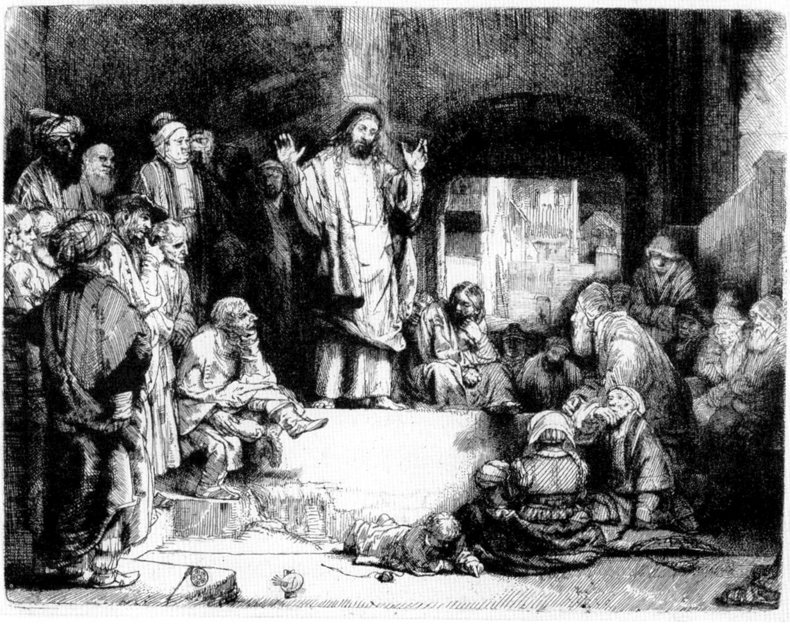

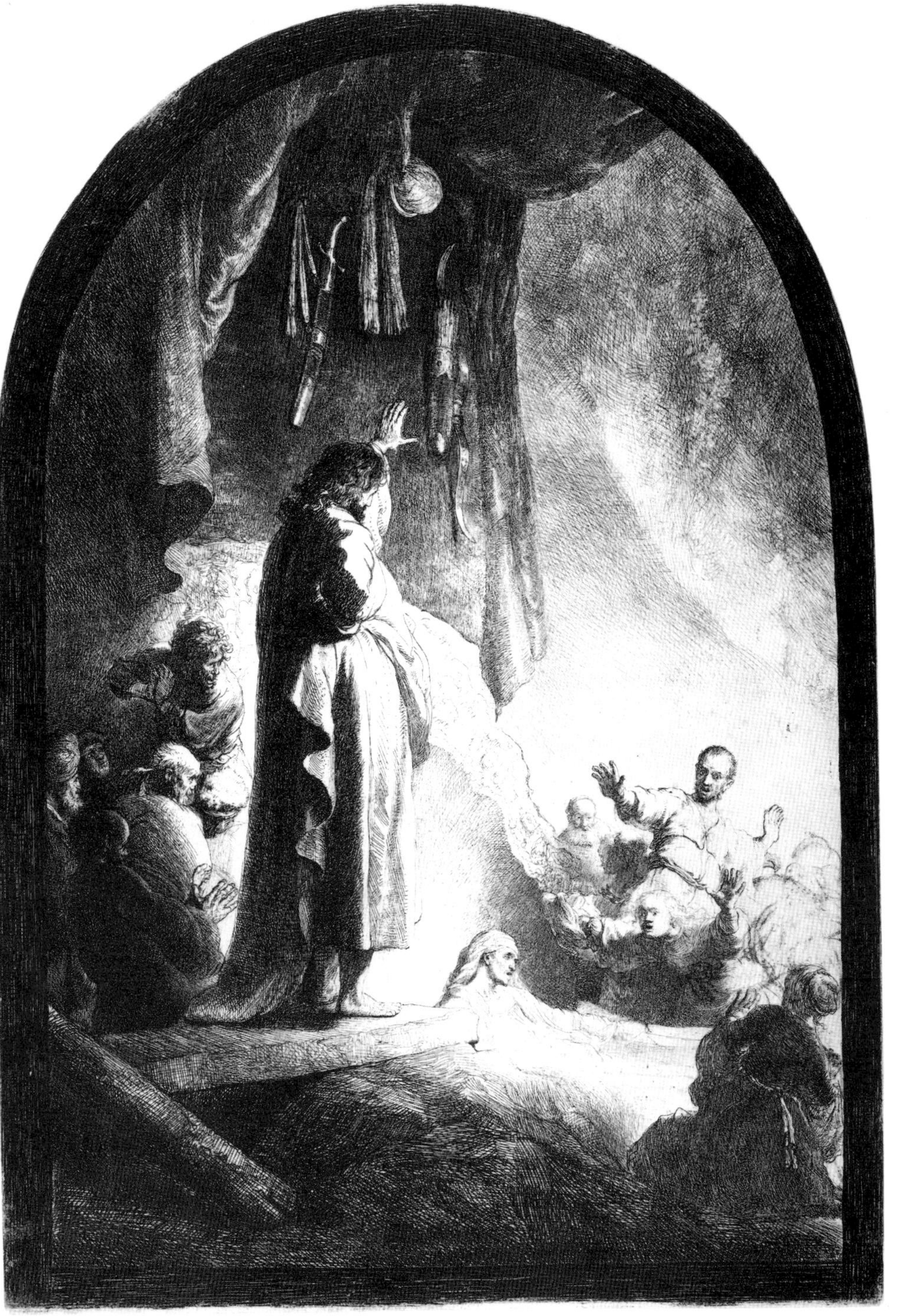

52 Rembrandt, *Raising of Lazarus*, c.1632. Etching, 36.6 × 25.8 cm. British Museum, London.

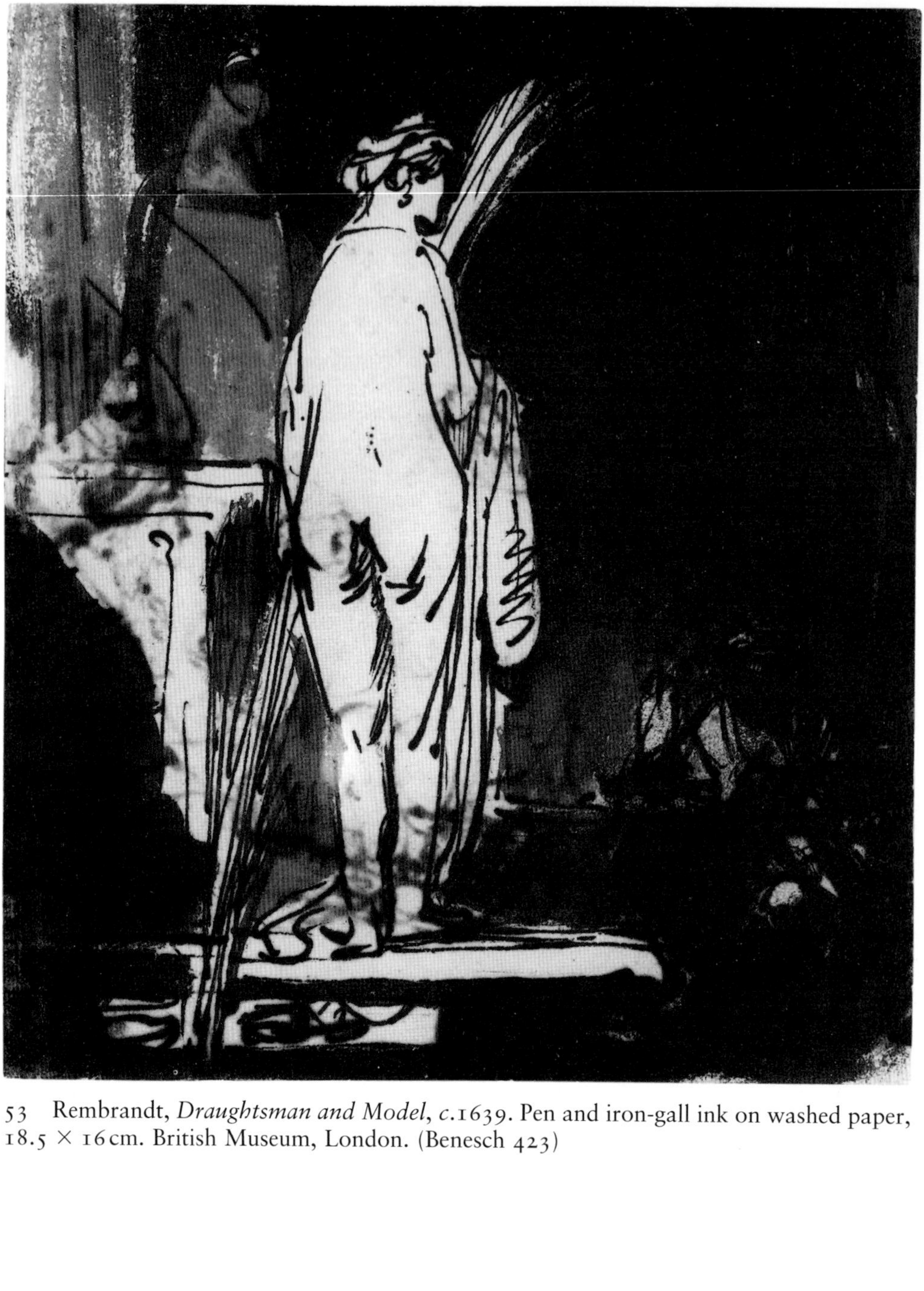

53 Rembrandt, *Draughtsman and Model*, *c*.1639. Pen and iron-gall ink on washed paper, 18.5 × 16 cm. British Museum, London. (Benesch 423)

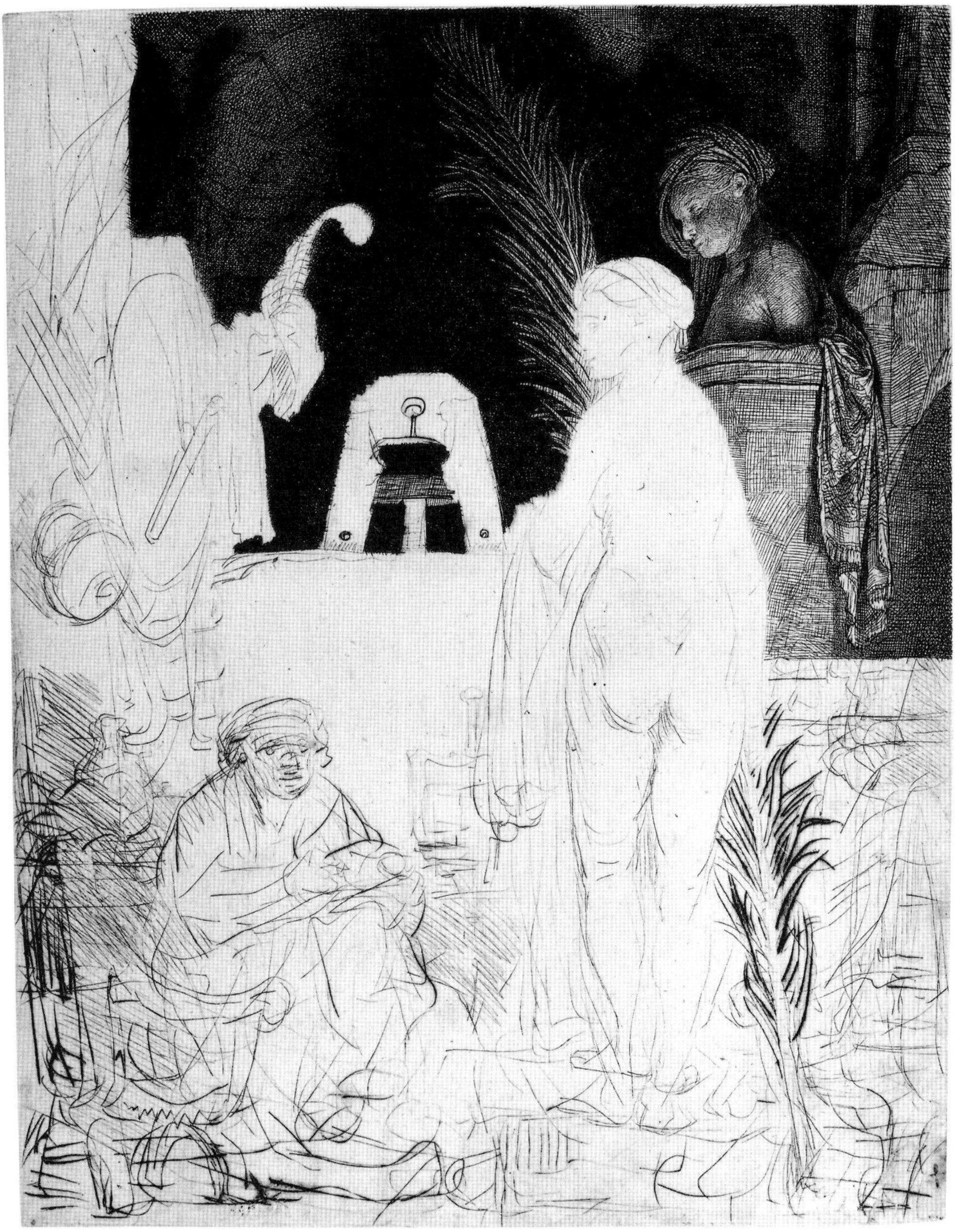

54 Rembrandt, *Draughtsman and Model*, *c.*1639. Etching, 23.2 × 18.4 cm. British Museum, London.

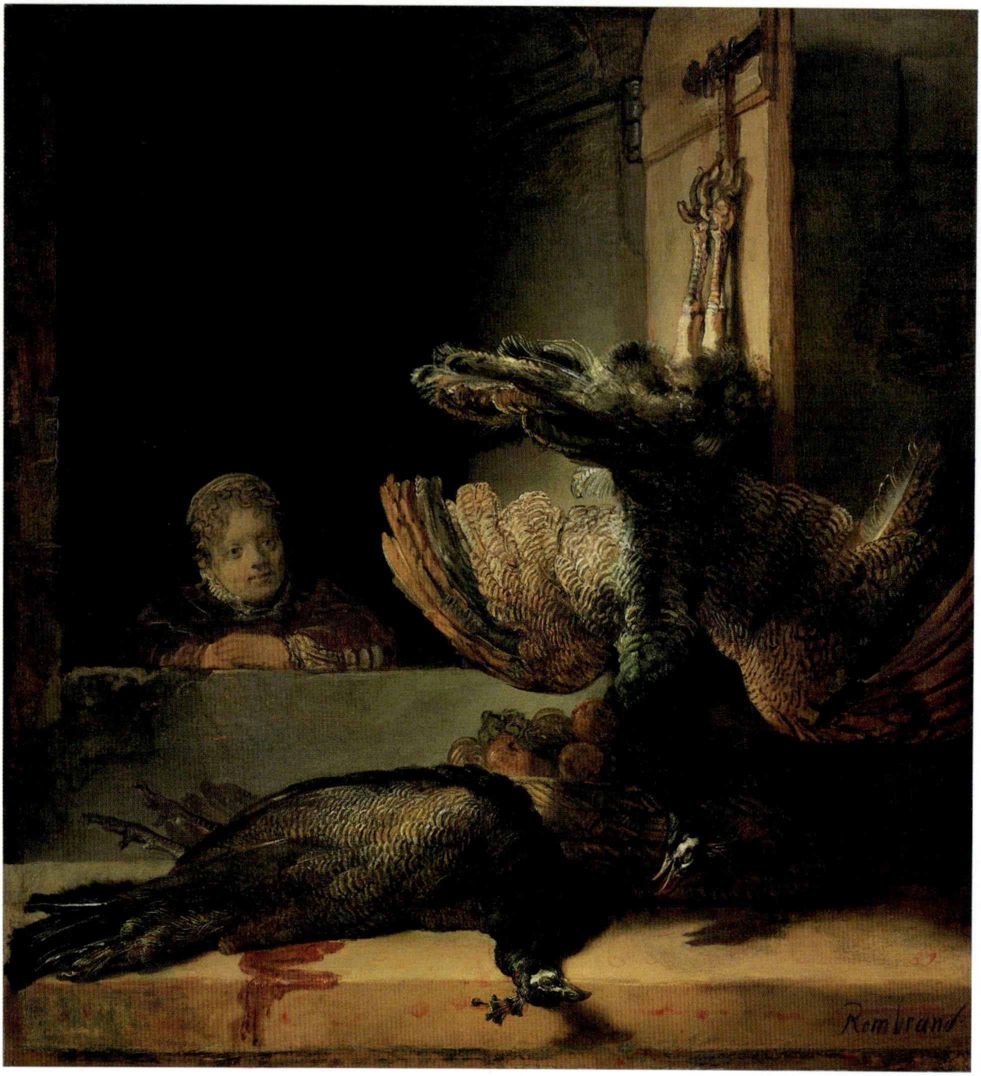

55 Rembrandt, *Girl with Dead Peacocks*, *c.*1639. Oil on canvas, 144 × 135 cm. Rijksmuseum, Amsterdam.

and this compositional thought is anticipated in his *Adoration* (fig. 2).) Both the spiral of drawing and the intimation of other orientations has the implication of making us aware of our view as one in a continuous series and the subject as independent of the viewer. In *St Jerome Reading in an Italian Landscape* (figs 61 and 62) the lion faces one way and Jerome the other, and they are so disposed to suggest the continuity of the space round the tree. The independence of the scene from any particular view is enhanced by the saint being casually placed and absorbed in his own thought, while the hatching by which the image is built up on the etching plate stops at the saint's reading eyes, the rest of his body only sketched in as though declining to complete the image for the viewer; we might compare this with *St Jerome beside a Pollarded Willow* (fig. 46) where the dominant object of attention is not Jerome and is not even something of which he appears aware. The sense that the depiction affords us an underprivileged view becomes thematic in the case of the etching of *Medea* (1648), made to accompany the publication of a play by Jan Six (fig. 63). The temple ceremony of the marriage of Jason and Creusa is seen from a dark ambulatory space behind the high altar, a viewing angle oblique to the orientation of the building and the ceremony itself from which we are, like Medea, excluded.

IV

The intimations of alternative orientations to the subject converge with other aspects of Rembrandtian depiction. For example, in a range of paintings from the late 1630s onwards the viewer's position is both invoked and disregarded. What is involved is the way in which we imagine ourselves in relation to the gaze and the action of the people represented. In the ordinary course of events, painting aside, as we look around us we are necessarily at the centre of our own world and at the same time we see others as at the centre of theirs. The basic condition of relating to other people is that we see them in a situation that is fundamentally symmetrical with our own with the possibility that we do not simply observe them but communicate with them. In ordinary experience we move naturally from observing others to reciprocal acknowledgement. In depiction – which is static – the shift is not really possible. Although figures depicted as turning to face outwards into the viewer's space may suggest this transition, the representation of people would seem to divide between those shown in communication with the viewer and those in which they are not. And the distinction holds even though it is only at a certain viewing distance and momentarily that we can imagine ourselves in reciprocal acknowledgement, in an interchange of looks. When

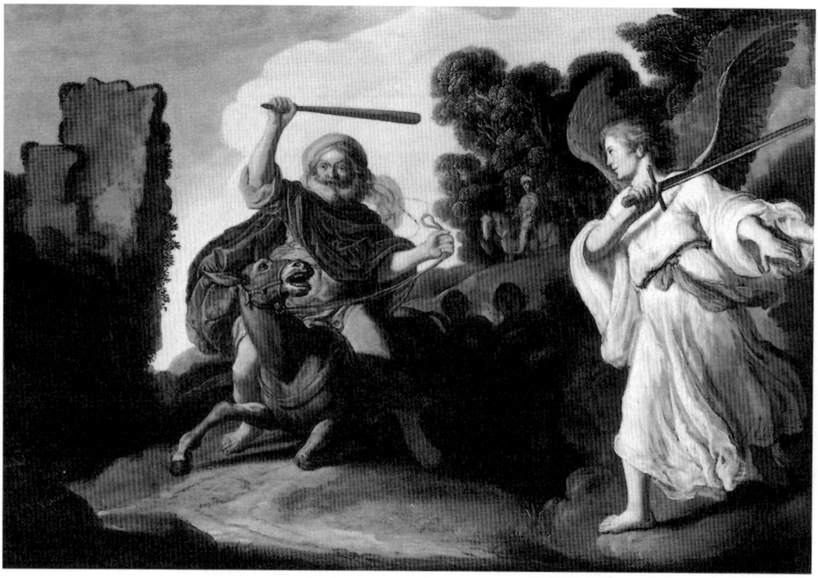

56 Peter Lastman, *Balaam and the Donkey*, 1622. Oil on panel, 40.3 × 60.6 cm. Israel Museum, Jerusalem.

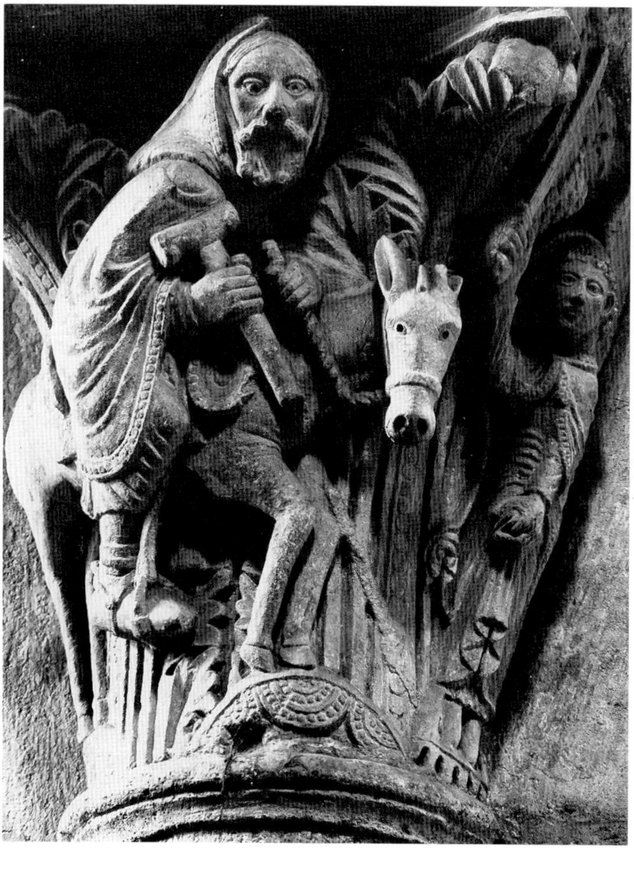

57 *Balaam and the Donkey*, c.1150. Historiated capital, St Androche, Saulieu.

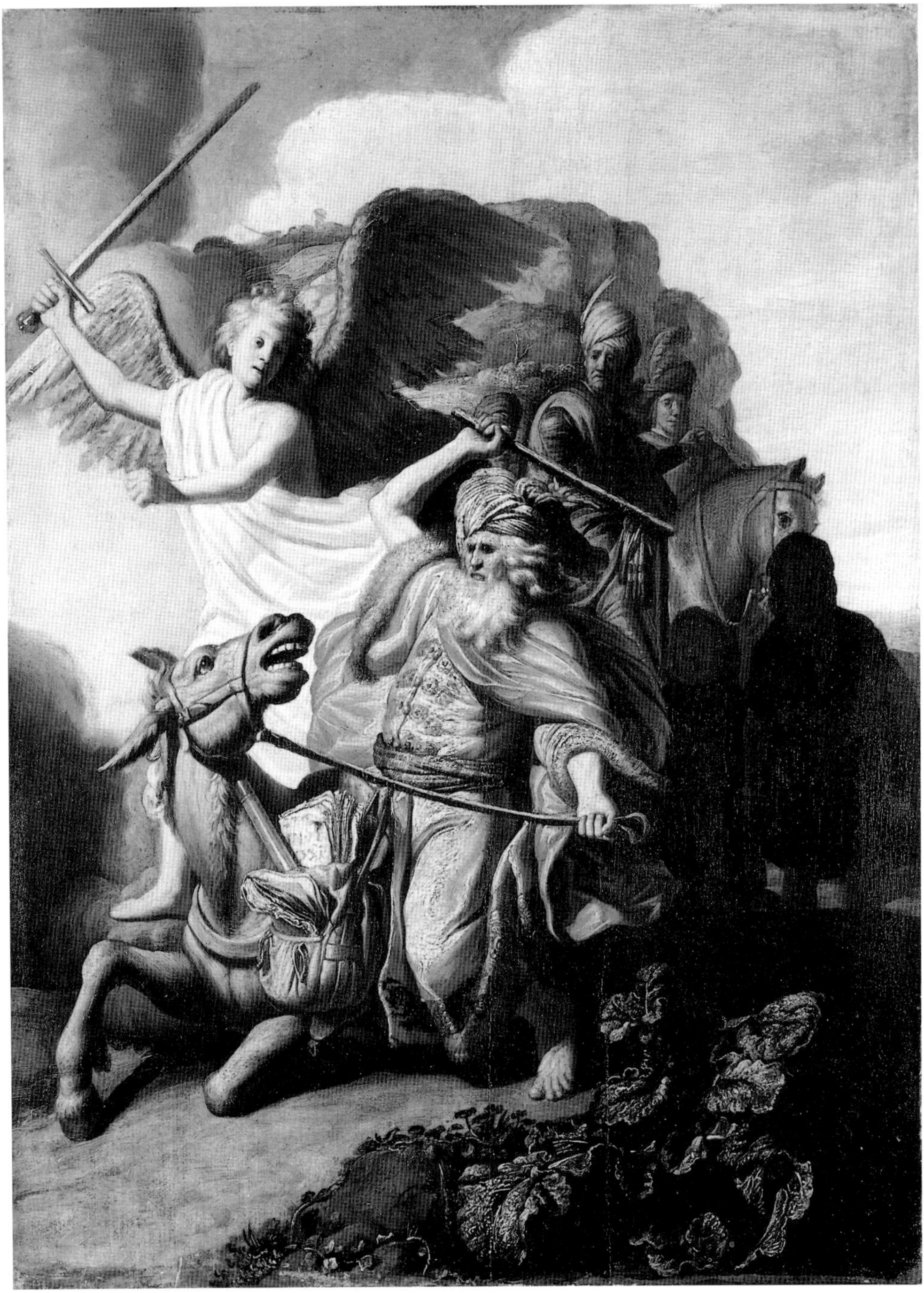

58 Rembrandt, *Balaam and the Donkey*, 1629. Oil on panel. Musée Cognac–Jay, Paris.

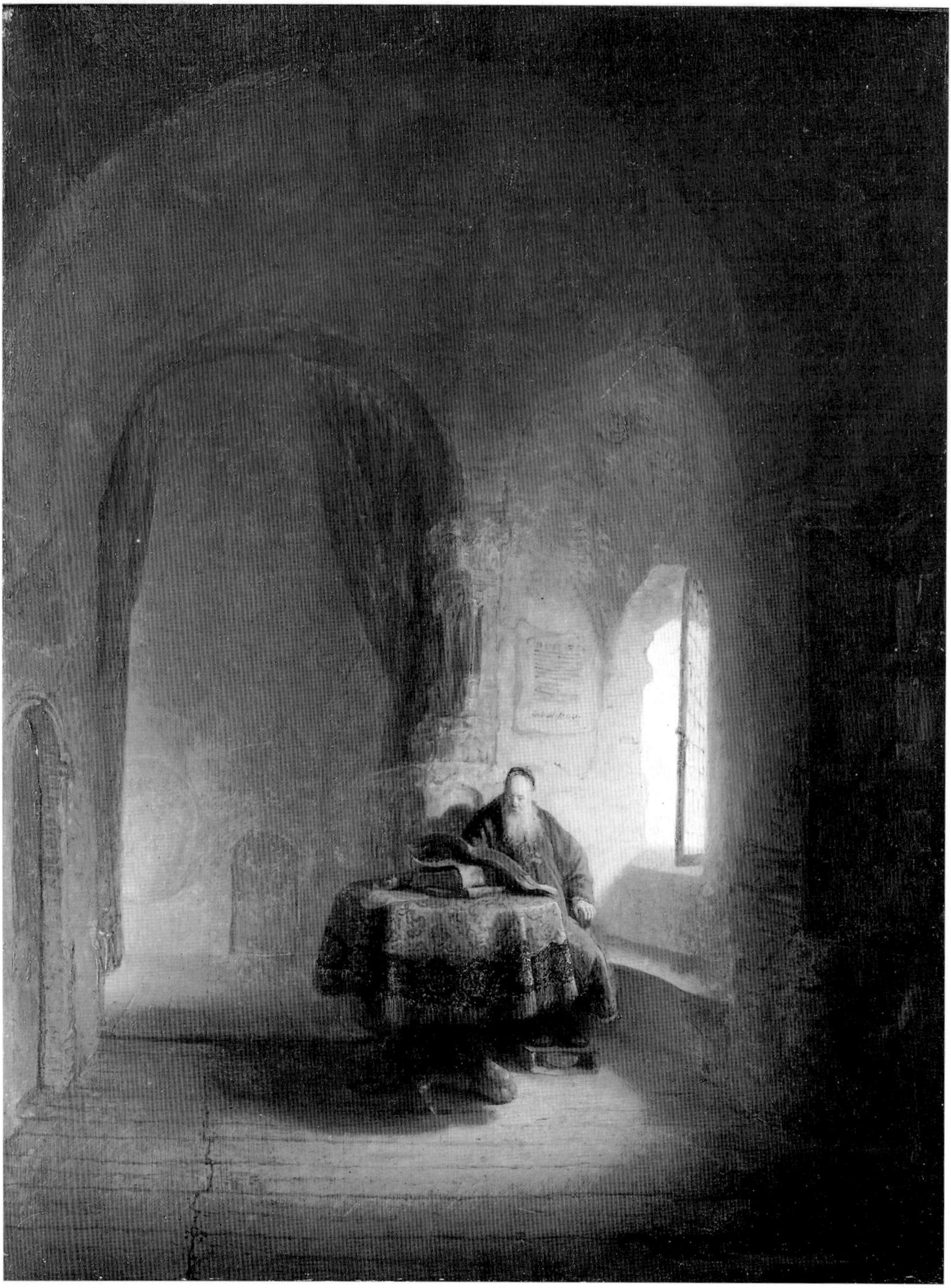

59 After Rembrandt, *Scholar in a Lofty Room (St Anastasius)*, *c.*1630. Oil on panel, 60 × 48 cm. Nationalmuseum, Stockholm.

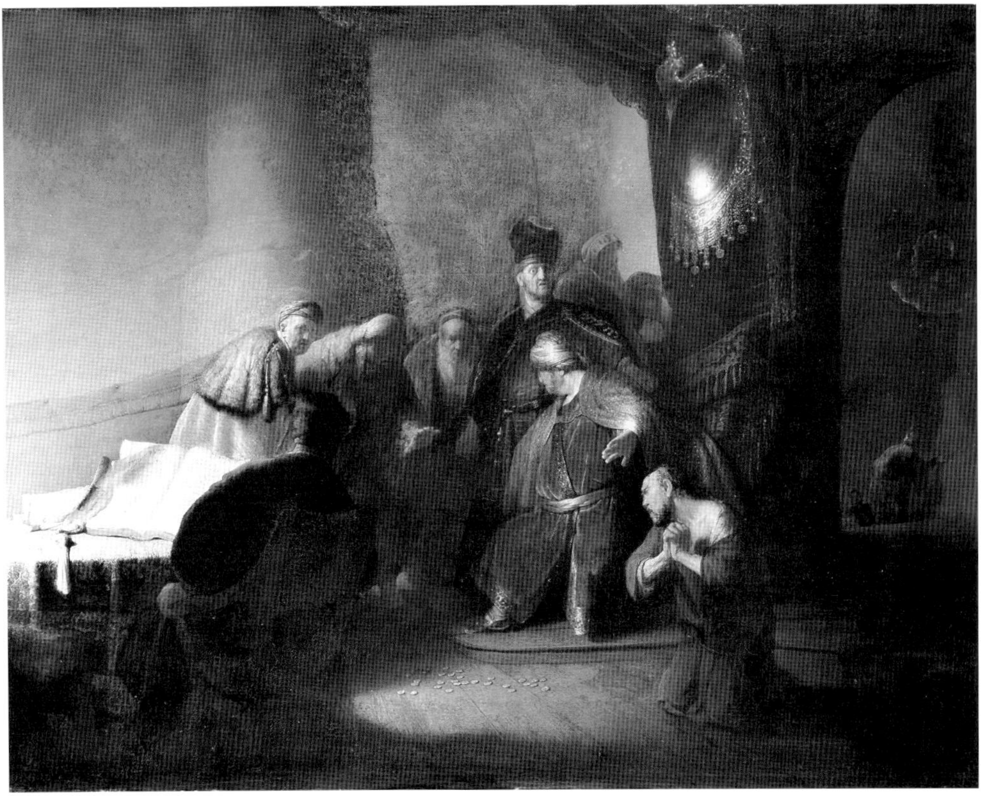

60 Rembrandt, *Judas Returning the Thirty Pieces of Silver*, 1629. Oil on panel, 76 × 101 cm. Private Collection.

we go too close we no longer experience their eyes as co-ordinating their gaze on us and they seem to look behind us; also if we keep looking for too long without ourselves scanning back and forth we will experience a loss of contact. (The very instability may enhance our sense of reciprocal adjustment – of eye contact, which is something we are naturally disposed to seek.) The problem of adjustment notwithstanding, we make a basic distinction between figures that we simply imagine ourselves as observing and others with which we imagine reciprocal cognizance. But, crucially, there is a group of paintings in which Rembrandt both avoids the sense of interchange between viewer and depicted figures while at the same time retains it as an imminent possibility; and this effect is closely related to the play upon orientation, as it involves imaginative transitions between the axes along which the represented figures do or do not look back at us.

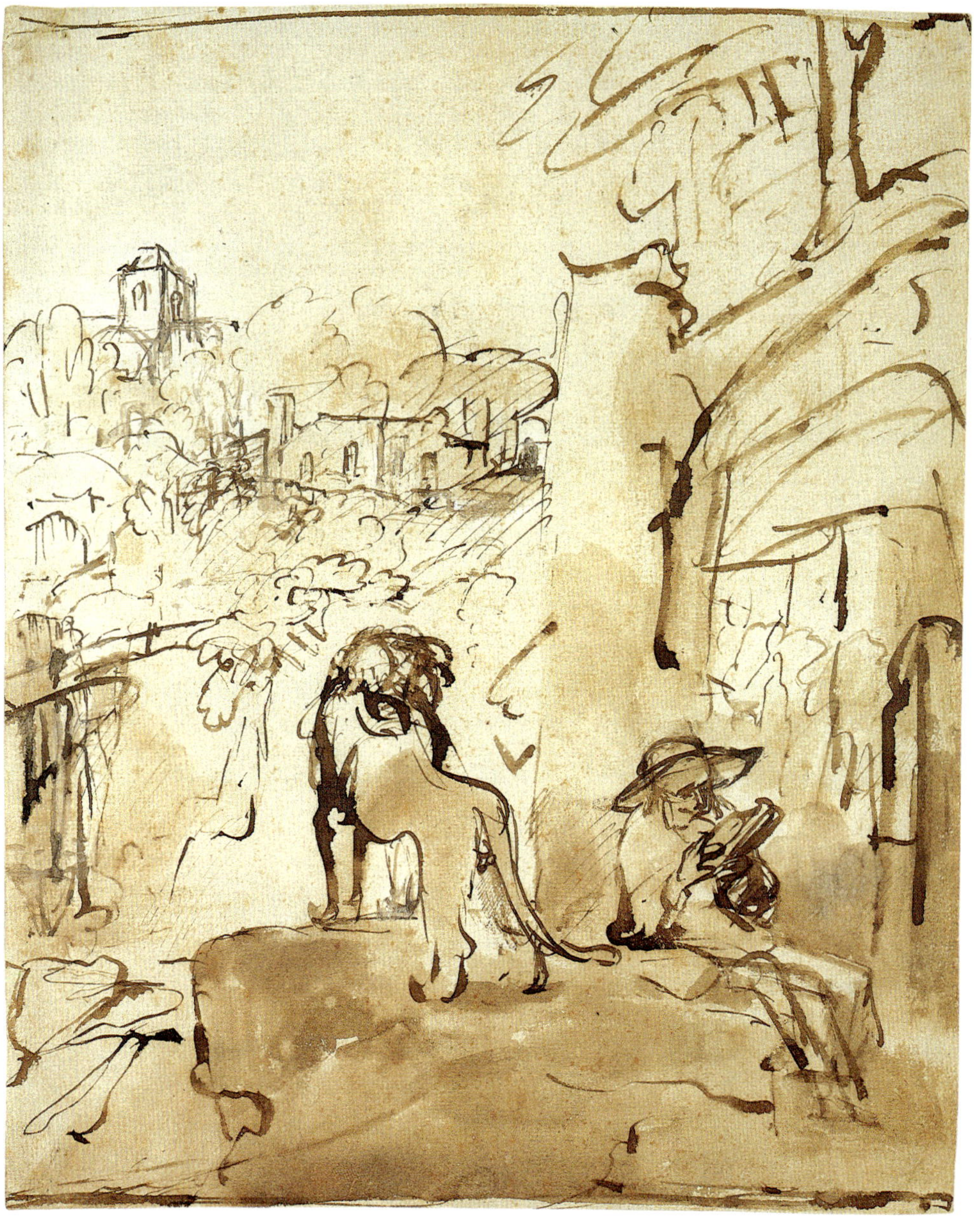

61 Rembrandt, *St Jerome Reading in an Italian Landscape*, *c.*1651. Pen and brown ink, brown and white wash. Kunsthalle, Hamburg.

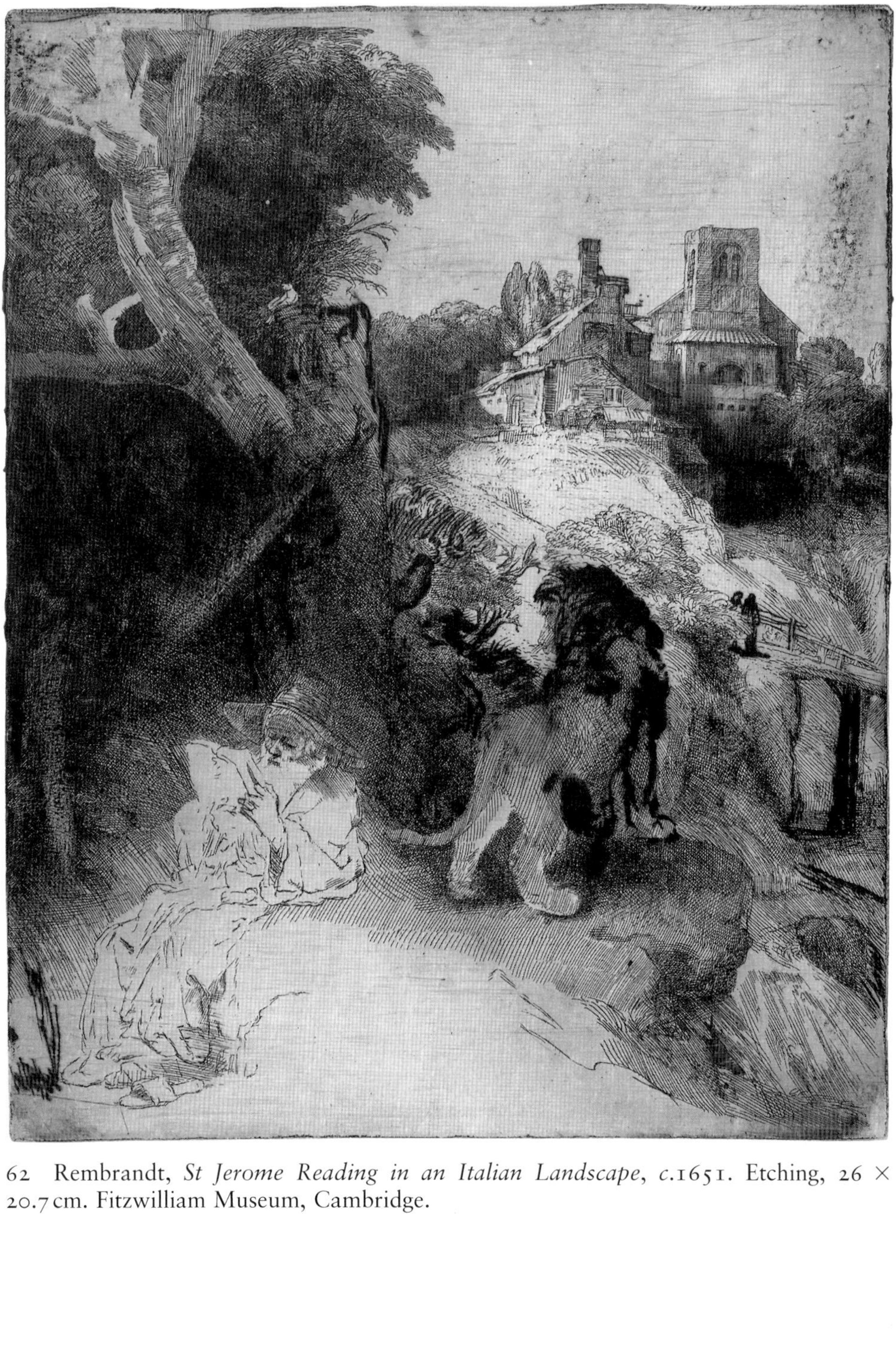

62 Rembrandt, *St Jerome Reading in an Italian Landscape*, c.1651. Etching, 26 × 20.7 cm. Fitzwilliam Museum, Cambridge.

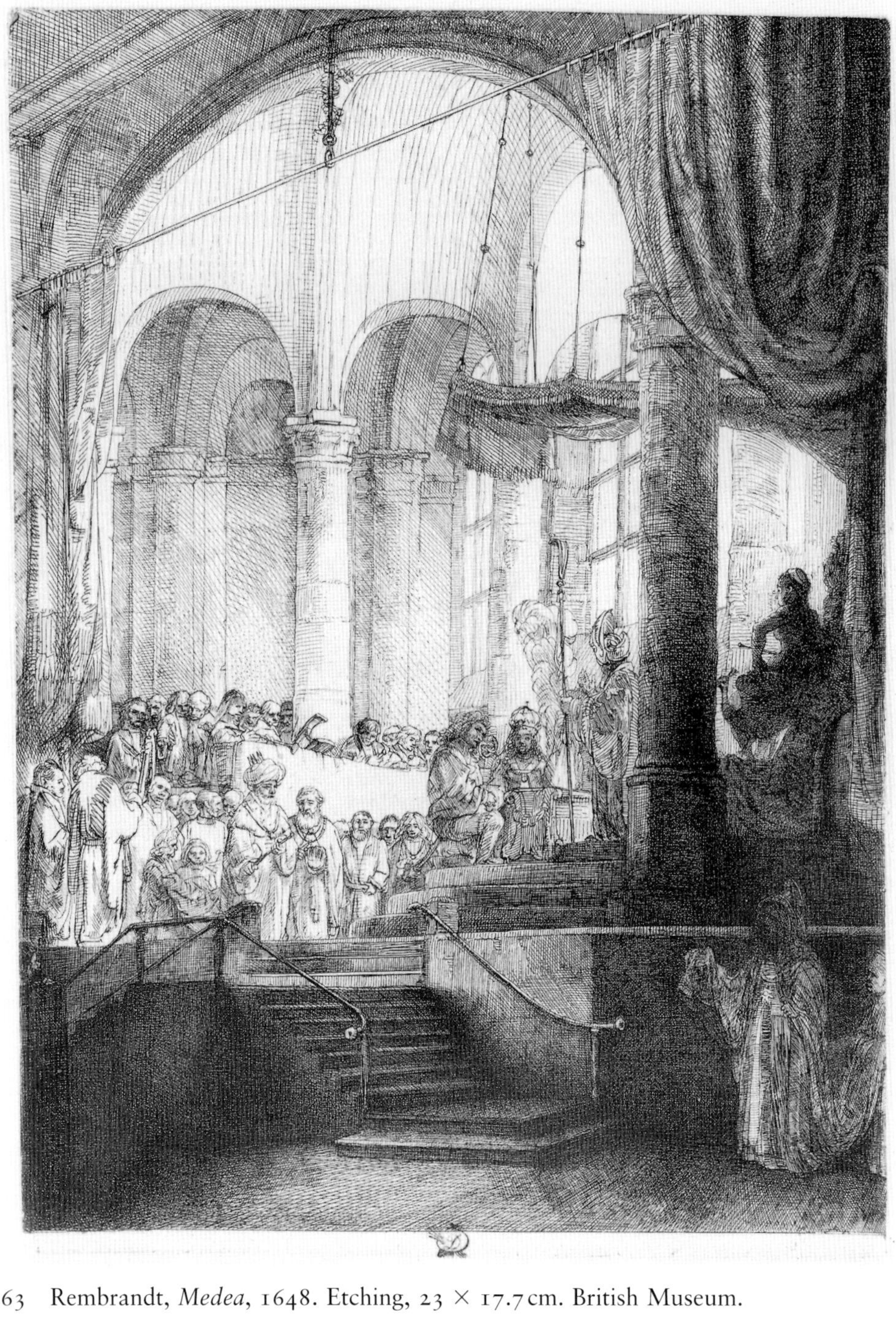

63 Rembrandt, *Medea*, 1648. Etching, 23 × 17.7 cm. British Museum.

V

The painting in Edinburgh (fig. 64) of the woman leaning out of bed has been interpreted as of Sarah the wife of Tobias, whose previous seven husbands had been killed by a devil, each on their wedding night (Tobit, 3 and 8). Under the tutelage of the angel, Tobias overcomes the devil by burning the entrails of his fish. Rembrandt's teacher, Lastman, had depicted this scene (fig. 65).[5] In Rembrandt's painting we seem to be observing someone who is earnestly watching an event we cannot see, and this does not depend on our having identified her as Sarah. We are aware of the woman observing an event that continues beyond the frame, in the space in which we stand, and because of the approximation of the fictive setting to the real frame and the proportion of the surface occupied by the figure we imagine her as seen from very close. What is arresting here is that despite the sense of closeness and imagining the scene thus extending into our space, we have no role and can imagine no position for ourselves in relation to her.

Other major paintings appear somewhat comparable. The preacher Anslo gestures out toward others looking past his attentive wife (fig. 66). Here again the scene psychologically extends into our space but in seeking out our relation to the depicted figures we are left with an undefined position although our role is presumably like that of his wife. The point can be underlined by the comparison with the earlier double portrait of the *Shipbuilder Rijksen and his Wife* (fig. 67) where there is no invitation to reflect on our orientation. In the Anslo double portrait we do so owing to the low viewpoint – which makes us reflect on our own position – and the preacher's gesture. Similarly in *The Syndics* – the assessors of the clothmakers' guild – our awareness of our orientation to the scene is called into play partly by the equivocation or uncertainty about the relation of the table to the bottom edge of the picture, and partly by the related uncertainty of how the figures are aligned to it and so to us (fig. 68). And here, too, our space is penetrated – as has been remarked from the early nineteenth century – since the scrutiny of the men seems to converge well to our side of the table while we find ourselves without a role, without being acknowledged within what is going on.[6] In each of these cases we have an equivocation on the boundary between the fiction and the viewer's space; the dominant axis of the action extends across the boundary, making us attendant at an uncompleted transaction

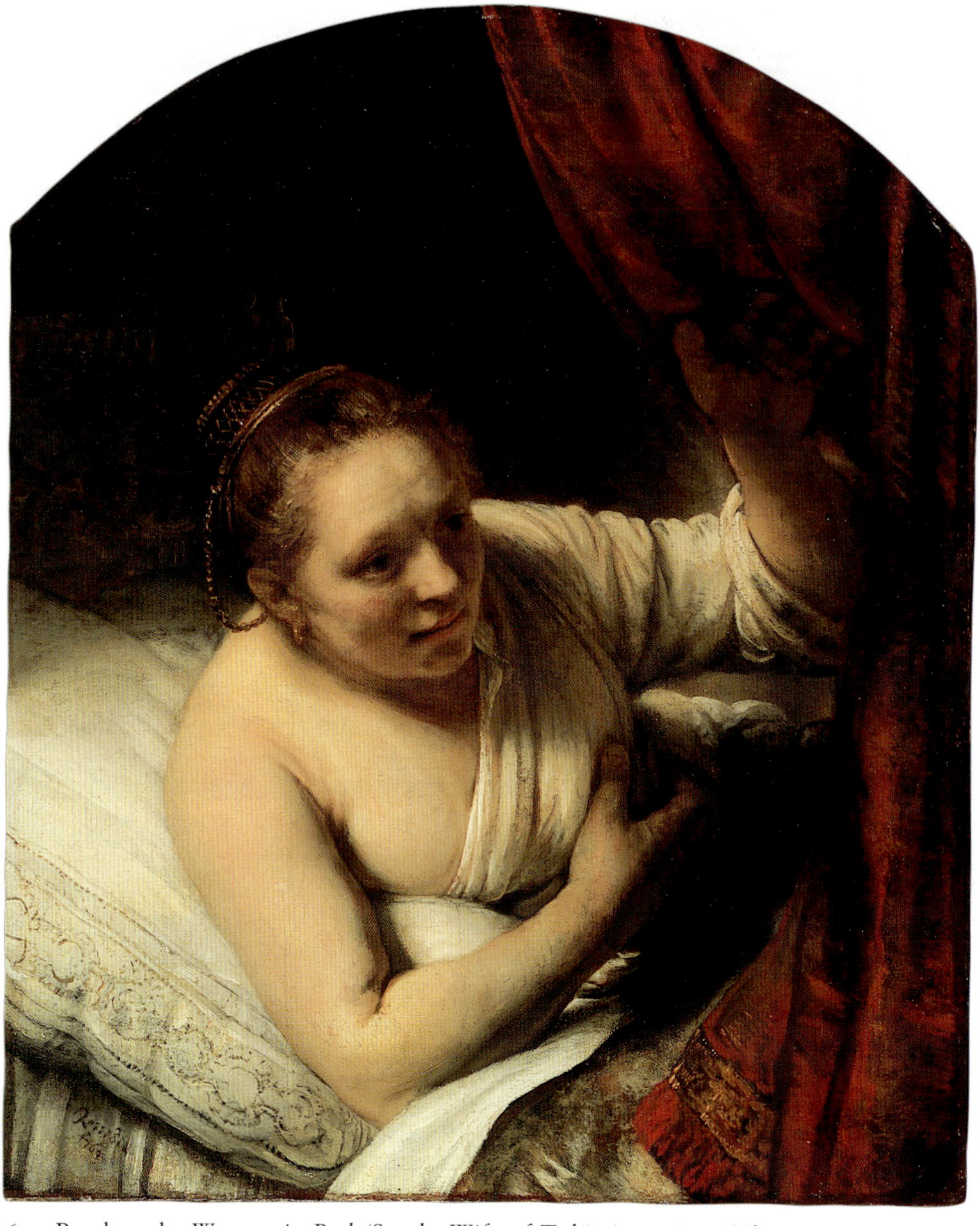

64 Rembrandt, *Woman in Bed (Sarah, Wife of Tobias)*, *c.*1645. Oil on canvas, 81.2 × 67.9 cm. National Gallery of Scotland, Edinburgh.

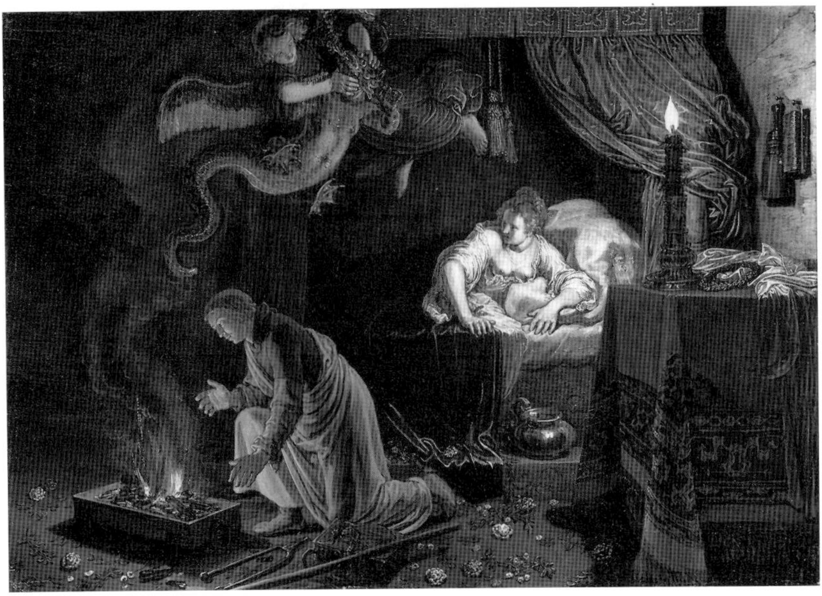

65 Peter Lastman, *The Wedding Night of Sarah and Tobias*, 1611. Oil on panel, 42 × 57 cm. Juliana Cheney Edwards Collection. Courtesy, Museum of Fine Arts, Boston.

which may or may not concern us. The distinction between our external onlooker's relation to the figures and a reciprocal engagement is insecure; something of the fluidity of nonpictorial life enters the picture, as in our search for acknowledgement in the eyes of others, or at least a sense of sharing the same object of attention.

In his history of critical responses to *The Syndics*, H. van der Waal argued that critics from the early nineteenth century to the present day anecdotalized the picture: they had assumed that the figures were on a dais, that they were to be conceived as facing some assembly or meeting, and that there had been some intervention from the floor to which they were responding.[7] Against this account he argued, first, that the group is depicted as if seen from below not for the literal reason that it is set on a dais but because of the painting's original viewing position; and second, that the arrangement of figures is to be accounted for not as the dramatization of a response to some sudden intervention but as the solution to the pictorial problem of representing a group of figures round a table without either putting them in a row as in a Last

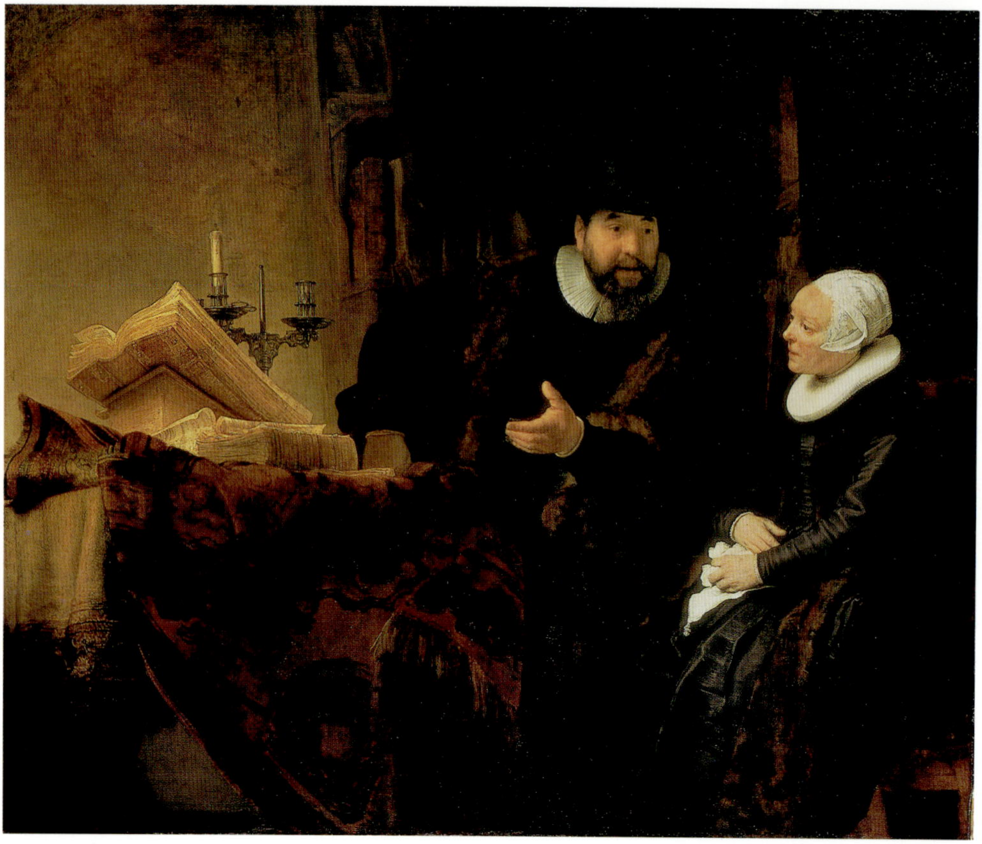

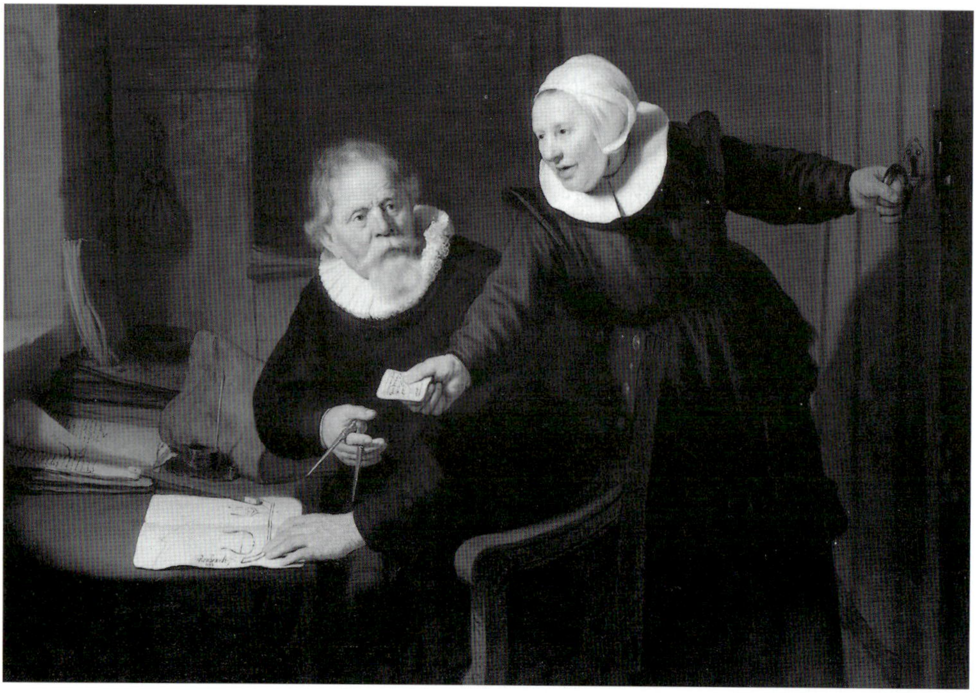

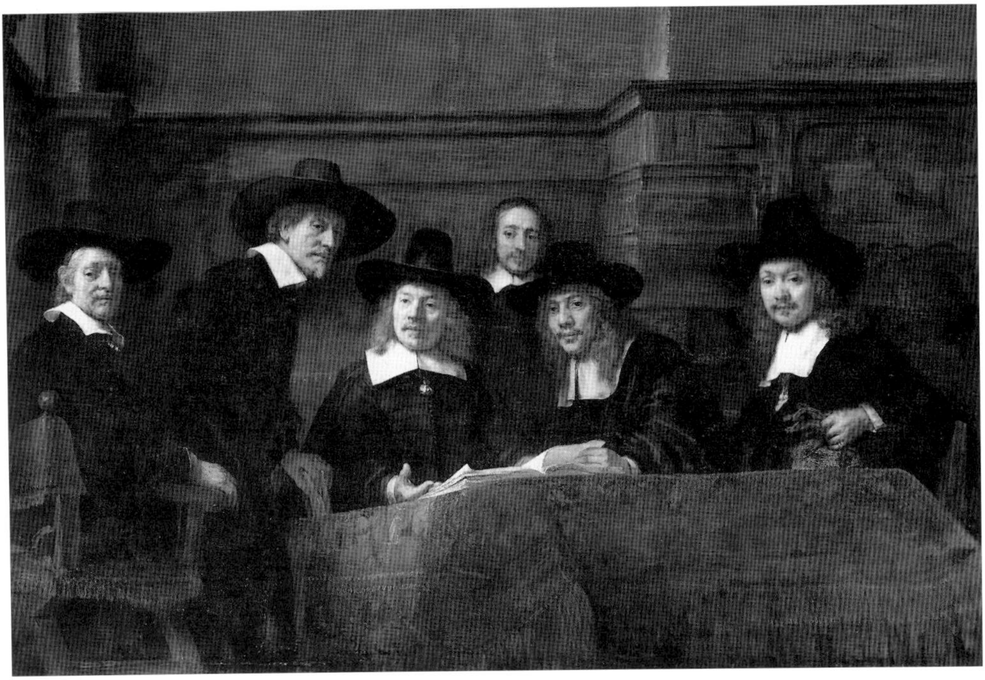

68 Rembrandt, *The Syndics*, 1662. Oil on canvas, 191 × 279 cm. Rijksmuseum, Amsterdam.

66 (*facing page top*) Rembrandt, *Double Portrait of Mennonite Preacher Anslo and his Wife Aeltje Gerritsdr. Schouten*, 1641. Oil on canvas, 176 × 210 cm. Staatliche Museen Preussischer Kulturbesitz, Gemäldegalerie, Berlin.

Supper or along two sides and so splitting the composition in two, foreground figures occluding those further back. While he is surely right in objecting to a very literal interpretation of the seating and disposition of the figures, he seems at the same time to deny the surely unavoidable dramatic effect of the way the figures look out into the viewer's space. He stressed the conventional nature of portraiture as opposed to anecdotal narrative, but within the conception of portraiture there had developed a quasi-dramatic sense of the presence of the sitter to the viewer – however determinate or indeterminate the role of the viewer might be: respectful subject, colleague or member of the family. The structure of this painting could not be conceived simply as the reconciliation between arrangements in the surface and disposition in space. Although van der Waal's objection to a simple anecdotal interpretation in which the spectator is addressed by the protagonist is

67 Rembrandt, *Double Portrait of the Shipbuilder Rijksen and his Wife, Griet Jans*, 1633. Oil on canvas, 115 × 165 cm. The Royal Collection © Her Majesty Queen Elizabeth II.

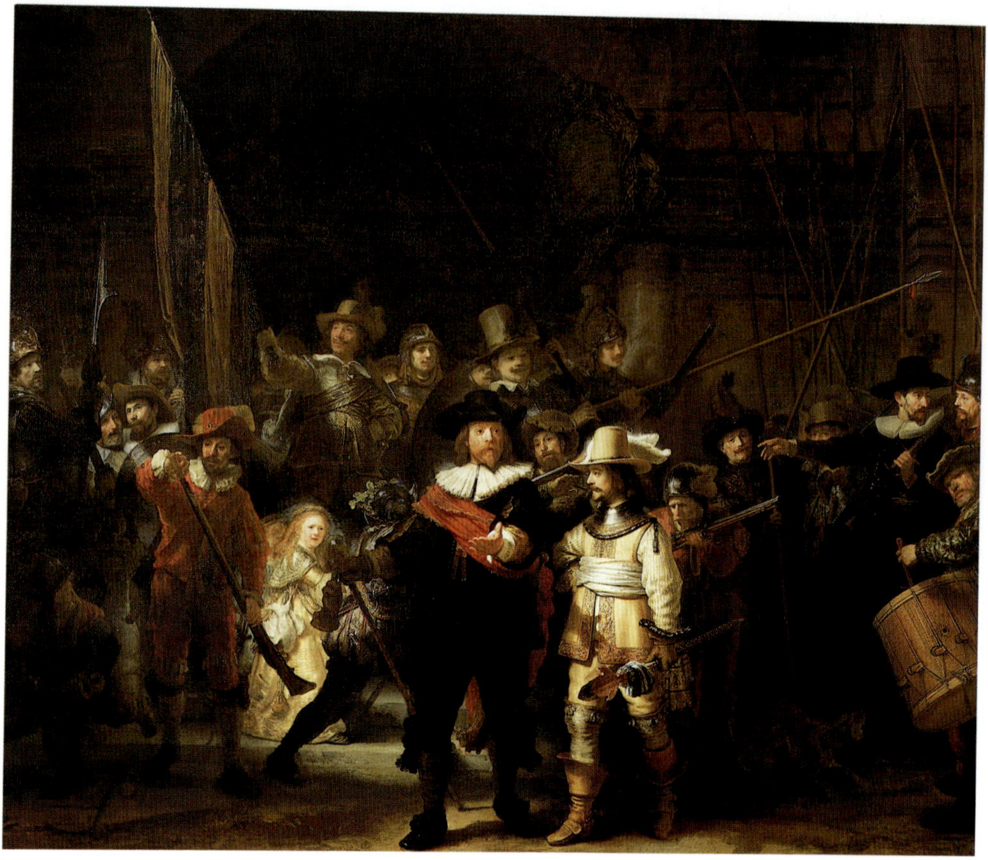

69 Rembrandt, *The Night Watch*, 1642. Oil on canvas, 359 × 438 cm. Rijksmuseum, Amsterdam.

surely right, it is a recurrent aspect of Rembrandt's painting that the action opens out into the spectator's space calling his or her relation to the protagonists into question.

This conception of a spectator as the addressee of the depicted figures should, therefore, be distinguished from the assumption of an implicit addressee as in the spectator's ambience, for Rembrandt plays on the possible transition between them. And this would seem characteristic of a wide range of Rembrandt's images. Thus, in *The Night Watch* (fig. 69) we are allowed no secure relation to the foreground figures of Captain Banning Cock and his yellow-suited lieutenant; we are aware of the outstretched hand through the shadow it casts, a gesture passing across our vision, neither addressing us nor presenting a clear gestalt; nor can we absorb these two figures in the overall scene: wild children, an antique shield and an old man playing at musketry form a dissociated screen in front of which they stride. The other figures look in all directions while the two officers advance towards us for all the world as if we were not there. We are not even like one of Anslo's listeners or a witness in front of the Syndics. This would have been underscored by the contrast with the other more orderly group portraits among which it was originally placed.[8]

We have observed a range of ways in which the viewer's orientation is called up imaginatively within a print or painting: for instance, where the viewer's relation to the depicted event has its analogue in a figure within the depicted space; or the way the viewer's position is felt as one of many possible positions for looking at the scene, and in certain cases, a specifically underprivileged one. A variant of this occurs in paintings where the border between the real and the fictive space is equivocal and, as viewers, our relation to the protagonists is made uncertain; we are led to imagine seeking and failing to engage their attention. These inflections in how we relate ourselves to the sitters or protagonists give us a sense of their independence, both in relation to their settings and in relation to us the viewers, an effect that converges with Rembrandt's treatment of physiognomic expression which frequently and peculiarly makes us aware of the inaccessibility of their thought.

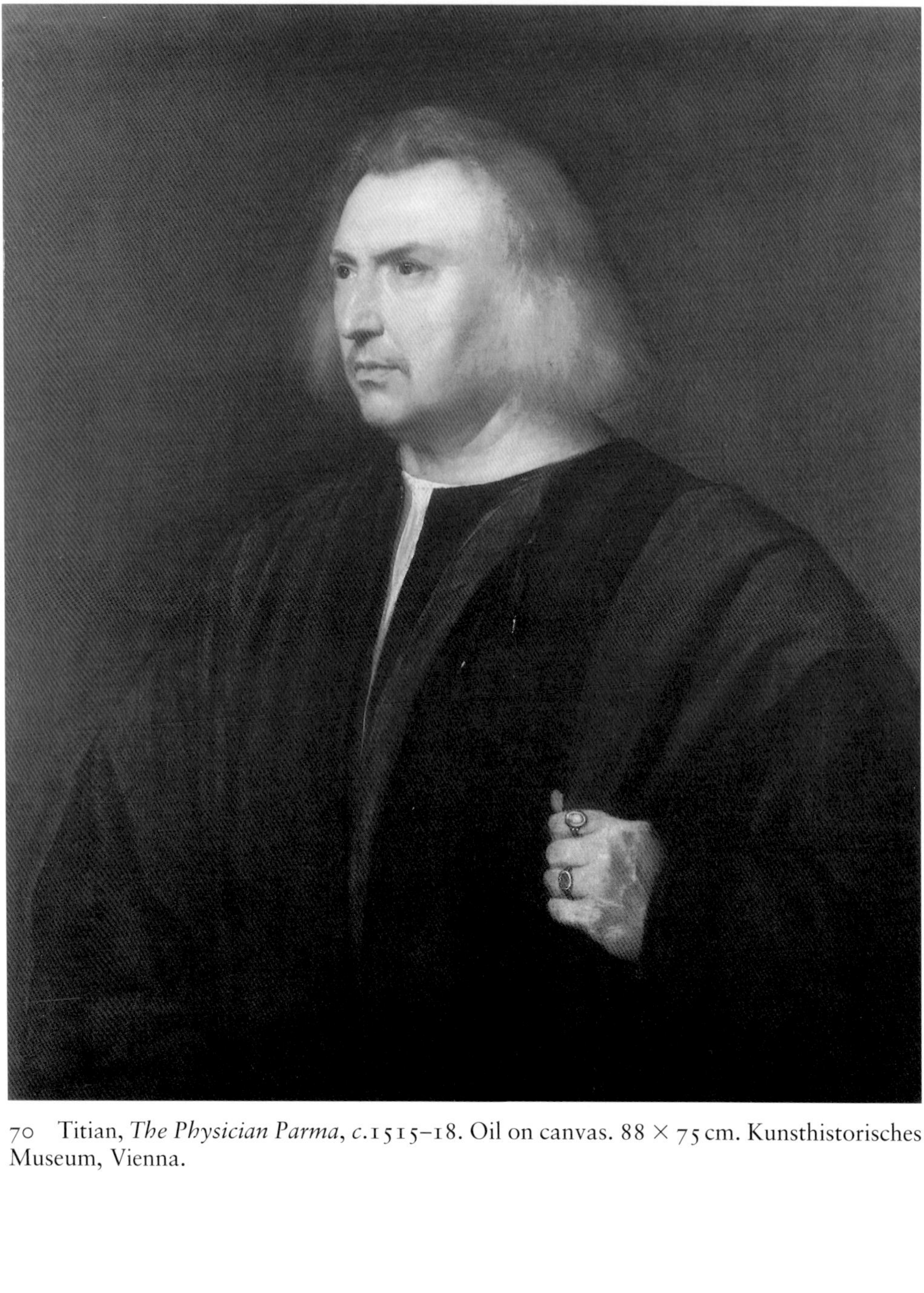

70 Titian, *The Physician Parma*, *c*.1515–18. Oil on canvas. 88 × 75 cm. Kunsthistorisches Museum, Vienna.

Chapter Four

Portrayal: Performance, Role and Subject

I

THE CONDITIONS OUT OF WHICH paintings emerge reappear more or less interwoven in their content; we seek out the procedures of painting in the subject and not only the subject in the procedures. Similarly, the wider conditions that lie beyond the technical procedures, the functions that the paintings serve or the life in which they participate may be recruited to the internal organization, the imagining that the painting prompts. Where the subject represented is the presence of another person, imaginary or real, this brings with it possibilities that occur for no other kind of subject and from the sixteenth century such possibilities converged and complicated each other, the painter miming, addressing or himself serving as his subject.

The notion of the painter acting the characters he depicts figures in traditional anecdotes and advice from the seventeenth century, and while it refers to history painting it has implications for portraiture. Annibale Carracci came unnoticed into a church where the painter Domenichino was working and watched him miming a man aggressively scoffing in order to paint such a figure in his fresco. Domenichino is reported to have held that one must not only observe the effects of emotions but feel them oneself in order to depict them.[1] Similar views were attributed to Annibale Carracci himself who was said to be a good actor. Bernini is reported to have made faces before a mirror to get the look of his St Lawrence and his David,[2] and in the seventeenth century the

Dutchman Samuel Hoogstraaten, theorist and sometime student of Rembrandt, held similarly that the painter needs to imagine the situation of his subject and then use a mirror; in this way he comes to know appearances both from within and without.[3] Hoogstraaten's mirror should give us reason to pause.

The notion that the painter uses a mirror to enable him to perceive an action both from inside and from outside is suggestive, but not without oddity. The notion may first be taken to imply that a mirror enables the painter to serve as his own model when depicting a figure in a particular emotional state. But in that case the mirror would be just a convenient replacement for a model and Hoogstraaten is surely saying more than that. For the implication is that by using his own reflection in the mirror the painter is enabled to correlate external manifestations with their internal states. But what sense are we to give to correlation here? Why should looking in a mirror be better than looking at another person being – or playing at being – angry or resentful? When we look at that other person we do not go behind the external expression in order to decide whether the person is angry or cheerful despite the fact that we may be wrong. What would give more point to the painter's use of a mirror would be that it enabled him to take up a second position outside himself, to be both his own actor and observer. What is gained by that two-sidedness toward his own action is imagining himself in action.

In general we have an awareness of how we appear to others, for some sense of this is built into all our expressive behaviour, perhaps all our behaviour; we have the sense of our being in a shared world in which our conduct has a shape and expressiveness for others. (Of course we may dissimulate or hide our feeling, but our doing so itself assumes this accessibility in principle.) But if, in general, each of us perceives the emotional attitudes expressed in the postures and gestures of others and some sense of how we appear to others, what would be achieved by use of the mirror? One analogy that comes to mind is the way we revise what we have written: we re-read our texts, or re-hear – in memory or in a recording – what we have said in order to discover whether it articulated or conveyed what we thought we had conveyed, whether what we had said was adequate or appropriate to the occasion; and in a corresponding way we may monitor our gestures. Although all our speaking and gesturing anticipates how it would be taken up by those we are appearing to, we might try to be more aware of how we appear so as to make our expression more effective. We might imagine Hoogstraaten as achieving with his mirror not a correlation of external expression and internal feeling, but an exploration of the two-sidedness of behaviour, of active appearing to others.

The particular relevance to painting beyond being simply a convenient aid for effective human representation is the parallel between the two-sidedness of behaviour on the one hand and the two-sidedness of depiction on the other: for as behaviour typically anticipates appearing to others (which it may aim to diminish to the point of invisibility or episodically forget), so depiction anticipates its own visiblility. This is of its essence. Thus, in the depiction of people we may ask: does the inherent expressiveness for others that goes with being a person relate to the way painting is presented to be seen?

We can imagine pictures that include people – say the figures seen at a distance and unresolved in which the sense of behaviour is diminished – appearing as part of a visible array without the sense of bodily poise or gesture. At another extreme there are paintings in which we are acutely aware of the behaviour of figures but where our awareness of the painting procedure is diminished to near zero or dissociated from the figures it depicts. In contrast to these, at the centre of the painting that will be the concern of this chapter is their convergence: the painting procedure is presented to be seen, and seen as a way of showing its human subject so that each infuses our sense of the other.

The convergence might be of different kinds, the painting procedure attaching itself either primarily to the role of the viewer or to that of the subject; the painting procedure on the one side seeming to rehearse the viewer's scrutiny of the subject and on the other to rehearse the sitter's behaviour, to act the sitter's part. (The point may be made in an exaggerated way by comparing Bellini's *Doge Loredan* and Titian's *Doge Andrea Gritti* (figs 71 and 72).)

The sense of the painter acting his subject may be less demonstrative than in the case of Doge Gritti: for example, in the portrait by Titian in Vienna, called *The Physician Parma* (fig. 70), where the sitter is shown as concentrating and yet not engaged in an action that we can grasp. He is a man with greying hair in three-quarter view and clutching an academic gown or surcoat, and there is a particularly lucid delineation of the volume of the head. But this is combined with a certain understatement: throughout

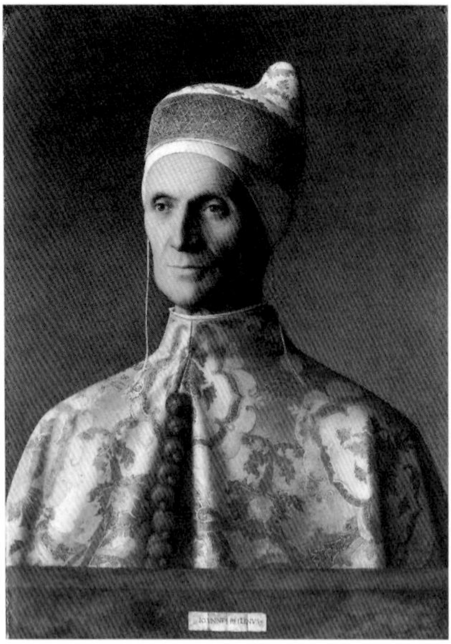

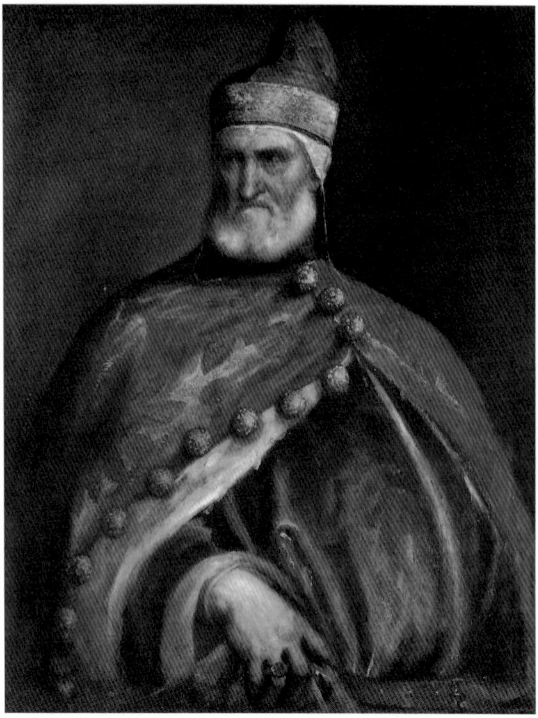

71 (*above left*) Giovanni Bellini, *Doge Loredan*, *c.*1501. Oil on panel, 61 × 44 cm. National Gallery, London.

72 (*above right*) Titian, *Doge Andrea Gritti*, 1535–8. Oil on canvas, 133.3 × 103.2 cm. Samuel H. Kress Collection, National Gallery of Art, Washington.

there are, seemingly, only slight changes in the homogeneous paint surface as we feel the brush against the grain of the canvas: the line of the nose against the far cheek is left implicit and the profile line, undisturbed by protruding features, forms a sharp boundary with the blank zone to the left. The concentration is matched by the grip of the veined hand, its abrupt squared-off foreshortening, and its disjunction from the arm and shoulder by the drapery. We utilize the understatement and compression in imagining not just his posture but his concentration. (The sense of the painting procedure as enriching and vitalizing our sense of the sitter is something pointed to, almost contemporaneously, by the Milanese artist and theorist Lomazzo. He described how drapery might be used to impart a sense of gesturing to the figure, which did not correspond literally to what the sitter was doing.[4] This, he says, should be restricted to portraits where it is not only a good but almost necessary enrichment, and it is something he regards as a distinctive feature of Venetian art as opposed to the art of Raphael. Lomazzo sees the subject's life as mimed by his clothes rather than the painting procedure, but he also makes a further analogy, comparing the painter imparting a sense of movement to the figure and the poet's creative urgency imparting life to his verses.)

We might be thought to utilize the sense of the painting procedure, in a way comparable to that in Titian's portrait *The Physician Parma*, in Tintoretto's *Vincenzo Morosini* (fig. 73) in the National Gallery in London; here the pull of the viscous paint mimes the skin across the forehead, and the brushstrokes marking the sleeves have an independent rhythm which informs rather than models the folds of the drapery and the posture of the figure, but there are some added factors. Both of these paintings are conducted within a tradition of portraiture where being made the subject of a portrait is a social usage. But within this tradition the sitter may be presented with greater or less formality. In Tintoretto's portrait the cropping of the figure at the edges, the concentration on the head and on its physiognomic accidents, and the ostensibly loose treatment of the drapery, which yet takes in the insignia of rank and honours, is informal. The painter's use of the conventions of portraiture are to make his and – by implication – our mode of address to the sitter attentive but unceremonial: it is to offer the distinguished sitter a means of presenting himself in a way that sustains his sense of rank while subordinating it to his personal presence. The painter, in controlling the portrait's mode of address within the social conventions of portraiture, is offering the sitter a means of presenting himself, but we may feel that there is no clear line between the painter's control and the authority of his subject. The painting urbanely acts the grandee it depicts. This indeterminacy between the character of the painting and the sitter was compared by Georg Simmel at the beginning of this century to that between the actor and the role: when we look at the portrait (he has those of Rembrandt in mind, but the point is more general) the sense of the painter's performance and the sense of the subject can be as inextricable as the personality of the actor and the protagonist he portrays.[5]

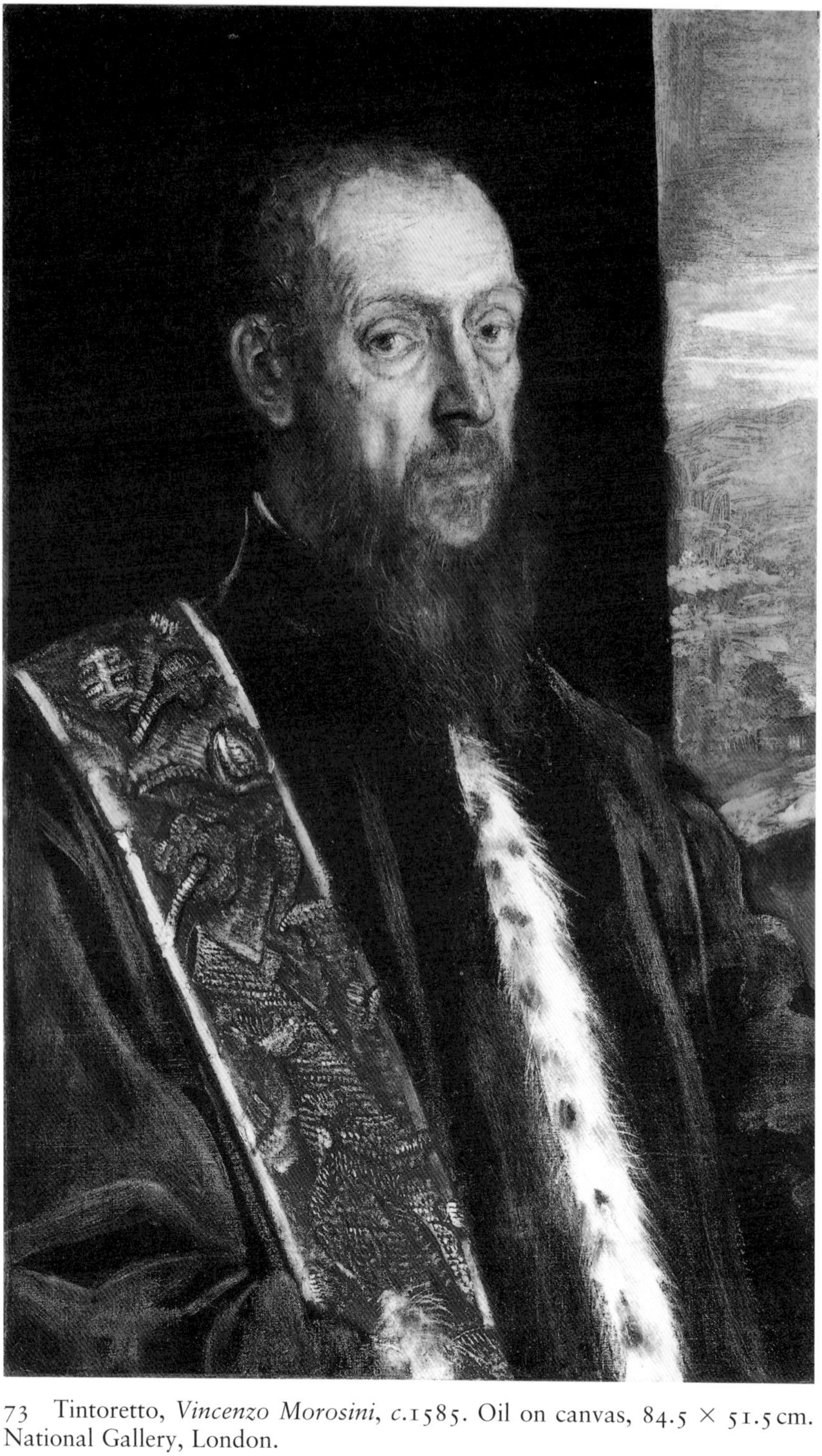

73 Tintoretto, *Vincenzo Morosini*, *c.*1585. Oil on canvas, 84.5 × 51.5 cm. National Gallery, London.

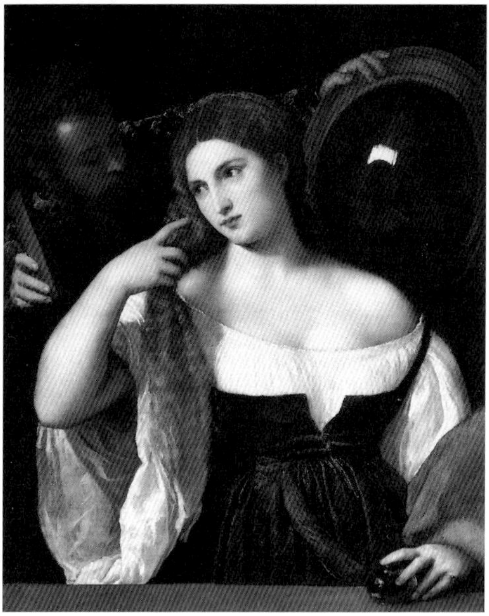

74 Titian, *Woman at her Toilet*, *c.*1515. Oil on canvas, 96 × 76 cm. Musée du Louvre, Paris.

We have so far observed three ways – or three kinds of emphases – in which painting relates itself to the figure or sitter it represents: the painter's procedure may rehearse scrutinizing the figure; in contrast to this it may rehearse the sense of movement within the figure; and thirdly the portrait may itself be a mode in which the sitter, with the co-operation of the painter, presents himself.

The notion of the painting procedure rehearsing or acting out the life of the sitter has application not only to such portraits as those of Parma and Morosini, but should be extended to Titian's paintings of women, like the *Woman with a Fur Wrap* (fig. 75) or the many Venetian paintings of women at their toilet. (That the subject was a model and not a commissioning sitter does not affect the issue.) It might be objected that here our sense of the painting procedure is used differently: it becomes an analogue of the (presumed) male viewer's delight in the physical and social presence of the woman. But if this is an ineliminable factor, it does not exclude our using the painting procedure to imagine the subject's sense of herself, as, for instance, in the painting of the *Woman at her Toilet* (fig. 74) where the modelling of her arm and shoulder with the finely layered gradients of tone suggest the sensitivity of the body's surface in the context of her self-absorbtion.[6]

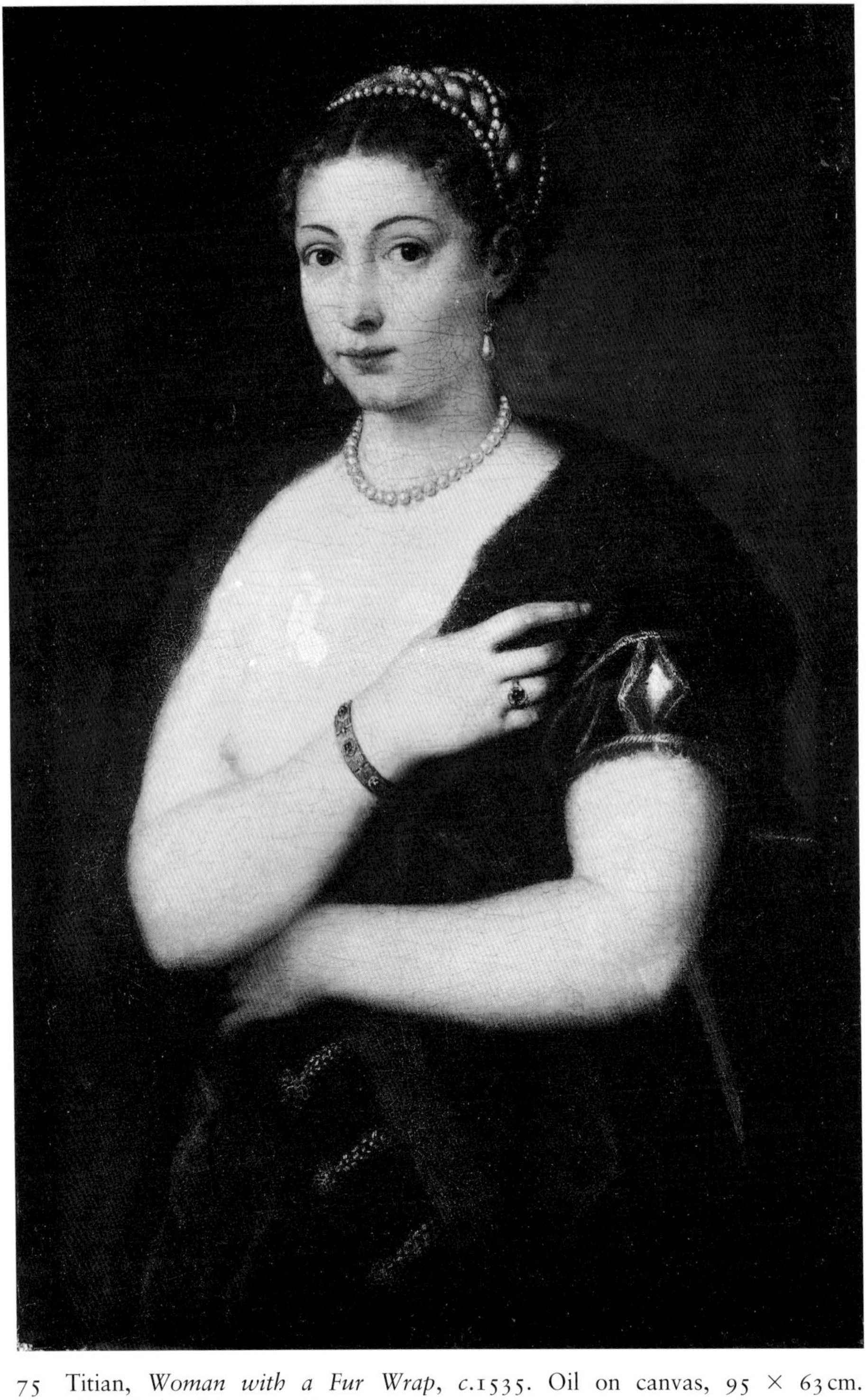

75 Titian, *Woman with a Fur Wrap*, *c.*1535. Oil on canvas, 95 × 63 cm. Kunsthistorisches Museum, Vienna.

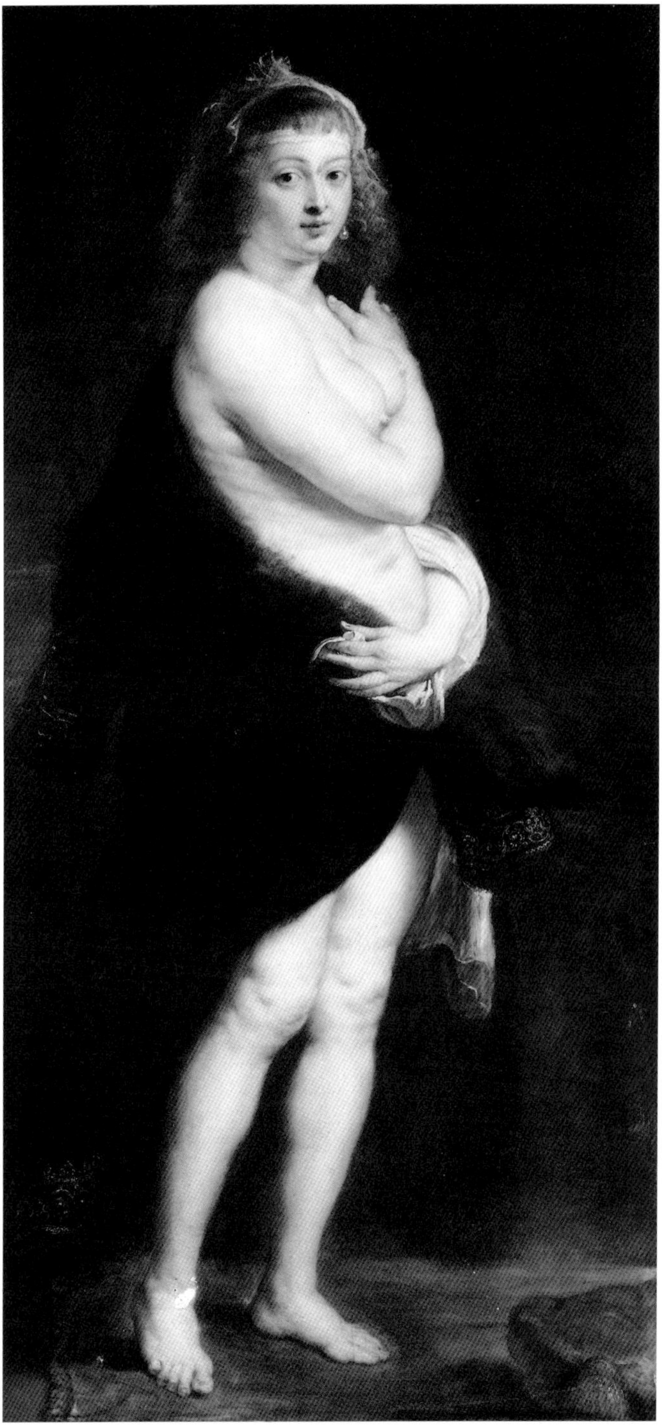

76 Rubens, *Hélène Fourment (Het pelsken)*, 1630. Oil on panel, 176 × 83 cm. Kunsthistorisches Museum, Vienna.

II

Let us now turn to the way in which the painter may be conceived not as observing or acting, but addressing his subject. In a painting that invokes Titian's *Woman with a Fur Wrap*, Rubens's *Hélène Fourment* (fig. 76), the painter was offering his young wife his vision of her in which she in turn could see herself. He offers her a sense of herself and of his admiration for her. Viewer and viewed have distinct roles and are re-related in a way that is brought about through the painting. Presumably this was already happening in the art of Titian but we do not have the corresponding information. Vasari writes that for Giovanni della Casa '. . . Titian did a beautiful portrait of a lady whom Giovanni loved in Venice, to which picture he wrote the sonnet beginning: "Ben vegg io, Titiano, in forme nuove/L'idolo mio, che i begli occhi apre e gira".'

The sonnet praises both the painter and the sitter. Titian's painting may have been conceived as a visual counterpart of, or at least naturally associated with, the sonnet writer's address to his mistress. Titian had produced his painting on behalf of della Casa, while Rubens had addressed his own wife in his painting. In each case the personal context of the painting mobilizes multiple potentialities of depiction: a convergence of addressing the figure, or looking at her with admiration, and of her seeing herself in the work that is being presented to her – the directedness of a painting to a viewer who is also its subject. The location of painting in personal or social relations becomes internal to the sense of the painting itself, while in its turn the painting gives focus to and elaborates the situation; it is not simply a reflection of it, or currency within it. Later there emerged a distinct register in which the procedure of painting seems caught up in a conversation.

III

Apart from the painter as an actor – acting, that is, through the presentation of his procedure – and taking the role of an unseen interlocutor he may appear as the visible protagonist. In the self-portrait properly so-called the painter presents himself, and he does so in two different senses: he presents his artefact, which is representative of his mind and skill and so of him as an artist, but

77 Nicolas Poussin, *Self-portrait*, 1650. Oil on canvas, 98 × 74 cm. Musée du Louvre, Paris.

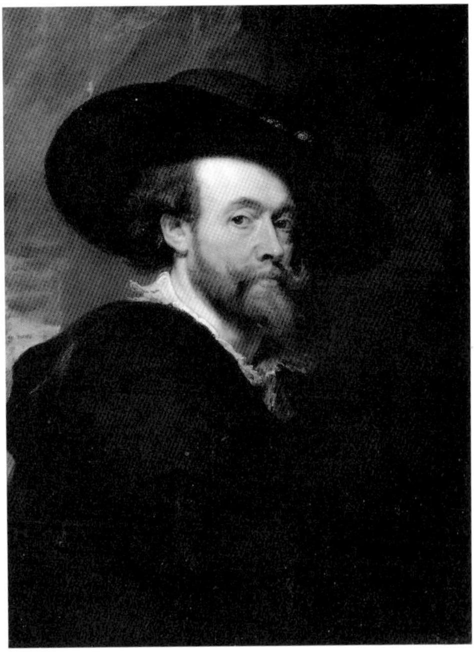

78 Rubens, *Self-portrait*, 1623. Oil on canvas, 86 × 62 cm. The Royal Collection © Her Majesty Queen Elizabeth II.

he also represents his social appearance. But are personal appearance and exemplary skill more than fortuitously or contingently related in the self-portrait? For the artist may exemplify his skill in depicting someone else, or in depicting the attributes of his art. What brings the two aspects of the self-portrait into an essential interdependence is the wider social context in which it is produced. For example, when the painter presents himself to his guild; an essential qualifying attribute is his skill, but he is also presenting himself socially, so the apt mode of self-presentation combines in exercising his skill with representing himself. The institution of the self-portrait as self-representation in the exercise of painting provides the framework in which these otherwise discrete elements are integrated. Thus Poussin presents himself to his patron friend, offering not merely his likeness as a memorial (and the sense of memorial here is very strong) but, in its elaborate construction, his very mind (fig. 77).[7] Rubens's self-portraits were in one case ordered by a royal patron, the prince who was soon to become

Charles I, and in another by a scholar friend, Peiresc (fig. 78).[8] The person and his skill were indissoluble in those contexts. The central cases of the self-portrait involve this address of the painter in his character as painter, to someone or group of people, his guild, his friend, or later – as in the case of Murillo – his family.[9] Murillo looks out across the frame and addresses his children as if from another world, and he addresses them in his role of painter with the attributes of his art. Hogarth, demonstrating his skill and aligning himself with the traditions of English literature (fig. 91), addresses not a single friend, like Poussin, nor a family, like Murillo, but London's literary world. In each case the appearance of the painter and the exemplification of his skills give focus to each other.

The address to the viewer may be made not only by the painter depicting himself in isolation. Titian sent Charles V a self-portrait carrying a painting of Charles's son Philip.[10] In *Las Meninas* Velázquez implicitly presented himself to Philip IV and his Queen (reflected in the mirror); he had included himself in the demonstration of his skill in depicting their daughter with her attendants, who is more directly presented to them, as Titian had depicted Charles's son, a connection already made in the early eighteenth century by Palomino in his biography of Velázquez.[11] These follow the logic of the self-portrait, the self-presentation through one's likeness, embodying one's skill.

In the self-portrait the painter is the protagonist and actor, but he can also become at the same time the person addressing and addressed. The centrality that Rembrandt has come to have in the conception of portrayal and in particular self-portrayal may lie in part in the extent to which he brought these distinct imaginative possibilities into a single focus. In the 1640 self-portrait and the etching of 1639 (figs 79 and 80) the world is addressed with splendid diffidence, the body drawn back, the painting of the grand costume of fine black and dark grey so markedly understated that the greatest discrimination is needed to discern its varying textures and shapes. Correspondingly in the depiction of the head the painter strokes in the ambiguities and elusive transitions without emphasis. Restraint is all, the restraint of the grandee. The sense of courtly presence is acted out by the posture and the painting. It is a self-portrait, and in the ambience in which Rembrandt worked it would surely have been recognized as such. But, as far as we know, Rembrandt was not presenting himself to a particular patron or friend with a demonstration of his artistry. It might at first seem to fall within a genre that developed in the sixteenth and seventeenth centuries, that of *tronies* – expressive heads. If we take a number of Rembrandt's early depictions of himself and others, and even single figures of, say, 'scholars', we can observe that they are, in their effect, dramatic; but the extensions or specific details of the drama are indeterminate, even with some suggestion that the drama is internal, a matter of thought. So we have a category of dramatic paintings without literary or narrative specificity: characters or characterizations. In depicting and acting such characters the painter is not placing himself within the social network that calls for painting a self-portrait. But if, for argument's sake, we think of this as self-depiction-as-character, there is the question of what kind of context we envisage for it.

Rembrandt's self-portrait of 1640 may not have been socially anchored like those of Rubens or Poussin, but it was surely anchored in the convention in which Rubens's own self-portraits participated and which was associated with a wider genre, the series of portraits of generals, nobles, men of letters and artists? Van Dyke's *Iconographia* (figs 81 and 82) which was being engraved in the 1630s was a series of this kind.[12] Constantijn Huygens, the scientist, humanist and courtier had been asked to write some verses for a portrait in this series, and a little later Rembrandt was in correspondence with Huygens over paintings for Prince Frederick Henry, offering Huygens a painting as a gift.[13] This is not to suggest that Rembrandt's self-portrait was that painting (it is anyhow dated two years later than the letter and the painting offered by Rembrandt is described as very large). But at the time the portrait of the artist as distinguished man was an established genre and Rembrandt was here adopting a pose suggesting Titian's *Ariosto* and Raphael's *Castiglione* (figs 83–5), which he had seen as they passed through the sale rooms of Amsterdam. The role that Rembrandt adopted here so grandly and with such grace of painting might appear to be that of the artist who presented himself for the collector of self-portraits or portraits of distinguished men; as Svetlana Alpers has argued persuasively, Rembrandt acted out these roles within the studio and without the context of patrons or institutions.[14]

When we turn to the late self-portraits (figs 86 and 87) we seem called upon to regard them rather differently. First we may

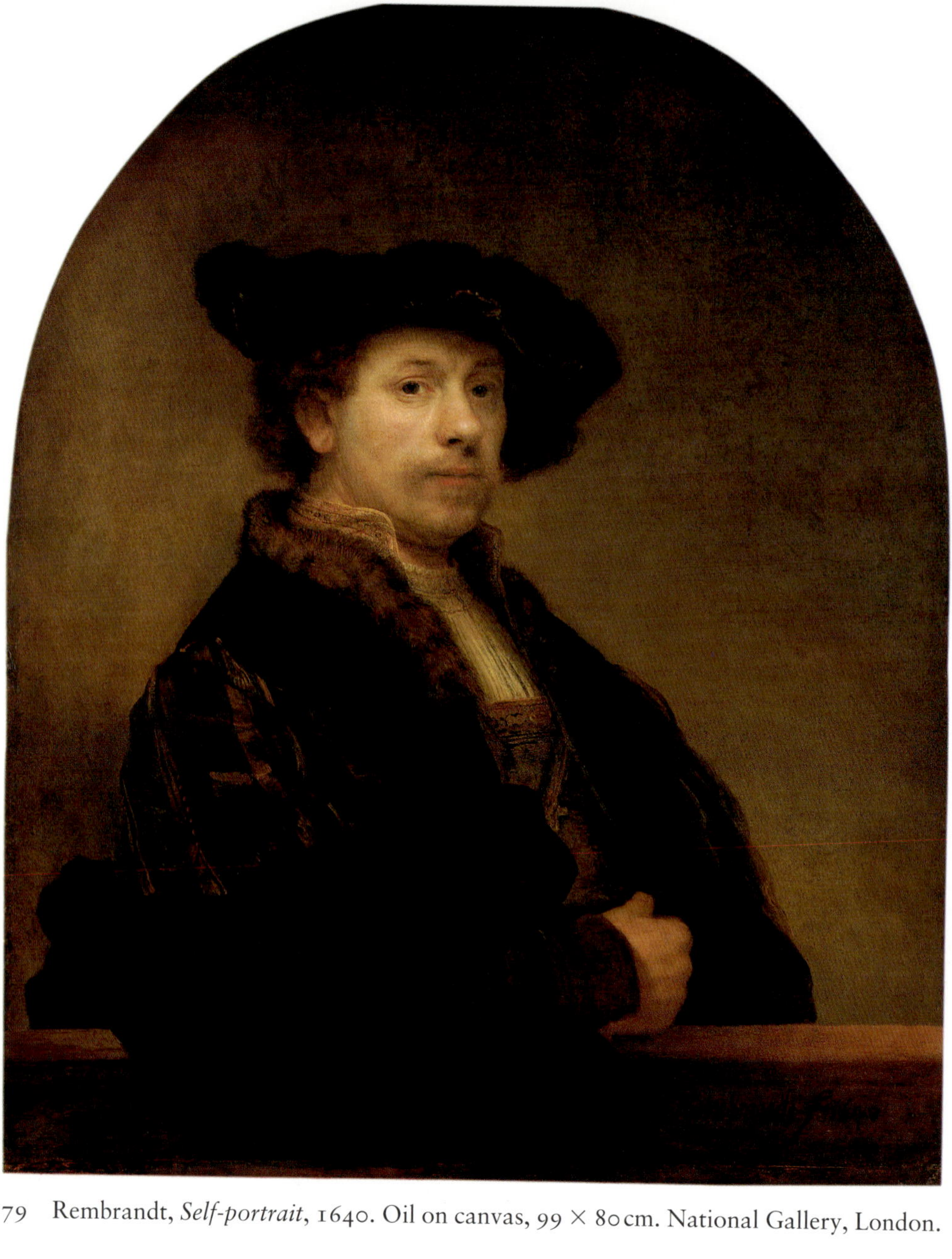

79 Rembrandt, *Self-portrait*, 1640. Oil on canvas, 99 × 80 cm. National Gallery, London.

81 (*right*) Anthony van Dyck (engraved by P. Pontius), *Constantijn Huygens* from his *Iconographia*.

82 (*far right*) Anthony van Dyck (engraved by L. Vosterman), *Jan Lievens* from his *Iconographia*.

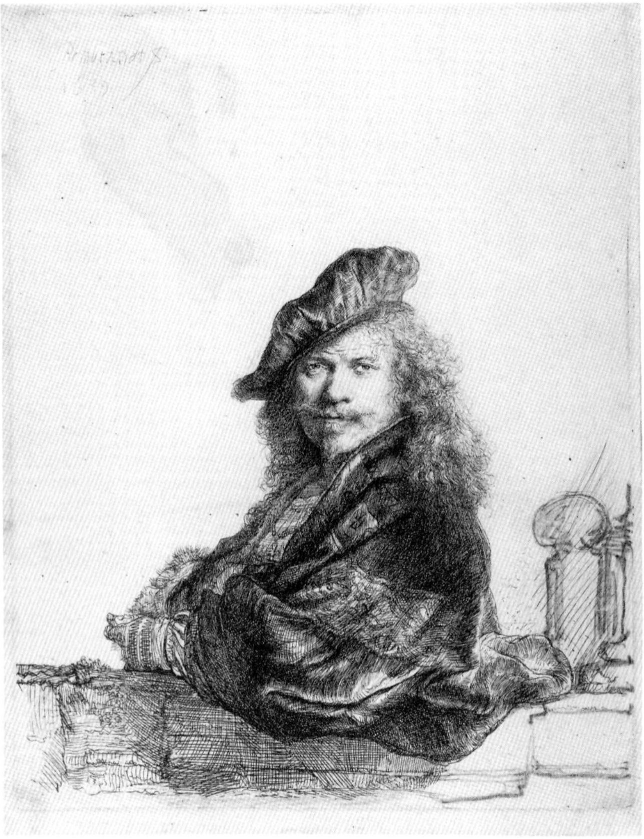

80 Rembrandt, *Self-portrait*, 1639. Etching, 20.7 × 16.4 cm. British Museum, London.

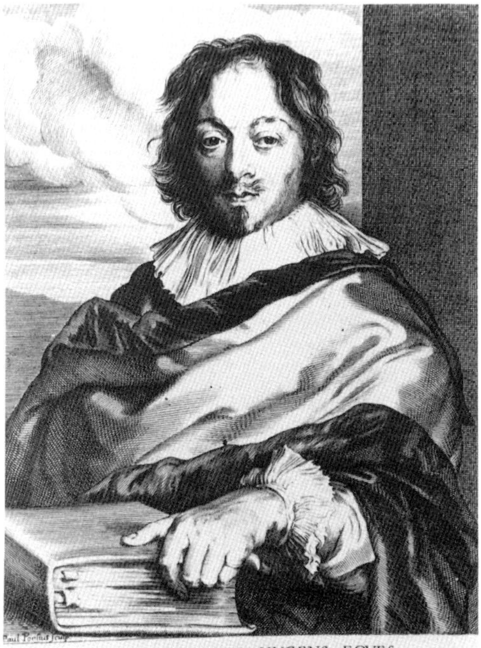

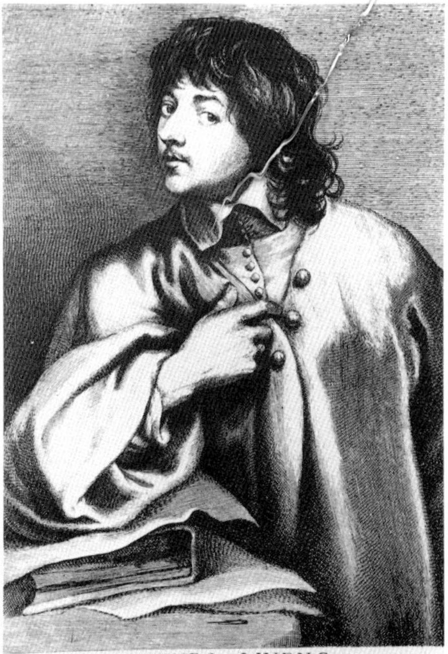

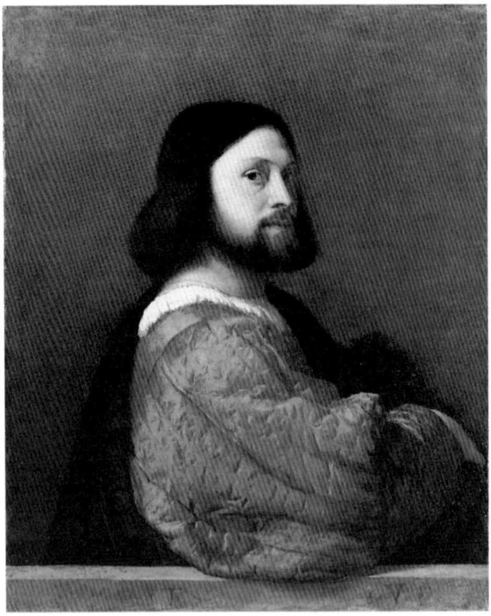

83 Titian, *Ariosto*, *c.*1512. Oil on canvas, 81.2 × 66.3 cm. National Gallery, London.

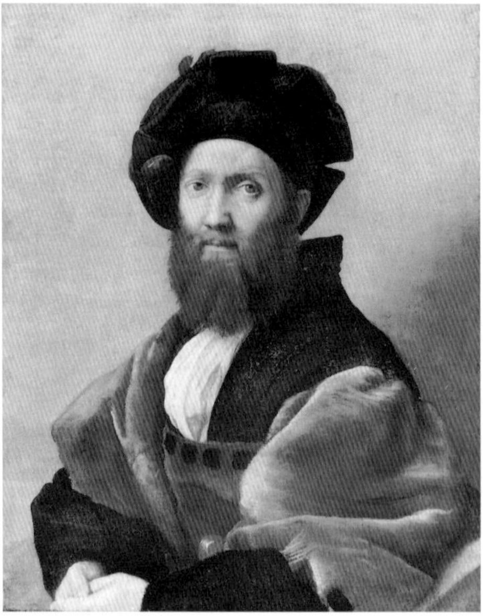

84 Raphael, *Castiglione*, *c.*1515. Oil on canvas, 81.5 × 51 cm. Musée du Louvre, Paris.

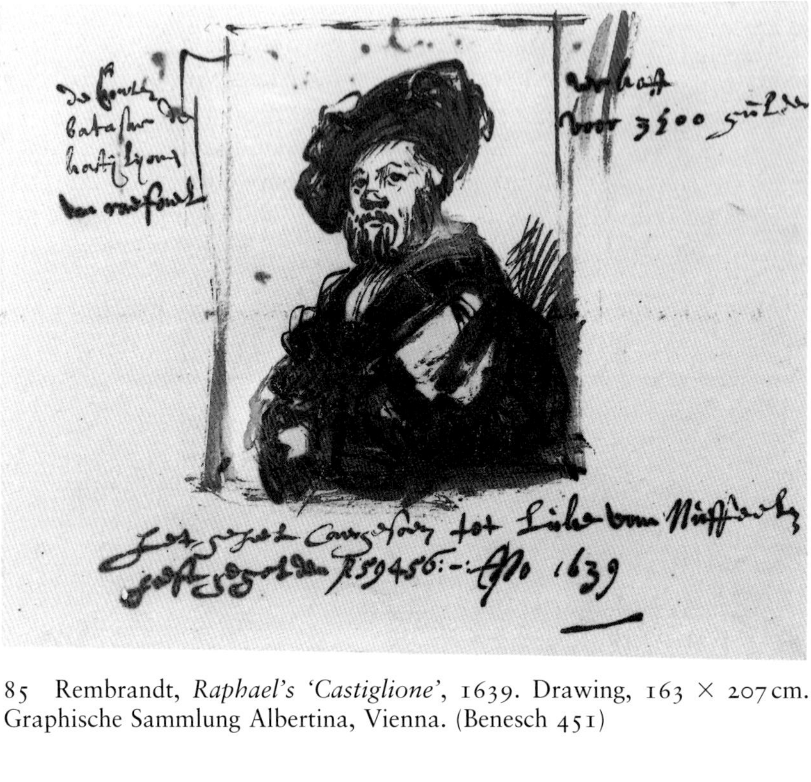

85 Rembrandt, *Raphael's 'Castiglione'*, 1639. Drawing, 163 × 207 cm. Graphische Sammlung Albertina, Vienna. (Benesch 451)

imagine him as divesting himself of roles. Once, as it were, he had been the actor in his grand paintings and comic etchings. But there came a point after which he often seemed not to be acting – to be presenting himself as *not* acting. He had come to know his own appearance so well over the years that he could scrutinize it in its deteriorations and inflexions – looking at himself from close to or further away, his lips now more, now less tensed – against a horizon of known possibilities richer and more complete than he, or anyone else, could bring to anything. Twenty years ago, in his penetrating essay on portrayal in Rembrandt, John Nash wrote:

> In his youth he drew his own features continually. He laughed, scowled, raged, enacting the gamut of the emotions, discovering the meaning of the human mask by examining it simultaneously inside and out . . . He also appears to have delighted in his youth in the inexhaustible protean variety of his being. He could become a beggar or a prince. By the transformations of his paint he could feign omnipotence. But as the years passed, as the 1650's gave way to the 1660's, it is evident that he grew impatient with the superfluity of these disguises . . . Impassivity was the true mask, through which and at which he peered in the daily confrontation at the twin mirrors of glass and canvas.[15]

In the Kenwood self-portrait (fig. 87) he stands against the large canvas, broadly – even perfunctorily – marked with the two circles of the *mappa mundi*, a painting with uniquely extensive areas unoccupied except by the sense of the painted surface, completely free of clutter, without distraction.[16] There are other late self-portraits where he does not appear to be addressing anyone and where we have something comparable with the structure of a Shakespearean soliloquy, as when Macbeth suddenly sees himself in the very actor, 'the poor player' who embodies Macbeth for us; we see the depicted Rembrandt seeing himself in the very painting that is the condition of our seeing him. This convergence of factors, as we observe what he observed in his own self-scrutiny, should not give rise to self-bemusing paradox of the *mis en abime* variety: it is not a matter of paradox but of many layeredness in which the roles overlap: the viewer of the painting; the viewer of the figure; the painter of the figure; the figure painted. These coincide in multiple ways. What those coincidences show us is the mobility of factors that are in play generally in portrayal. Having aligned them like this, having made them thus coincident or convergent, a new kind of concentration entered painting.

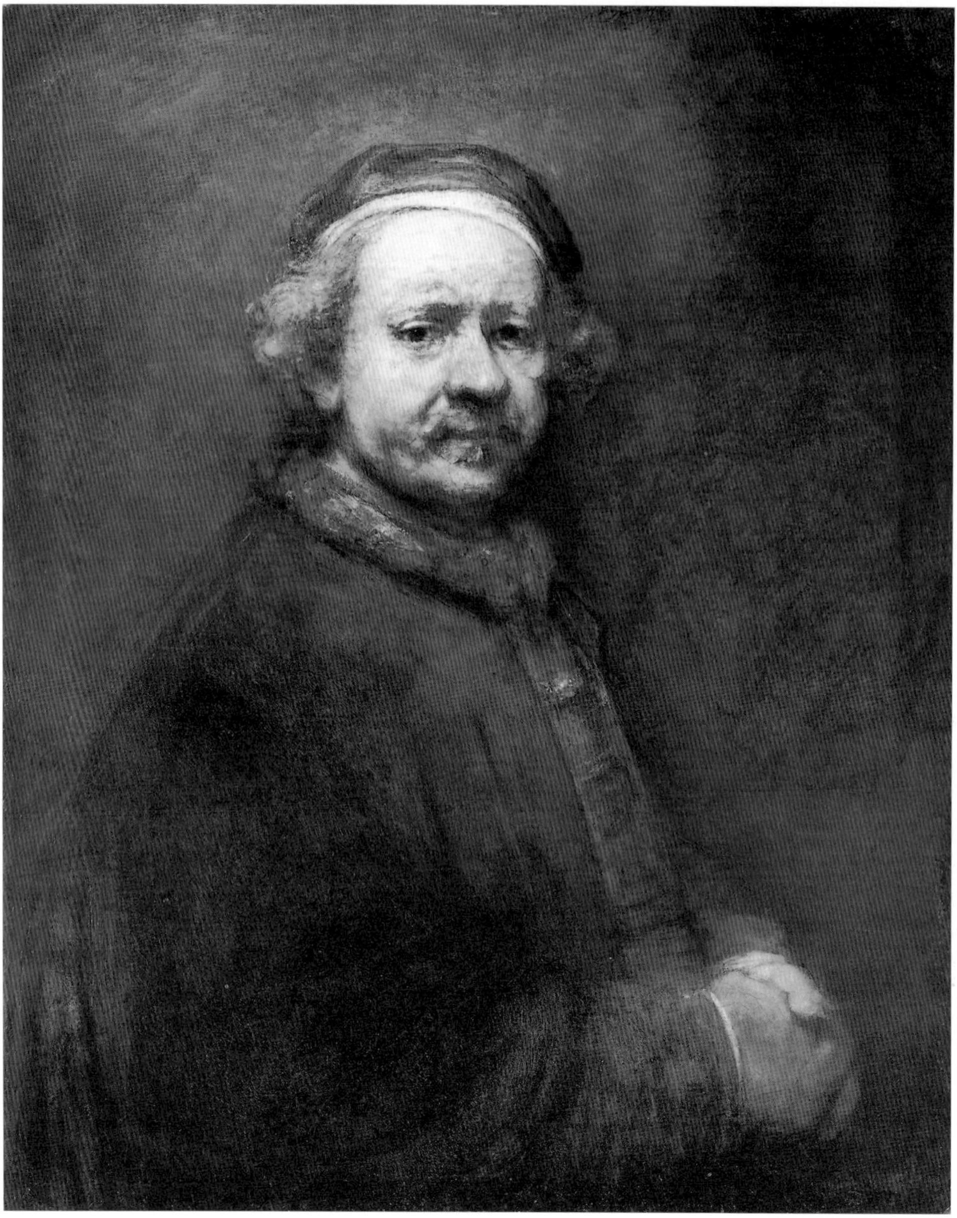

86 Rembrandt, *Self-portrait*, 1660. Oil on canvas, 83 × 69 cm. National Gallery, London.

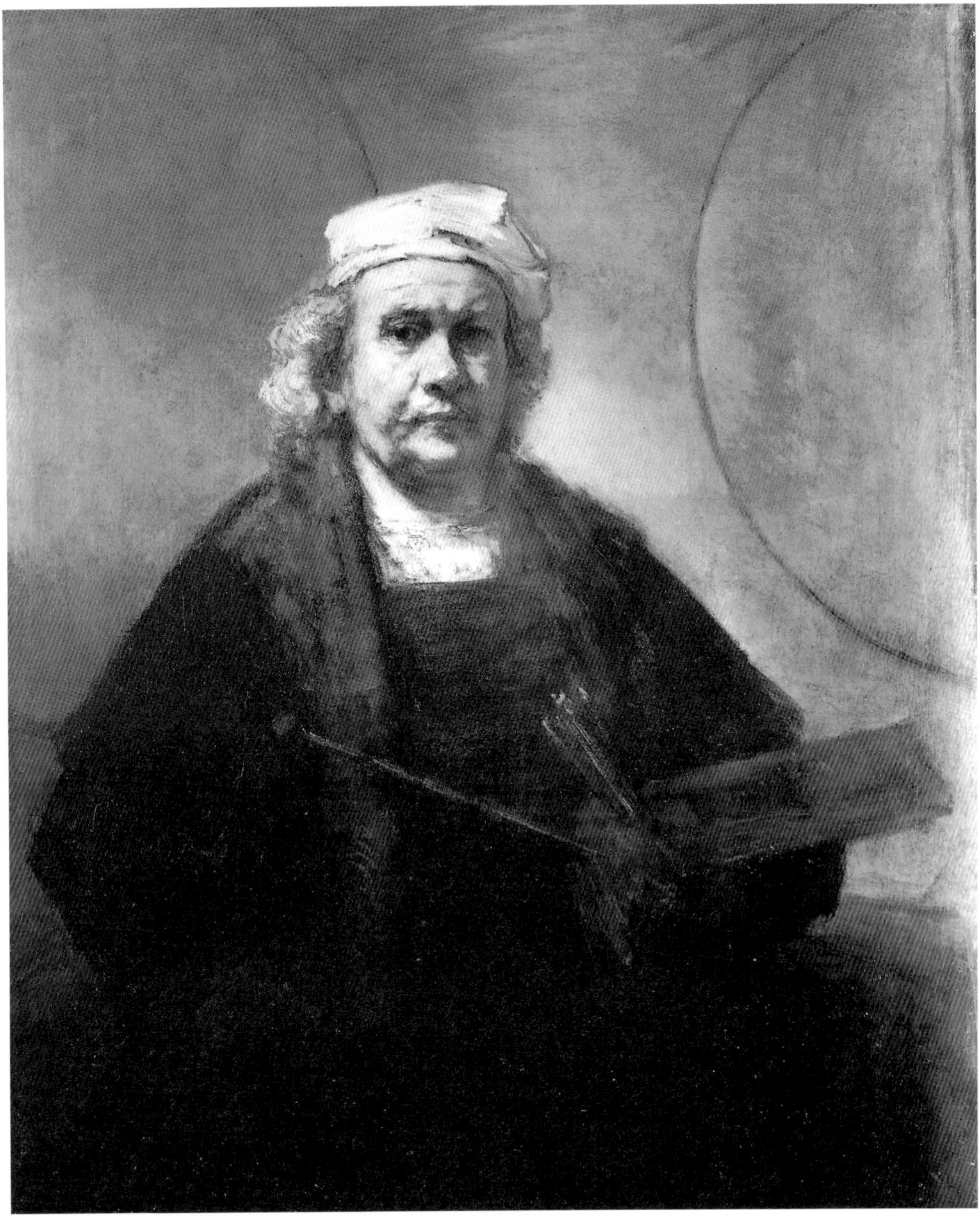

87 Rembrandt, *Self-portrait*, *c*.1665. Oil on canvas, 144.5 × 94 cm. Iveagh Bequest, Kenwood, London.

This convergence of factors no longer seems surprising. The portrait that implies reciprocity with the sitter (radically unlike the profile of the medal) and even intimacy (unlike the state portrait), as well as the self-portrait itself are now central to our conception of the art. The art itself has developed, since the sixteenth century, continuously shifting ways of registering and nurturing intimate reciprocity, playing off courtly formality against informal friendship or familial relations. But at the core lies the relation of the viewer and the viewed, and the way each may identify with and address the other while the painter by turn takes all the parts.

Part Two

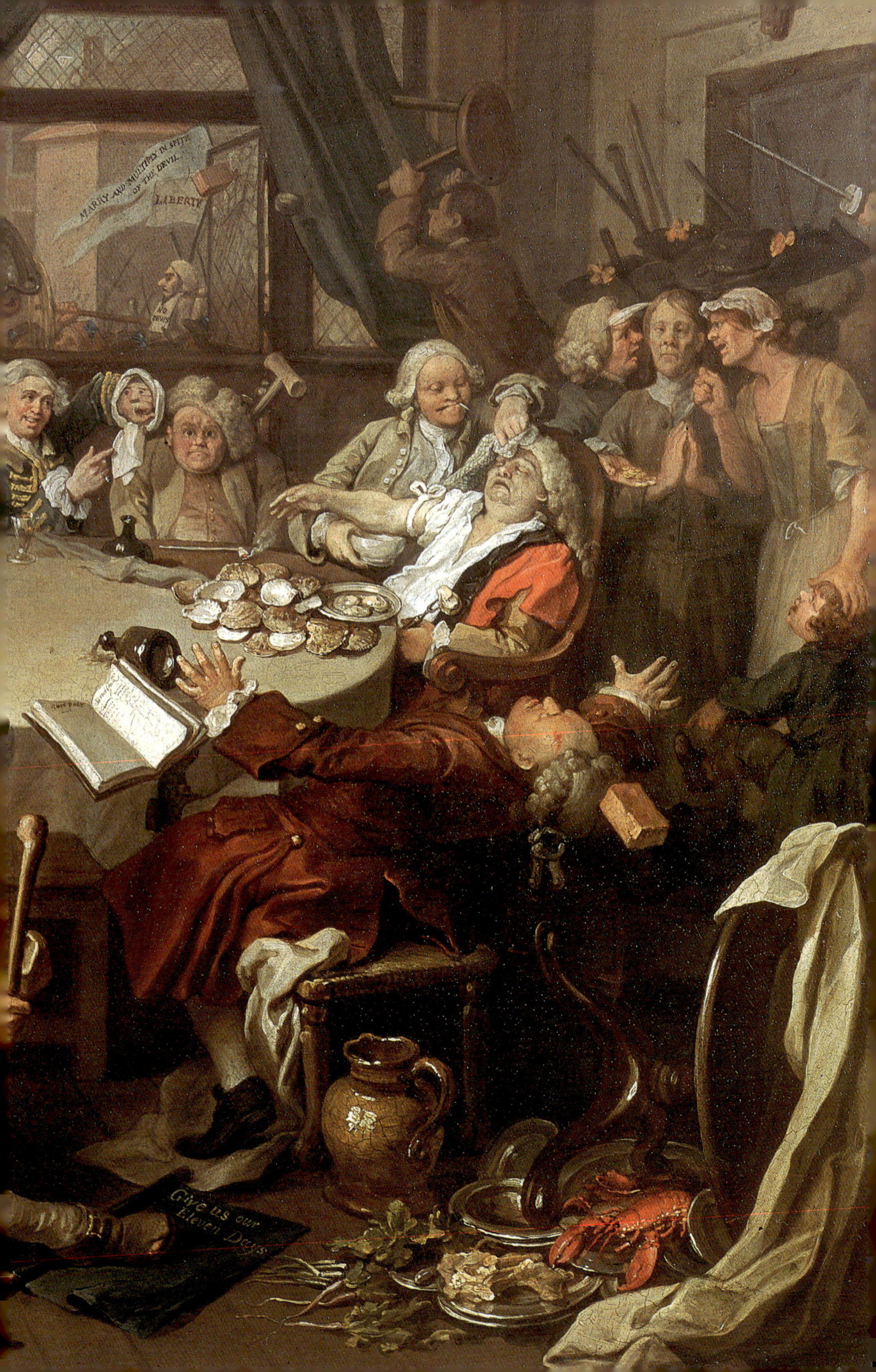
MARRY AND MULTIPLY IN SPITE OF THE DEVIL
LIBERTY
NO JEWS
Give us our Eleven Days

Chapter Five

Hogarth's *Analysis* and its Application

THE PREVIOUS CHAPTERS HAVE BEEN CONCERNED with how the painter transforms his subject and with his recursive use of depiction's psychological as well as its material conditions. The next chapters, which form the second part of this book, are on Hogarth and Chardin respectively, examining how this process takes on two further kinds of implication: on the one hand how it becomes a mode of social behaviour and on the other a mode of private self-reflection. Not only were these possibilities developed in the work of these artists but they were articulated in related writing, by Hogarth himself and by theorists in the ambience of Chardin.

I

Hogarth's *Analysis of Beauty* examines aspects of depiction that have nowhere else been so fully articulated.[1] For Hogarth the painting or the print does not merely represent and reconstitute its subject, but opens up a distance between the subject and its representation so that the painting takes on a separate voice, at its clearest when the implied attitude of the painting is ironic, refusing to be complicitous with how depicted figures or institutions like the Church or Parliament would present themselves.

The context in which Hogarth wrote was the literary and political world in which, as a painter, he had already gained a distinctive status. He had established himself, after his early years, without inherited means, working progressively less for print-makers and publishers, or painting portraits merely to survive, and

88 Hogarth, *The Election Entertainment*. Detail of fig. 107.

never acting as an agent for rich clients buying pictures. He was an entrepreneur who created his own merchandize. By first becoming in 1731 the dealer for his prints of *The Harlots's Progress*, avoiding, as he claimed, the exploitation of the printsellers, he then further secured his position by getting the visual artist's copyright act through Parliament, estabishing his professional and economic status.[2] One way of regarding the *Analysis* within his career is as a further stage in confirming the comparability of the painter's authorship to the writer's. In the campaign to gain copyright for printmakers it had been argued that the artist added his intellectual labour to the paper on which he drew and this earned him his right to the work as his property; in the *Analysis*, that insistance on the role of the painter became a matter not only of claiming authorship of his invention but a challenge to the authority of the men of letters or theologians in the sphere of visual art. Arguing for its own irreducible mode of thought, he was not isolating painting from the world of issues beyond itself – of morality, money, sexuality and religion – but showing how it engaged with them through its own distinctive constitution, and he did this by demystifying the procedures of the painter.

The diagrammatic images [figs 1 and 2]* accompanying the text of the *Analysis*, he wrote,

> will never be imagined to be placed there by me as examples themselves, of beauty or grace, but only to point out to the reader what sorts of objects he is to look for and examine in nature, or in the works of the greatest masters. My figures, therefore, are to be considered in the same light, with those a mathematician makes with his pen, which may convey the idea of his demonstration . . . Nay, so far was I from aiming at grace, that I purposely chose to be least accurate, where most beauty might be expected, that no stress might be laid on the figures to the prejudice of the work itself. [p. 22]

He contrasts his approach with the 'more fashionable introduction to the mysteries of the arts of painting, and sculpture'. To a remarkable extent he honours his promise. In a broad sense his argument might be thought Lockian, isolating the relatively simple elements out of which the complexity of art is produced. But the

* Page, plate and figure numbers given in square brackets refer to Hogarth, *The Analysis of Beauty*, 1753.

elements are not simple ideas of sensation, rather they are procedures of thought and execution.

II

The Arguments of the *Analysis*

1 Hogarth's 'Introduction' starts with the kind of advice that drawing instructors give their students; it is unmistakably part of a pedagogical procedure and we may assume that Hogarth developed it while teaching at the St Martin's Lane Academy and in instructing others who, it seems, consulted him.[3] He tells the student to conceive of the object that he is trying to draw as a hollow shell, the volume of which is defined by wires or threads; he should then think of his own outline of the object as corresponding to one such wire. In this way Hogarth sets out to overcome two of the new student's most basic difficulties:

> in the common way of taking the view of any opake object, that part of its surface, which fronts the eye, is apt to occupy the mind alone, and the opposite, nay even every other part of it whatever, is left unthought of at the time: and the least motion we make to reconnoitre any other side of the object, confounds our first idea, for want of a connexion of the two ideas, which the complete knowledge of the whole would naturally give us. [pp. 8 f.]

The purpose of imagining the hollow shell is first to enable the student to disengage himself from seeing the object he is drawing as a flat shape; he must learn not to hug the outline but on the contrary to probe it for what it can be made to reveal about the volume; and secondly he must disengage himself from his own drawn line, which could prevent him remaining flexible and alert, so that – as Hogarth said – 'the least motion we make to reconnoitre any other side of the object confounds our first idea'. The young draughtsman must learn to use his line to imagine the volume of the object, avoiding fixation on silhouette or his own marks. This is the kind of advice still found in the life room where drawing instructors recall the dictum – which had been repeated by Cézanne – to draw by the cone, the cylinder and the sphere, or tell the student to go for the spatial structure, and not merely to

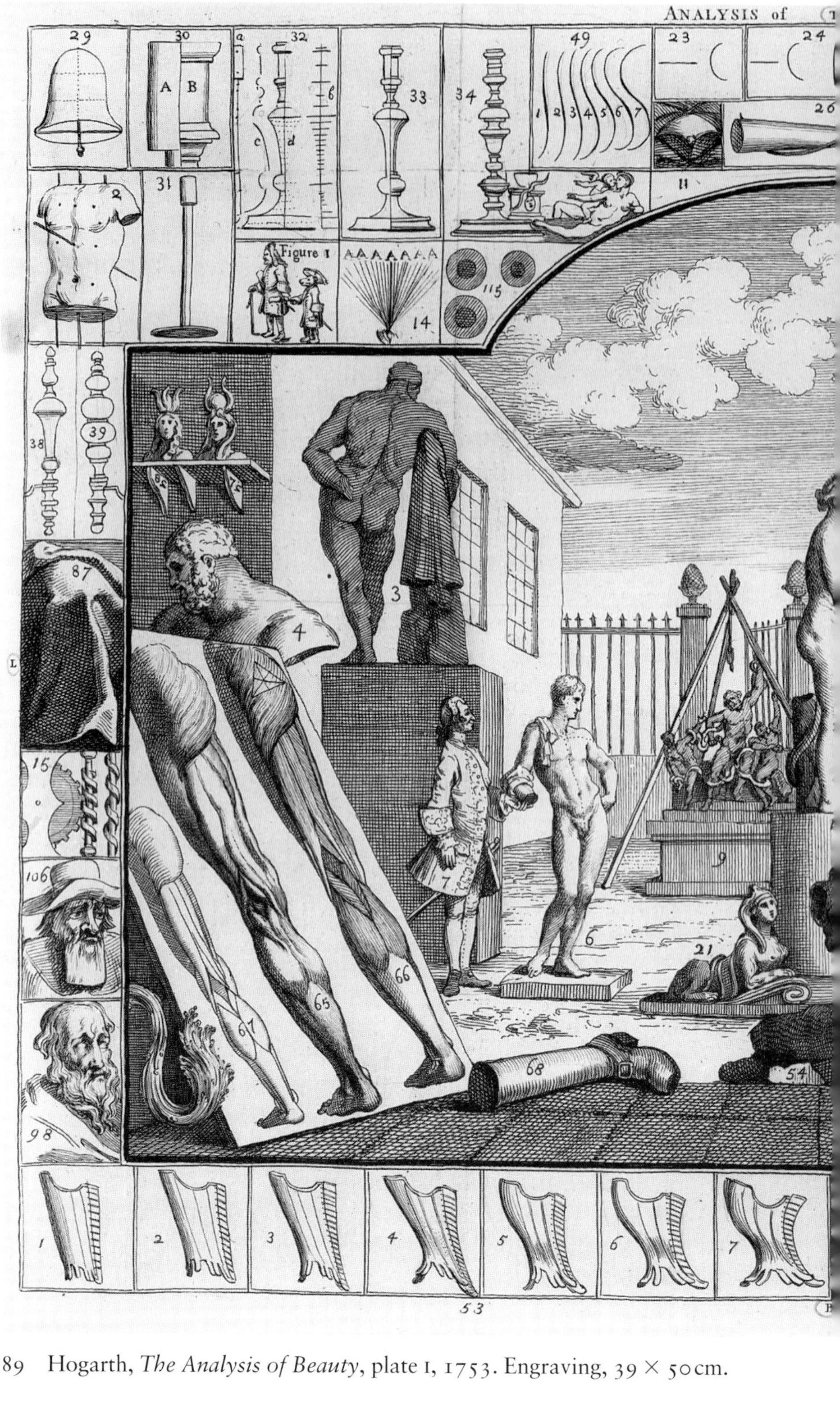

89 Hogarth, *The Analysis of Beauty*, plate I, 1753. Engraving, 39 × 50 cm.

AUTY, Plate I.

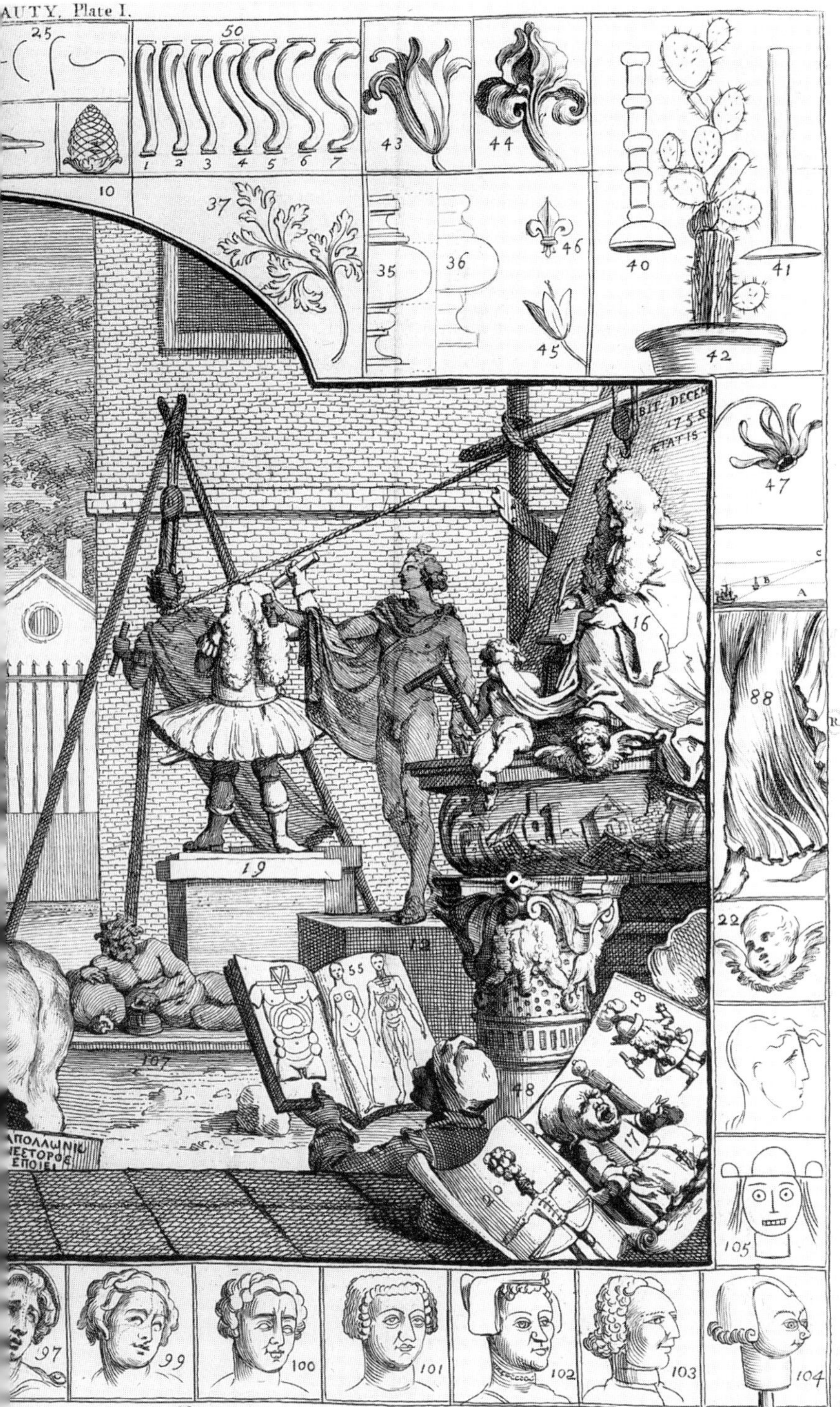

Designed, Engraved, and Publish'd by Wm. Hogarth, March 5th 1753, according to Act of Parliament.

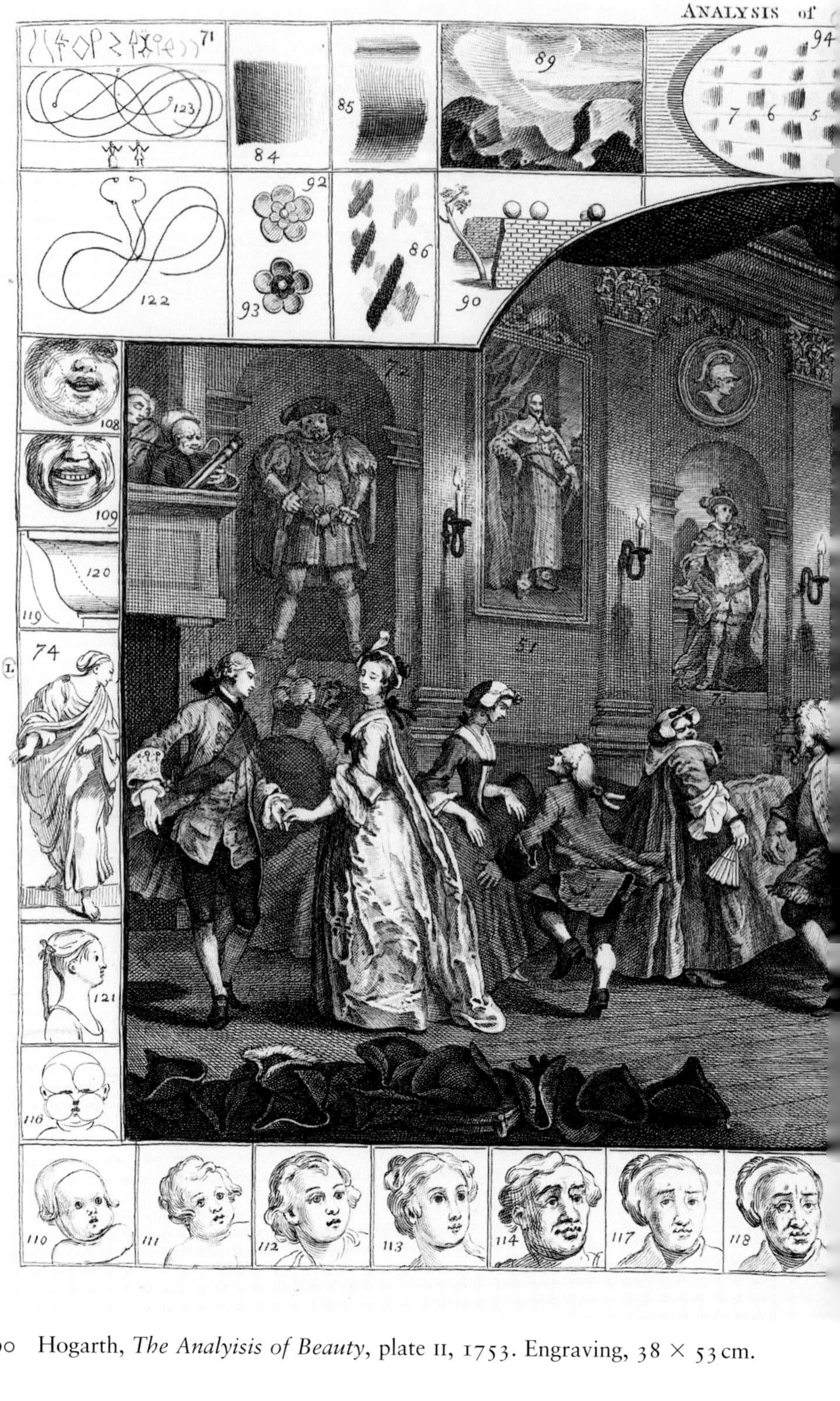

90 Hogarth, *The Analyisis of Beauty*, plate II, 1753. Engraving, 38 × 53 cm.

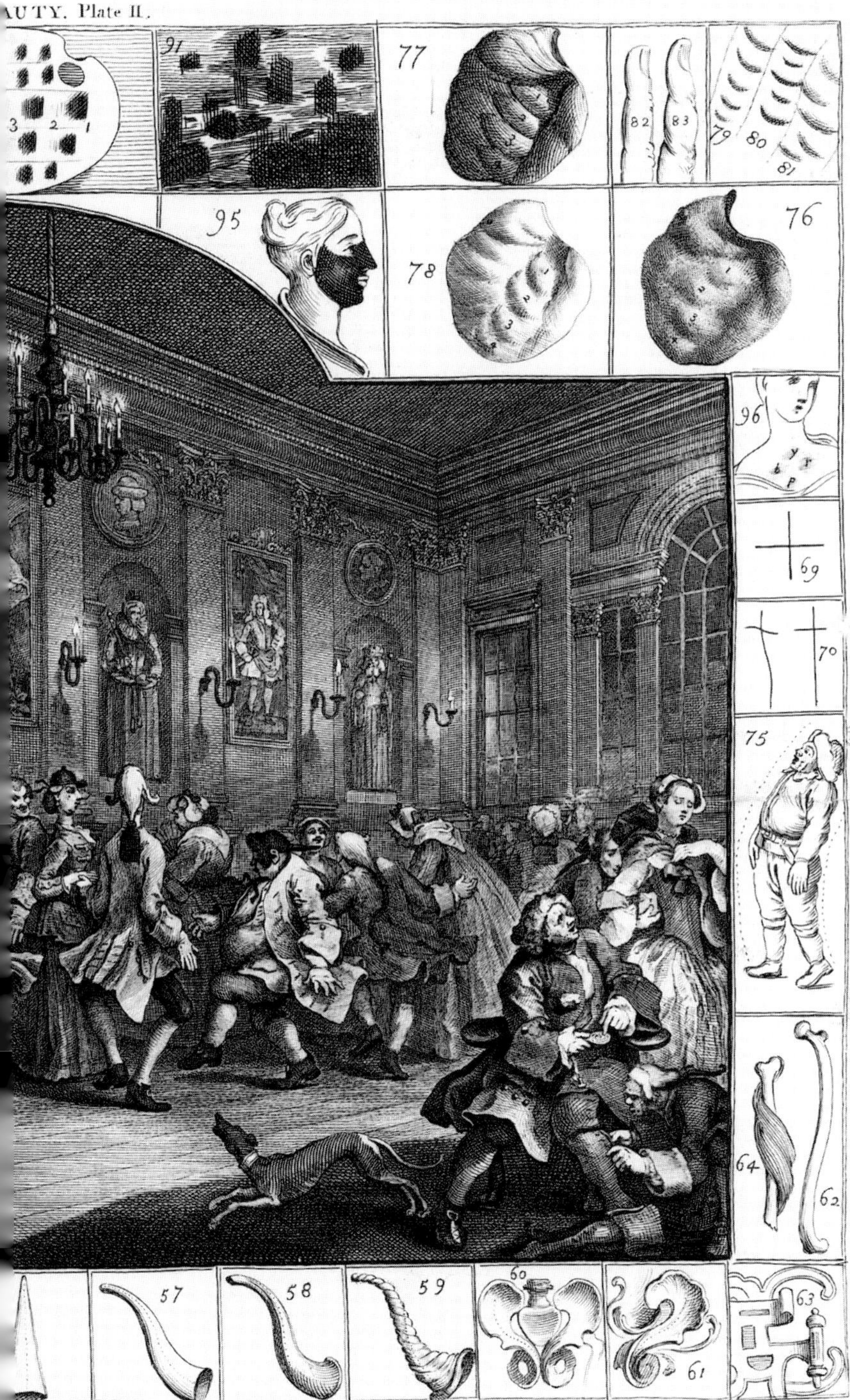

Designed, Engraved, and Publish'd by Wm. Hogarth, March 5th 1753, according to Act of Parliament.

mime edges. In other remarks the point is enforced by insisting that drawing is not a matter of copying but understanding, even understanding the grammar of objects:

> there were many disadvantages attended going on . . . continually copying Prints and Pictures altho they should be those of the best masters [,] nay even drawing after the life in the academys. For as the Eye is often taken off the original to draw a bit at a time, it is possible to know no more of the original when the drawing is finish'd than before it was begun. Thus it is common with the Hackney writers to know no more of what they have been copying than if they had not wrote a line, unless they have paid attention to it with that design . . . more reasons why I should not continue copying objects but rather read the Language of them and if possible find a grammar to it.[4]

2 But there is a further implication of the wire shell: by use of it we will not only 'facilitate and strengthen our conception of any particular part of the surface . . . [and] . . . acquire a more perfect knowledge of the whole to which it belongs: [but] the imagination will naturally enter into the vacant space within the shell, and there at once, as if from the centre, view the whole from within . . .' [p. 8]. The young artist must not only be the observer of what he draws but imagine what he draws as if from the inside; to draw convincingly is not to map surfaces nor simulate appearances, it is also to imagine being situated mentally within the object.

3 The most cited and discussed idea in Hogarth's theory, what he himself made its emblem, is the serpentine line. He placed it on his palate in the self-portrait of 1745 (fig. 91) and on his title page, returning to it throughout his book. It is sometimes treated by commentators as if it were an eccentric doctrine or personal signature like Whistler's butterfly or as it were itself an explanation of the beauty of form. It is neither. It is a paradigmatic example, the effect of which he sets out to explain and analyse rather than leave as a mystery. The serpentine line had already been the subject of a substantial literature;[5] Hogarth cites in his preface Dryden's translation of Dufresnoy's *De Arte Graphica* with the commentary by Roger de Piles, where a good deal of Hogarth's thought is anticipated. The serpentine line functioned not only in drawing the figure but in ornamental decoration of the kind Hogarth must

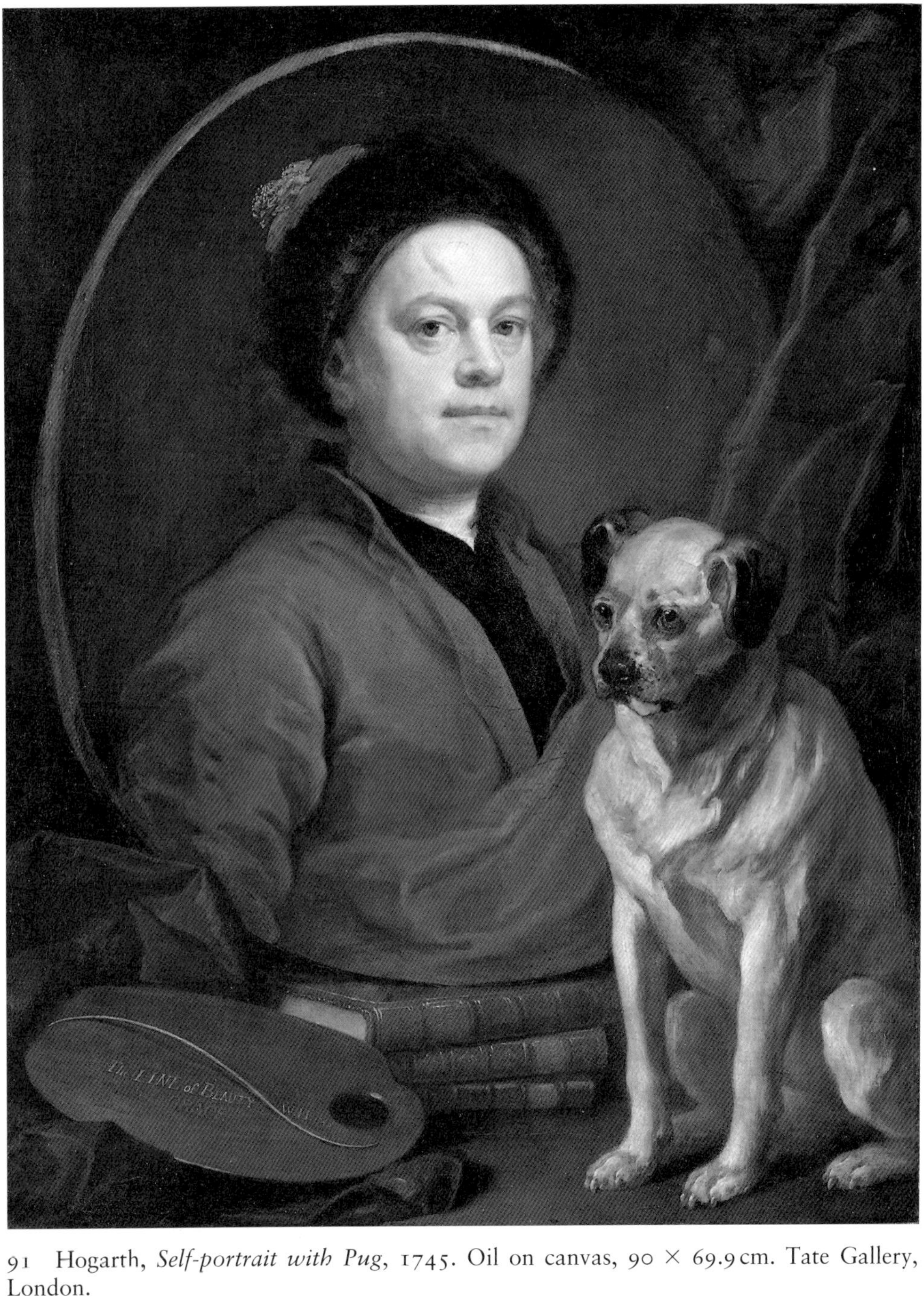

91 Hogarth, *Self-portrait with Pug*, 1745. Oil on canvas, 90 × 69.9 cm. Tate Gallery, London.

himself have rehearsed in his years as an apprentice silver engraver. But in taking up the notion he does not simply advocate the line as a principle but sets out to show why it could take on this paradigmatic status.

> that serpentine line, by its waving and winding at the same time different ways, leads the eye in a pleasing manner along the continuity of its variety . . . and which by its twisting so many different ways, may be said to inclose (tho' but a single line) varied contents; and therefore all its contents cannot be expressed on paper by one continued line, without the assistance of the imagination, or the help of a figure. [pp. 38f. and plate I, fig. 26]

In a further diagrammatic illustration he shows the fertility of the line: he leads us to see not only the continuity between the line's two-dimensional shape and its three-dimensional implication, but between its variety and informativeness:

> In the first of these figures, the dotted line down the middle expresses the straight lines of which it is composed; which, without the assistance of curve lines, or light and shade, would hardly show it to have contents. The same is true of the second, tho' by the bending of the horn, the straight dotted line is changed into the beautiful waving-line . . . But in the last, this dotted line, by the twisting as well as the bending of the horn, is changed from the waving into the serpentine-line; which, as it dips out of sight behind the horn in the middle, and returns again the smaller end, not only gives play to the imagination, and delights the eye, on that account; but informs it likewise of the quantity and variety of the contents. [pp. 51f. and plate II, figs 56–8]

Hogarth then adds – with obvious pleasure at the potentiality of his example [plate II, fig. 59] – a horn with a spiral running round its surface, 'with yet more variations (and therefore more beautiful)' [p. 53]. He then invites us to imagine that twisted horn cut in half down the middle so revealing the inside surface of the half we would not see; thus making manifest to us what we had all the time imagined – the continuity of the spiralling line as it becomes occluded from view.

4 And beyond this informativeness and complexity the line has yet a further value, a further appeal to our imagination: 'That

waving line, or line of beauty, varying still more, being composed of two curves contrasted, becomes still more ornamental and pleasing, insomuch that the hand takes a lively movement in making it with a pen or pencil' [p. 38]. Crucially, we have the sense of participation in the form of the object, not only by our attention being led to follow the twists of the form but by our own gesture informing it.

5 These four factors come together in representing the human body: 'Almost all the muscles and bones, of which the human form is composed, have more or less these kind of twists in them [as the horn which twists as well as bends] . . . There is scarce a straight bone in the whole body.. Almost all of them are not only bent different ways, but have a kind of twist in them which in some of them is very graceful' [pp. 54–5]. Hogarth's argument here, broadly, is that the human body is potentially the supreme exemplification of beauty and the prevalence in it of the serpentine line confirms our intuition of the beauty of that line: our intuitions converge and – as he says regarding the more serpentine character of the woman's body over the man's – this 'enhances the merit' of his principles.

The beauty of the serpentine line coincides not only with the morphology of the human body but with its movement: Hogarth consistently ties the sense of form to the sense of movement; 'it is plain and evident that nature has thought fit to make beauty of proportion, and beauty of movement necessary to each other . . . he who is exquisitely proportioned is most capable of exquisite movement . . .' [p. 76], and he later goes on to elaborate on 'our usual feeling, or joint sensation, of figure and motion'. He brings the sense of form and movement together in his example of the ceremonious gesture of handing a lady a snuff-box or a fan, which traces the serpentine form through the air. And Hogarth finesses his game by pointing to the way in which the movement of the hand in making that elegant gesture corresponds to the movement of the hand in drawing the two-dimensional line of beauty onto a curved architectural moulding. The form, its movement and the movement of the draughtsman are seen through each other. [p. 143 and plate II, figs 119 and 120]

6 Hogarth goes on to examine a phenomenon wider in scope than the realm of painting: how we distinguish between the forms that provide visual satisfaction, those that 'please and entertain the

eye' from those that do not, inviting us to discriminate between various candlesticks [p. 41], various drawings of the thorax or of the musculature of a leg. Even where there is no serpentine line the same general principle obtains: we take pleasure in the variety in unity, in separate forms retaining their distinct and varied characters within a comprehensive overall shape. But this capacity to entertain the eye is not merely a matter of shapes; we do not occupy a world of ornaments. Whether a lever is strong enough to lift a weight, a column sturdy enough to support its load or the body to move swiftly is internal to how they look, or how they can be made to appear. These factors 'cooperate in the production of beauty, mutually correcting and restraining each other occasionally' [p. 12]. The appearance of function and the elegance of shape limit each other in the cause of beauty. (Here Hogarth's thoughts about beauty of forms considered in themselves and then considered in relation to function corresponds to that of Francis Hutcheson, who also saw beauty as lying in Unity amidst Variety: 'Cubes or square Prisms are generally chosen for Pedestals of Statues, and not any of the more beautiful solids, which do not seem so secure from roll . . . The like Reason may influence Artists, in many other Instances, to depart from the Rules of original Beauty, as above laid down. And yet this is no argument against our sense of Beauty being founded, as was above explain'd, on Uniformity amidst Variety, but only an Evidence, that our sense of Beauty of the Original Kind may be vary'd and over-balance'd by another kind of Beauty'.[6]) Hogarth's corresponding acknowledgement that the beauty of form requires a sense of propriety or function prompts the question of what kind of beauty and what kind of unity is possessed not just by a single form or figure but by a painting or an image taken as a whole.

7 For Hogarth this cannot be identified with some overall morphology, nor even a compromise between morphology and characterization. Rather it is a matter – to use Hogarth's term – of pursuit relating one group or figure to another, by searching out connections and continuities of both form and significance.

> The active mind is ever bent to be employ'd. Pursuing is the business of our lives; and even abstracted from any other view, gives pleasure. Every arising difficulty, that for a while attends and interrupts the pursuit, gives a sort of spring to the mind,

enhances the pleasure, and makes what would else be toil and labour, become sport and recreation. [p. 42]

And this pleasure in pursuit is not a matter merely of serpentine lines, but plots and 'labours of the mind' in working out riddles and allegories.[7]

Previous writers, pre-eminently Roger de Piles, had also presented theories of how painting structured the viewer's attention to his subject. There is a considerable amount that Hogarth takes over from de Piles, but where de Piles had conceived this structure as achieved primarily by the distribution of light, giving concentration to a single central feature and subsuming discrete forms into an overall tonal effect, Hogarth says virtually nothing about visual emphasis and little about the tonal unity of the image.[8] Where Hogarth talks of tonal and colour gradients he is primarily concerned with local transitions in modelling or spatial effects in landscape and not with bringing the disparate objects in the picture into a unified form [pp. 111 f.]; nor does he take up de Piles's sense of *coloris* with its distinction between the surface hue of objects and the colour and handling of paint by which they are represented. Hogarth conceives the structuring of the image less sensuously and less a matter of momentary impact. However strong the dramatic element in Hogarth's painting, it requires extended deliberation on parts, gestures, motifs, details: it engages a reflectiveness that is never subsumed in a striking effect – it never allows withdrawal from the continuities of argument, comparison or causal connection.

This is something on which Hogarth prompts his reader to reflect with plate II of the *Analysis*. There is a contrast between the elegant dancers on the right and the remainder of the company, which may be in themselves inelegant but do not fall outside the order of the image; Hogarth indicates the unity in the multiplicity of the image as a whole by giving us a ground plan of the dance [p. 147 and plate II, fig. 122]. He has also correlated the scene with a mnemonic schema, a visual shorthand used, he says, to recall something seen for future use in painting [fig. 71]. In effect the mnemonics constitute a set of analogies which could work only because we use them to suggest figures, and including them here sets the mind off in yet another pursuit.

8 The sense of unity within Hogarth's images, so it might be

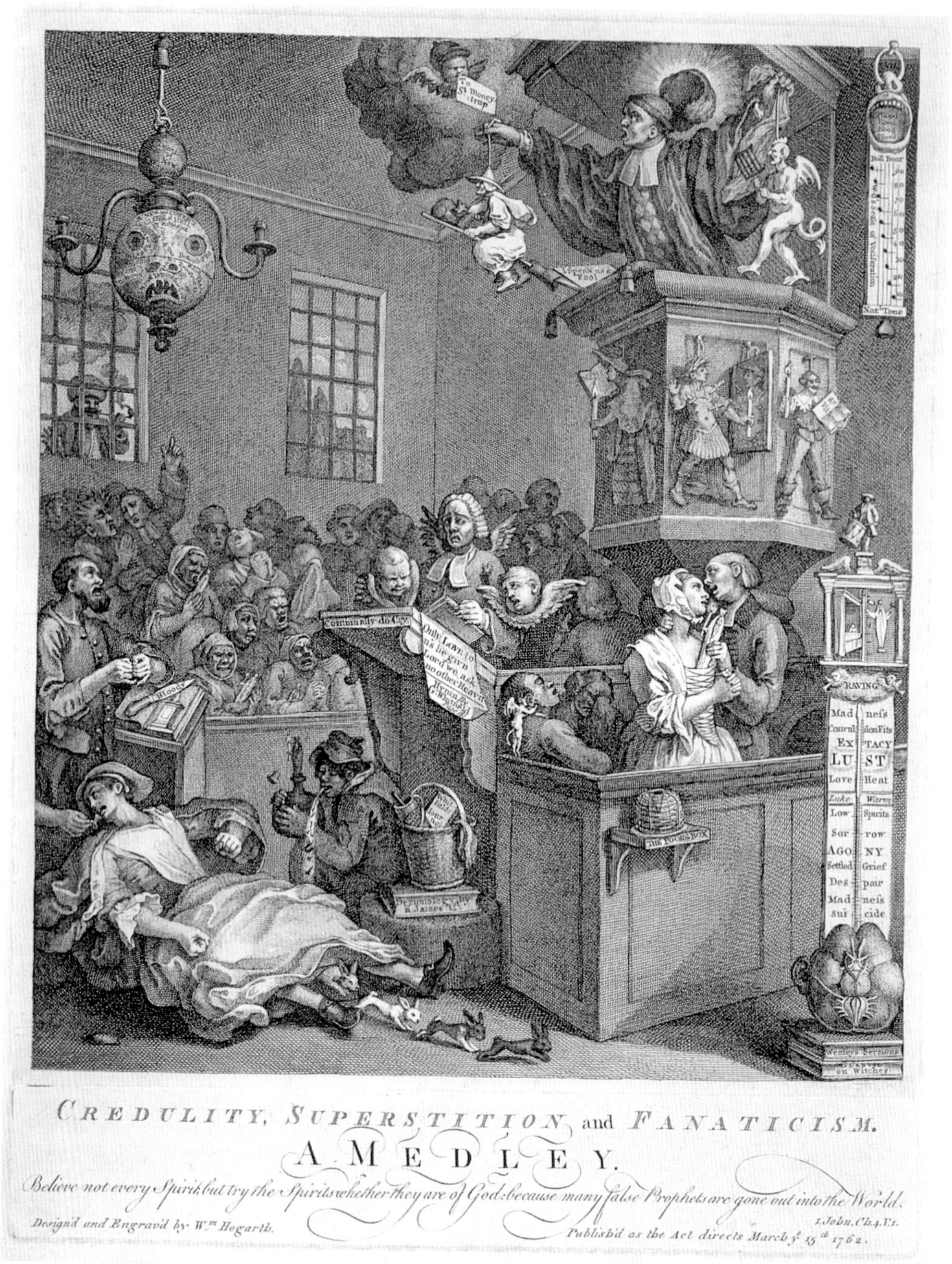

92 Hogarth, *Credulity, Superstition and Fanaticism*, 1762. Engraving, 38 × 31 cm. British Museum, London.

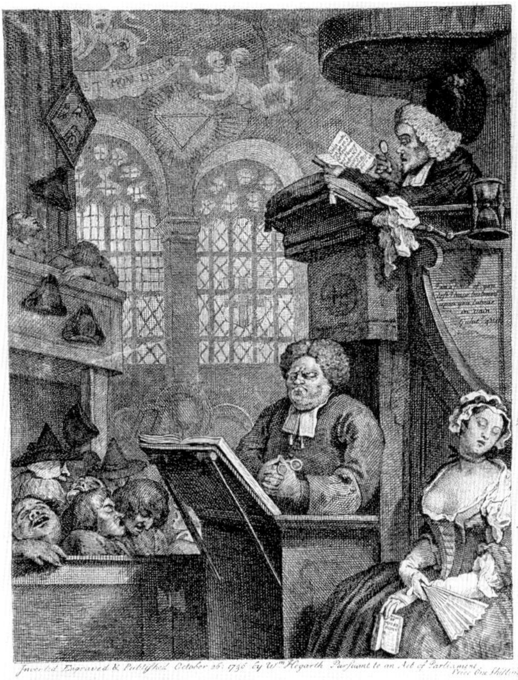

93 Hogarth, *Sleeping Congregation*, 1736. Etching and engraving, 25.4 × 20 cm. British Museum, London.

argued, is typically more conceptual and less visible than this would suggest. For instance in *Credulity Superstition and Fanaticism* (fig. 92) he condensed into a single plate an unparalleled density of interrelated images, returning here to some of his own earlier prints, the *Sleeping Congregation* (fig. 93), *Cunincular* – the woman who claimed to have given birth to rabbits – and a variant on his 'Lustometer' now used to measure rising religious enthusiasm, a transition that picks up on a Swiftian conceit in *The Battle*: 'Persons of visionary Devotion . . . are in their complexion most amorous; for *Zeal* is frequently kindled from the same spark with other fires . . .' and Swift goes on to talk of 'the height and Orgasmus of their spiritual exercises';[9] while the figure of the preacher himself complies with a complex description in Butler's *Hudibras* (which he had twice illustrated early in his career, although not this figure): 'This Zealot/Is of a mongrel, diverse kind/Cleric before and lay behind kind/A lawless linsey-woolsey brother? Half of one order, half another . . .'[10] and there are many more references that relate to his past reading and image making. This is revealing not only biographically – as one sees Hogarth's past thoughts and images being reconnected – but because it demonstrates what unity in mutiplicity would have meant for him in practice: the theological transition from Catholic to Dissenter in a single irrational figure – invoking both Butler and Swift – and the variations on Enthusiasm in relation to the church (the Church of England) hardly allows us to separate the conceptual and the formal play.[11]

If it were argued that some of these connections were not made visually but only in thought, one might first of all accept the distinction while feeling that it is a very nice psychological matter where the borderline is crossed in particular cases, and such uncertainty may be part of the interest. But beyond the question of how fully the conceptual and visual conceits are integrated there is a further issue; it is whether the conceptual play is more or less marginal to any particular print. It may be that the triangle in the *Sleeping Congregation* invokes the mystery of the Trinity, although upside down, as well as the sign of the Tetragamaton and Freemasonry, as Paulson has suggested recently, but if it does so it can hardly be more than mocking the whole use of mystic symbols; the print does not give focus to the theological controversies as *Credulity Superstition and Fanaticism* elaborates on the theme of Dissenters in *Hudibras* and *Tale of a Tub*.[12]

The border between visual and conceptual conceit is something that Hogarth seems to allude to in his presentation of the *Analysis* (fig. 94). The serpentine line of traditional art theory brings to Hogarth's mind Milton's description of the serpent of Genesis, the line in the frontispiece becomes a snake: 'So vary'd he, and of his tortuous train/Curl's many a wanton wreath, in sight of Eve,/To lure her eye . . .' But the notion of 'variety' also calls up, later in the text, Shakespeare's description of Cleopatra. It would seem part of Hogarth's sense of his own intellectual independence that he can go on making connections in this centrifugal way, which are both visual and conceptual and leave space for us to question how far each takes up the other. The visual/conceptual divide does not mark the border of his art but lies within it.

* * *

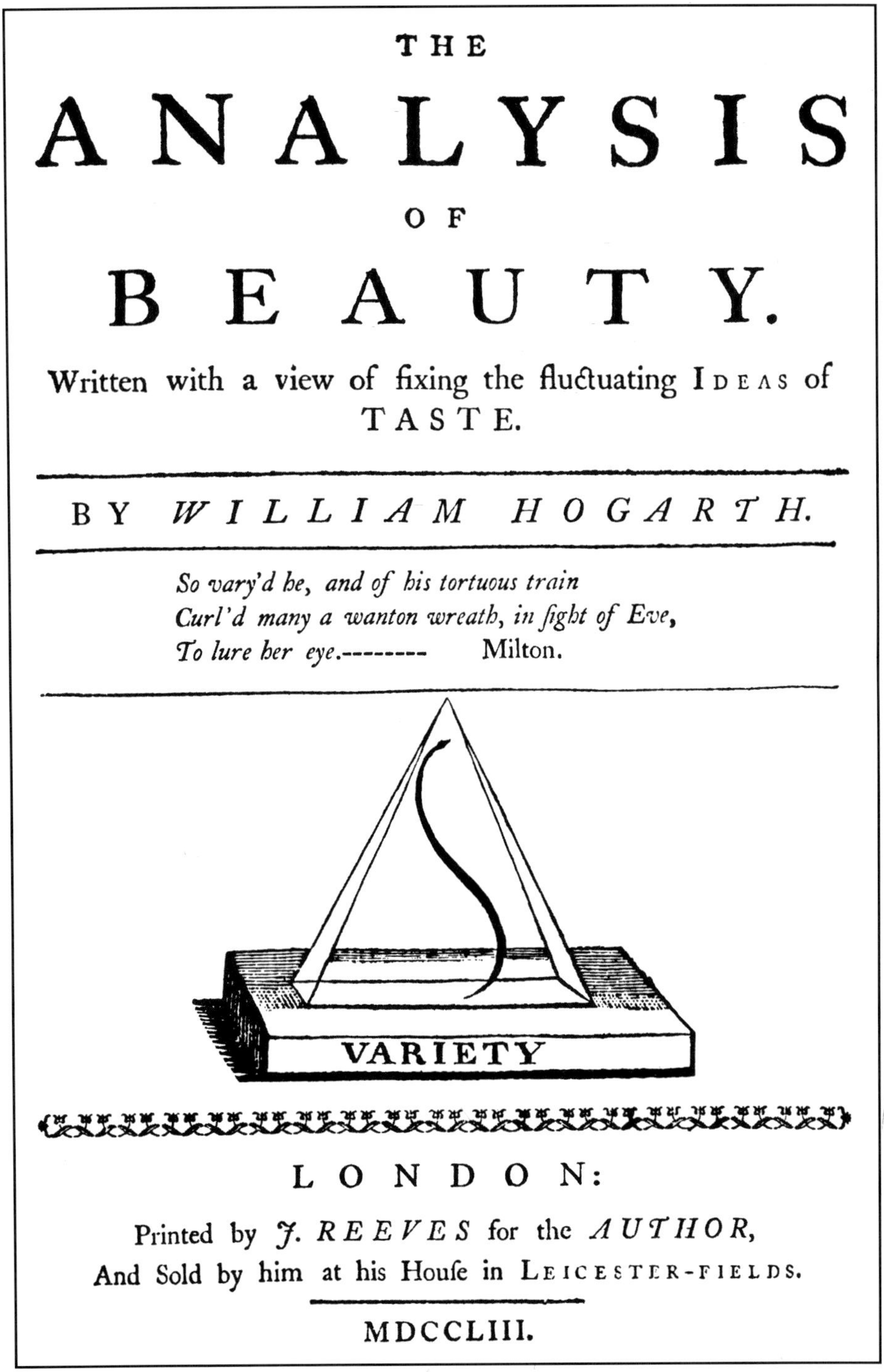

THE

ANALYSIS

OF

BEAUTY.

Written with a view of fixing the fluctuating IDEAS of TASTE.

BY *WILLIAM HOGARTH.*

So vary'd he, and of his tortuous train
Curl'd many a wanton wreath, in sight of Eve,
To lure her eye.-------- Milton.

LONDON:

Printed by *J. REEVES* for the *AUTHOR*,
And Sold by him at his House in LEICESTER-FIELDS.

MDCCLIII.

94 Title page of *The Analysis of Beauty.*

III

The *Analysis* and the Boundary of Beauty and Morality

The wider implication of Hogarth's independence of mind is intimated if not spelled out by remarks in his preface: 'For though beauty is seen and confessed by all . . . It is no wonder this subject should so long have been thought inexplicable' because 'it actually requires practical knowledge of the whole art of painting (sculpture alone not being sufficient) and that too to some degree of eminence'; failing that, 'those ingenious gentlemen who have lately published treatises upon it (and who have written much more learnedly than can be expected from one who never took up the pen before) would not soon have been bewildered in their accounts of it, and obliged suddenly to turn into the broad, more beaten paths of moral beauty' [p. ii]. It is not obvious how narrowly focused or directed Hogarth's remarks about philosophers should be taken. His attack could as well be against the deist Shaftesbury as against his opponents like Bishop Berkeley, for what is at issue for him is not what is at issue for them; for them it was the authority of revealed religion and conformity to the regulations of the Church of England, but for him – as near as one can judge an anti-mystical Church of England man – the central concern was not theology but the status of art, and this required resisting the encroachments of theology and moral philosophy. He confronts the mere men of letters for not understanding what can be learned only from the experience of the painter – not even that of a sculptor would do, presumably because the two-dimensional transformation of three-dimensional forms was seen as essential to the thought process. But there is a more radical argument: that current notions about the relation between art and morality were misconceived. Hogarth was resisting a range of overlapping positions that obscured or denied the distinctive interest of the painter's image making.

In a much cited passage of the *Second Characters*, Shaftesbury wrote: 'The moral part of painting lies but little in the forms . . . but is expressed in the air, feature, attitude, action, motion, and this is therefore wholly lodged in the part of painting called movements, where action, passion, the affections are shewn. The characters which in paintings are mere forms are not moral'.[13] One might think that Shaftesbury here had divested so much from mere forms – attitude, action, air – that there was little left over. And a great deal of what he says makes the moral world seem sensuously immanent and its beauty the manifestation of virtue. But Shaftesbury allows no intervention of the visual artist, no special beauty that his artistry brings to the work; for him the painter is a mere illustrator of moral ideas. Shaftesbury himself gave a famous example of the subordination of the painter to the moralist when he instructed a painter on how to represent the 'Choice of Hercules' so as to convey its moral significance – taking the stony path of virtue rather than being seduced by luxury. The disvaluation of painting as an art is explicit in 'Advice to an Author',

> poetry and the writer's art, as in many respects it resembles the statuary's and the painter's, [but] There is this essential difference . . . between the artists of each kind: that they who design after bodies, and form the graces of this sort, can never, with all their correctness and accuracy of design, be able to reform themselves, or grow one jot more shapely in their persons. But for those artists who copy from another life, who study the graces and perfections of minds . . . tis impossible they should fail of being themselves improved, and amended in their better part.[14]

It was precisely the capacity of painting to reach a moral nerve that Hogarth himself would claim, but do so at the same time as rejecting the fusion of morality and beauty that was the common currency of the time.[15]

Hutcheson, in some ways a follower of Shaftesbury was the philosopher whom Hogarth seems to have found useful; first, he had distinguished the capacity for pleasure in formal order and distinguished it from the perception of moral quality, ('Tis true, that what chiefly pleases in the Countenance are the indications of Moral Dispositions . . . but that would not lead us to like the form.'[16]); what linked beauty of form and of moral disposition was their independence of 'Advantage', self-interest. Secondly, following Addison he distinguished the beauty of objects from the beauty of representation; thirdly, in a later series of papers he extended his sense of pleasure in analogy to satire; and fourthly he, like Hogarth, regarded formal beauty as itself subject to the conditions of fitness. But although formal beauty had been given a central role within his theory, Hogarth might have thought himself at least somewhat at odds with it for two reasons: first, Hutcheson's conflation of the visual beauty of geometrical forms, of natural forms and those of art allowed no special place for the artistry of the painter and rigidified the beauty of nature; and second, because his analogy between beauty and virtue might be read as making beauty itself an intimation of virtue, a position which Hutcheson sometimes suggests rather than argues for, as where he writes 'it is *regular* and *beautiful* to have *stronger Benevolence* toward the *morally good* parts of mankind, who are *useful* to the *Whole*'.[17] Despite the divergences Hutcheson provided an armature of concepts around which Hogarth could elaborate his own position.

In an unpublished draft for the preface to the *Analysis*, Hogarth sketched his opposition to the conjunction of beauty and morality as part of a divine order:

> The chief steps that hath hitherto been taken by writers, to dispell the clouds of uncertainty, and error, with design to fix some true ideas of taste, upon a surer basis; have been first, those set forth by the natural philosophers, who by their extended contemplations, on universal beauty, as to the harmony and order of things, were naturally led into the wide Roads, of uniformity and regularity; which they unexpectedly found cros'd, and interrupted, by many other openings Relating to a kind of Beauty, differing, from those they were so well aquainted with. They then, for a while traverse these, seeming to them contradictory paths, till they found themselves bewilder'd in the Labyrinth of variety; not considering it was necessary first to go through the province of painting . . . before it was possible, to get into right Road, of Nature's superficial beautys, of sportiveness and Fancy, if they may be so term'd, and which differ so greatly from her other beauties, of order, and usefulness. Thus wandering a while in a maze of uncertainty, without gaining ground; they then to extricate themselves out of these difficultys; suddenly ascend the mound of moral Beauty, contiguous with the open field of Divinity, where ranging at large, they seem to lose all remembrance of their first pursuit.[18]

Despite its awkwardness, this summarizes his sense of the literature to which he responds; it does so with some further specificity beyond the preface as it was actually published. The draft makes clear that his resistance is not merely to the conflation of beauty and morality – pointing to the possibility of their divergence – but to the facile teleology encompassing morality, beauty and regularity in the 'open field of Divinity'. For Hogarth there is 'play' in the system, in the sense of fluidity and indeterminacy and not only in the sense of wit or irony. Beauty and virtue may converge but they cannot be read off from each other. In his rejected draft Hogarth had the following schema for his work: 'Fitness { uniformity and regularity { Fitness excites a pleasure equall or similar to that of truth and Justice, uniformity and regularity are pleasures of contentment' (this looks very like an adaption of the scheme of Berkeley's position, but without the divine purpose); it is complemented or opposed by 'Variety' and this 'excites the lively feelings of wantoness and play' and 'Intricacy like the joy of persute'.[19] When Hogarth seeks out his basic concepts at their most abstract they are contesting values.

The separation of values points to the artist having a distinct role, contributing a distinct and irreducible interest in what he produces and revealing something otherwise unrealized in the visible world. But it is also integral to Hogarth's thought that beauty as a distinct principle *engages* with morality, for his conception of beauty is always in reciprocal play with fitness, and that includes moral fitness. What is crucial for Hogarth is that beauty does not emanate from morality or divinity but reponds to them with its own voice, from its own position. But how can painting do this? It cannot of course respond with its lines and figures to their theoretical maxims; what it can do is respond to the behaviour in which virtue and vice make themselves manifest; it can do this by rehearsing the postures, movements, affectations and extravagances of its subjects in its own procedure; not only miming but evaluating them by virtue of its innate sense of what is natural and what is exaggerated. (Although Hogarth remarks 'It is strange that nature hath afforded us so many lines and shapes to indicate blemishes of the mind, whilst there are none at all that point out perfections of it beyond the appearance of common sense and placidity . . . Nor are gravity and solemn looks always signs of wisdom . . .' [p. 131])

Confidence that there is such an innate sense, however limited and fallible, is reflected in the writing of his friend Thomas Morell (fig. 95) who had helped Hogarth with the final preparation of the *Analysis*. Morell had rejected Locke's denial that we had innate ideas, arguing that unless the mind had innate concepts both of

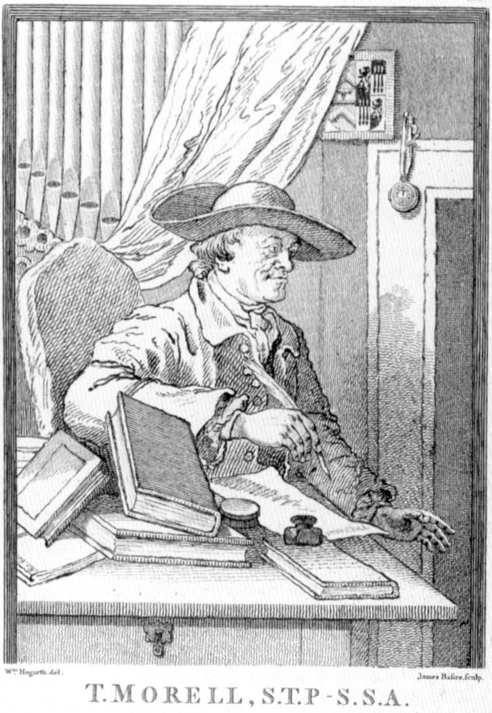

95 Hogarth (engraved by Basire), *T. Morell*, 1762. Engraving, 19.5 × 15 cm. British Museum, London.

spatial and mathematical relations and of morality it would never have been able to develop them.

> All these arguments [at the start of Locke's *Essay*] are so far from convincing me that there are no truths but what are *acquired*, . . . that as it is in painting, and all sorts of manufactures, the nearer they come to the imitation of nature . . . the nearer they come to those *innate* or *natural* truths . . .[20]

Whatever the epistemological difficulties, we can understand Morell when he says that there is an experience of such certainty 'as it is manifest in painting'; that is, in painting we recognize what is represented without recourse to some prior sensations or to making comparisons with the objects represented. Our innate capacities are enough to satisfy us as to the naturalness of the representation, and in the case of other 'manufactures' our innate capacities are enough to enable us to judge the fittingness of parts to each other or to their function. We have that innate capacity to judge, notwithstanding the fact that in exercising this capacity we cannot ourselves tell where our imagination ends and perception begins because we never confront simple ideas.[21] Morell extends this innate capacity to moral judgement; 'there is conscience prior to law', despite the differences between different societies. If this may appear as dangerous moral intuitionism, Morell counters, as Hogarth on the evidence of *Credulity* would also have done: 'It is not conscience (whatever is pretended) but some *irregular passion*, mingled with *religious phrenzy*, that oftentimes proves so venomous and mischevous'.[22] Conscience, properly so-called, is an innate sense of moral normality.

To talk of painting being critical of behaviour implies that painting already has a moral character within itself, from the start, and this might seem inconsistent with Hogarth's separation of values. But the difficulty is avoided if we follow Hogarth and do not assume that virtue is the exclusive and all consuming purpose in human affairs; to assume this, to be a moralist, is a theoretical stance which Hogarth explicitly resists. He is opposed to the position of the moralist not because he holds an amoral view of the world but (i) because the moralist scans the world for virtue and vice as isolatable and exclusive values (in this respect Hogarth is close to Mandeville[23] who held that a single-minded pursuit of virtue would lead to general misery and vice to prosperity, although Hogarth does not draw Mandeville's paradoxical consequences) and (ii) because he rejects the pretentions of a moralizing stance that in practice is likely to involve meanness, self-regard – its emblem is the woman going to church in 'Morning' from *Times of the Day* (fig. 96) – or at the very best the virtuous absurdity of Fielding's Parson Adams. Explicitly separating the sportiveness of painting from morality and religion he shows that sportiveness as responsive to moral character. (Where Hogarth takes up the conflict of virtue and vice as it was represented in Shaftesbury's 'Choice of Hercules' it appears in parodic form, Macheath in Gay's *Beggar's Opera* between the two women claiming him as their husband (fig. 97) and, a development of this, in *The March to Finchley* where a Catholic and a Protestant woman lay claim to the bemused English soldier (fig. 98). The project of judging between virtue and vice has been redirected into a world where choices are not made against a zero background but are caught up in a historical and social world where the vices and bad judgements of the past already prejudice the future; thus, in the

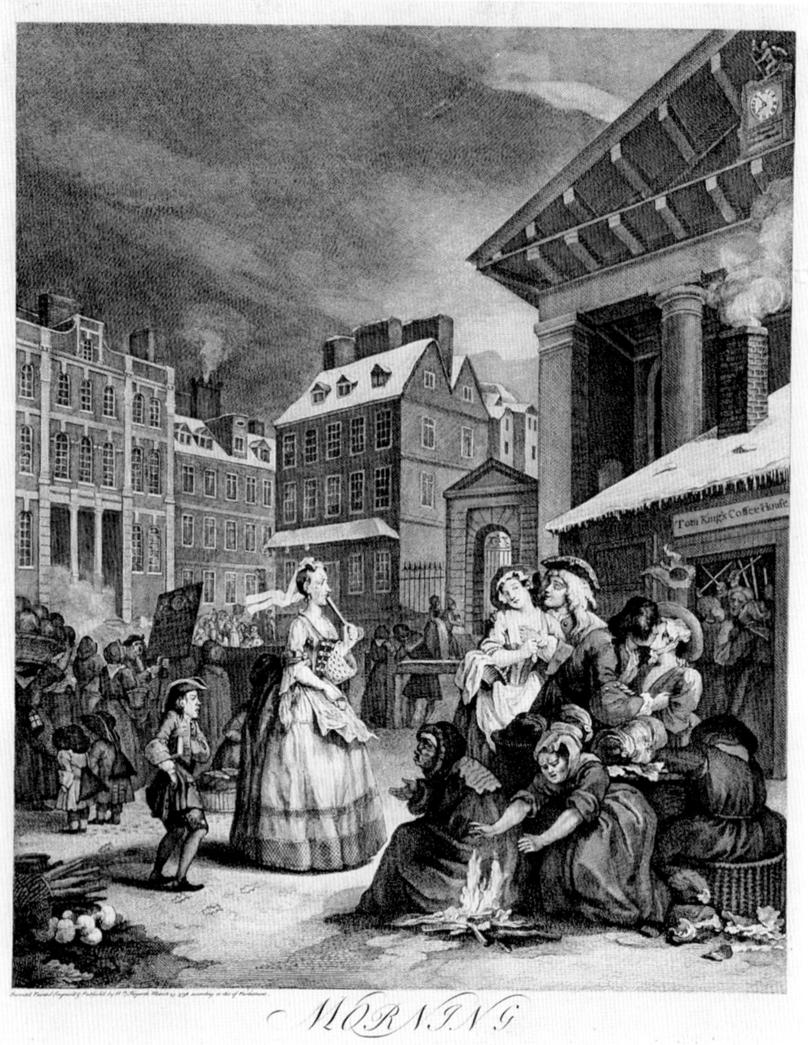

96 Hogarth, 'Morning' from *Times of the Day*, 1738. Engraving, 45.4 × 38 cm. British Museum, London.

Progresses the protagonists' disasters have parental irresponsibility as initial conditions and the subsequent actions are embedded in institutions that are themselves corrupt. The protagonists are never exonerated but nor are their actions seen as temporary disruptions of a divinely ordered world; rather they are part of its perennial character. Like Mandeville, Hogarth resisted

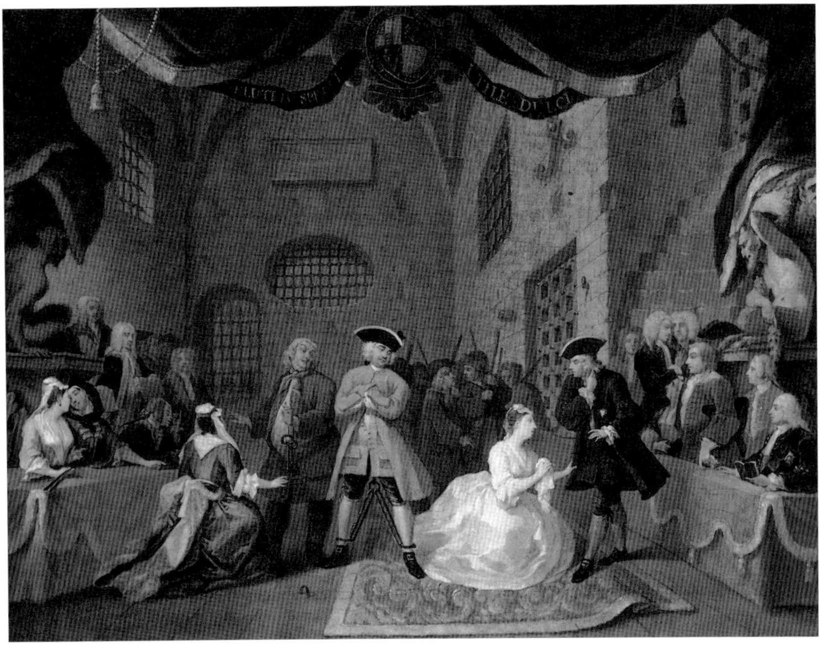

97 Hogarth, *The Beggar's Opera* VI, 1731. Oil on canvas, 57.2 × 76.2 cm. Tate Gallery, London.

98 Hogarth, *The March to Finchley*, 1750. Engraving, 39 × 56 cm. British Museum, London.

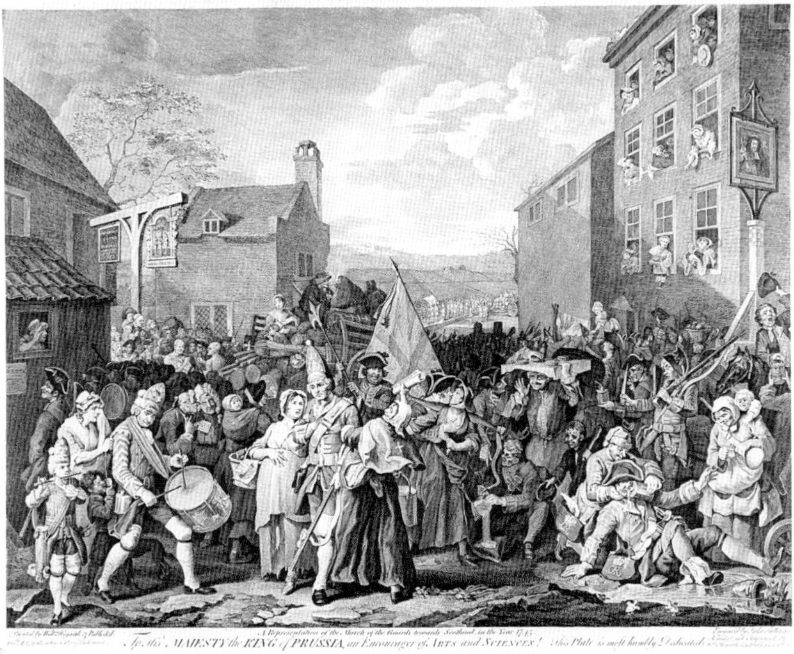

both the teleology of Berkeley and the aristocratic moralism of Shaftesbury, each marked by complacent disregard of the world's contingencies.

IV

The Progresses and the *Election*

We may trace two kinds of emphasis in Hogarth's response to moralism: on the one hand his rejection of a sense of divine teleology governing human affairs, as in the Progresses, and on the other his celebration of human vitality and diversity without worrying over praise or blame as in *The Election*.

The final episodes in each of the Progresses give no intimation of

99 Hogarth, *The Rake's Progress* (final scene), 1753. Engraving, 31.5 × 38.7 cm. British Museum, London.

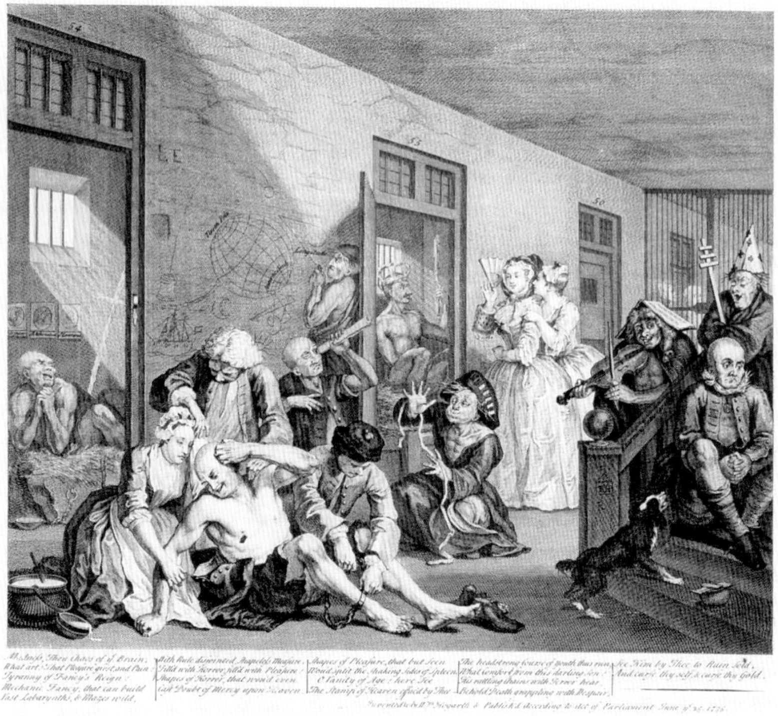

redemption, in contrast, say, to the story of the Prodigal Son. If the last scene of *The Rake's Progress* (fig. 99) recalls the 'Lamentation' it does so discordantly, not allowing our response to settle, opening the gap between the religious resonance and actuality. In the last two plates of *Industry and Idleness* (figs 101 and 102) the triumph of the industrious Goodchild is paired with the journey of Tom Idle to Tyburn, whom Goodchild has condemned in a tainted trial where, as magistrate, he looked away when the witness was bribed.[24] The moral niceties are lost in the distance of the festive crowds. In the *Marriage à la Mode* there is a marked shift between the satiric mode at the beginning and at the end (figs 103–6) from hyperbole to understatement; in the first scenes there is the enjoyment of characterization: the verve of the painting mimes the count preening himself, the affected dignity of the earl and inelegance of the alderman; in the second the count's exhaustion is evoked by the way his shirt runs over the line of his waist and the frogging of his coat immobilizes his arms in contrast to the countess's motility. But this humour gradually gives way to what Hutcheson would have called grave wit: in the third scene the cynicism of the splay-legged count, the razor-wielding procuress with the flashes of red in contrast to the pallid child prostitute and the leering pox doctor. Hogarth's diffuse humour of the earlier scenes has become the 'serious wit . . . no more apt to move laughter . . . than heroic poetry'.[25] In the last scene Hogarth registers with peculiar exactness the father removing the ring that would otherwise be forfeit as the property of a suicide; this painting precludes the earlier scenes' expansive game of analogizing to focus attention on the small act of meanness. Hogarth's resistance to moralism lies not in ignoring the moral qualities of the protagonists but in the independence of his response; how he lights on them, rehearsing their strutting, hunching, drooping, stretching and with these their cynicism, indifference or self-delusion; as he does so the virtuosity turns the feelings and thoughts it arouses into components of his own performance.

The series in which the balance between morality and the pleasures of wit and virtuosity tilts most fully toward the latter is *The Election* (figs 107–10). The series takes up the theme of a highly publicised election campaign in an Oxfordshire constituency that continued for two years until the election was due in 1754. It was the custom for the magnates on both sides, the country Tories and the governing New Interest, the Whigs, to arrange matters so that there was no expensive recourse to public opinion. What was unusual about this episode was that it brought into the open the conduct of politicians. The actual election was so corrupt that the result had to be reviewed and the decision actually reversed. Hogarth was not concerned with the specific vices of one party or the other, nor in the circumstantial details of the Oxford election; his subject was the system and the aspects of human nature that it exploited. Let us first observe some details and then consider the overall attitude they sustain.

In the first scene, the 'Election Entertainment', a banquet is thrown by the Whig interest to seduce the voters, the opposition having done the same in the same place the night before. A mob protests outside the window about the 'Jew bill' – limited emancipation for those living in Britain – while in the foreground a banner, lying on the floor and presumably wrested from the mob, carries its demand 'Give us back our eleven days' (outrage at the change of calendar stealing that period of time from their lives). This lies beside a figure falling back – almost out of the picture – as his head is struck by a brick; the remarkable pictorial feat depends on our sense of the brick's trajectory while our eye momentarily loses the figure below the line of the table. The effect – perhaps aided by the wild thought of the banner – involves a consummate control of texture, colour saturation and brightness: in the surface of the painting above our falling man is the expiring figure at the head of the table with his scarlet gown, white sleeves and a gleaming heap of oyster shells in front of him; lower and to our right of him, the sumptuously painted still life; both distract and hold our attention so that between them we are afforded a less determinate zone within which the figure falls. There is a further factor: the fluency and agility of the loaded brush keeps an unarrested interest and momentum running through the forms. And although this effect occurs at the lower margin of the painting we link it to the mob at the window, so implicitly cutting across the horizontal composition. This horizontality is itself varied by the shapes of the two tables, the analogies they set up elsewhere in the painting and, crucially, by the variety of the action which flows round them. The diners rivet attention by the physiognomic energy of their aggressions and discomfitures as we are drawn back and forth between them individually and from group to group, meeting the most extravagant demands that we, primed by the *Analysis*, could make for Variety and Multiplicity in Unity.

In the last scene of the series 'Chairing the Members' the precariously elevated candidate is given numerous causes for alarm, including the vision of a skull with spectacles which seems to have caused the girl to faint – yet another visual distraction for him – while rival factions fight with staves easily confused with chair poles and bloodying one of the bearers on the side of the head; in the midst of bearers and combatants a woman, just perceptible, has fallen, her blue stockinged-leg sticking in the air under which swine dash as if they had, like the rabbits of the notorious rabbit woman, run out of her skirts. Through the density of episodes the eye is led in numerous kinds of chase, including one running back to the shadow of the second member cast on the sunlit wall of the town hall behind. Beyond the visual intricacies there are oblique political and historical references, the parodic use of the Last Supper in the first scene and in the last the Triumph of Alexander – a goose instead of an eagle flying over the hatless member, such references being denser in the two middle scenes which are visually less complex.

In Hogarth's own terms the relation between *The Election* and the Progresses would have involved two propositions: Fancy and exuberance have their rights and do not depend on or stem from morality; but, at the same time, those rights are not unlimited and where the limits are reached Fancy has to negotiate with morality. This was Hogarth's point in writing of the convergence of fitness, unity and variety 'mutually correcting and restraining each other'. In the *Election* there is negotiation between beauty and fitness at the level of characterisation but any sense of moral enormity is general and abstract, as in the breakdown of the coach of state; the painting is responding to festivity, to naive cupidity, to absurdity in an area where moral seriousness has become suspended because the corruption of electoral politics was, as in Fielding's play *Pasquin*, so established as to be taken for granted, but also because it did not involve what counts as morally serious for Hogarth: self-delusion, weakness of the will, cynical personal relations and injustice. What Hogarth is responding to is not, centrally, the morality of the political system but the opportunity it offered to wholeheartedly disrespectful, amoral ingenuity for participants and painter.

* * *

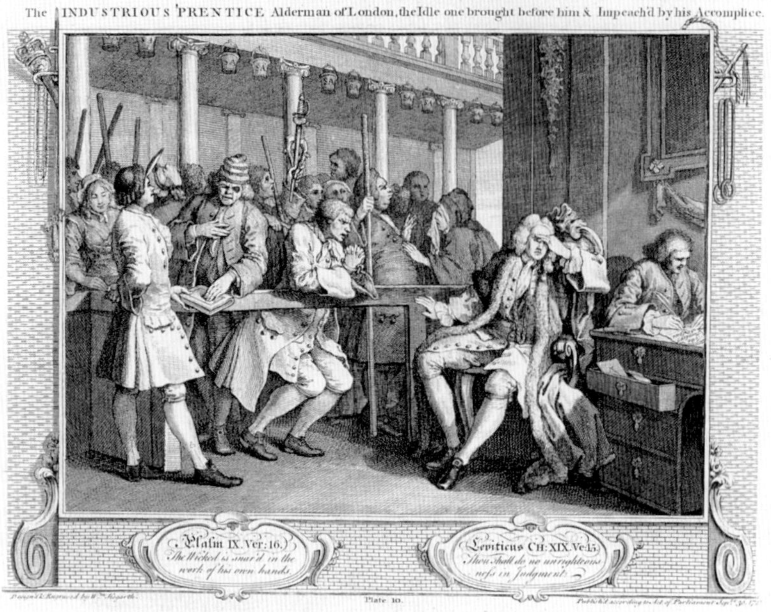

100 Hogarth, *Idle 'prentice Impeached . . . by his Accomplice*, plate 10 of *Industry and Idleness*, 1747. Engraving, 25.5 × 35 cm. British Museum, London.

101 Hogarth, *Idle 'prentice Executed at Tyburn*, plate 11 of *Industry and Idleness*, 1737. Engraving, 25.5 × 40.5 cm. British Museum, London.

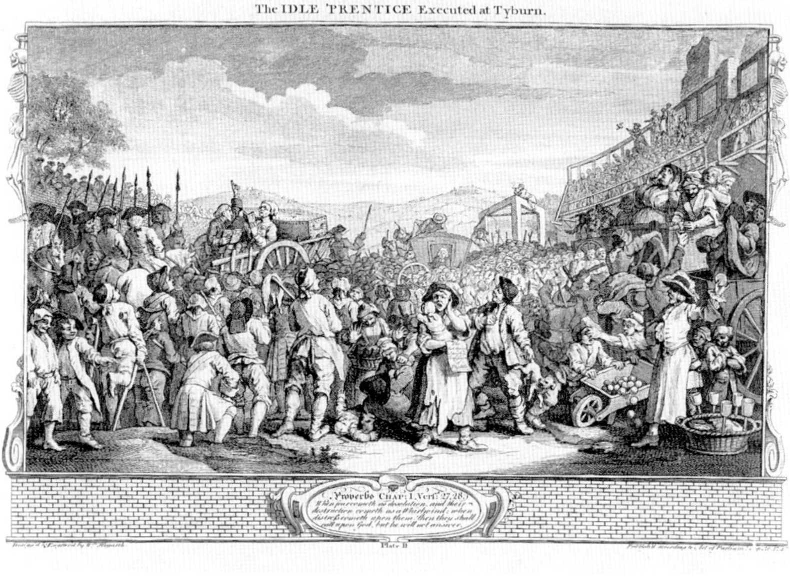

VI

Hogarth's theory in the *Analysis* has been branded as 'formalist' for two mutually supporting reasons. One is that Hogarth deviates from the project of history painting which carried with it moral and religious purposes, the *Analysis* being an attempt to provide a theory without such commitments; the other is that the theory has a psychological rather than cultural basis. The conjunction is invoked in the recent study of eighteenth-century art by Werner Busch: he treats the *Analysis* as offering a formalist doctrine seeking to recover some authority for painting in the wake of a cultural break down: the earlier theory of art, according to Busch, had presupposed a hierarchy of genres in which the nobility of subject matter and ideality of form had coincided. He thought that the problem for Hogarth and other eighteenth-century painters arose from a conflict between the aspiration of high art and unheroic modern subjects.[26] Busch sees the 'formalism' of Hogarth as an alternative to a concern with transcendent ideas, religious meaning and moral nobility for which painting had been the expression. It would be an answer to one aspect of Busch's argument – but only one – that Hogarth's so-called formalism

102 Hogarth, *The Industrious 'prentice Lord Mayor of London*, plate 12 of *Industry and Idleness*, 1747. Engraving, 26.4 × 40.5 cm. British Museum, London.

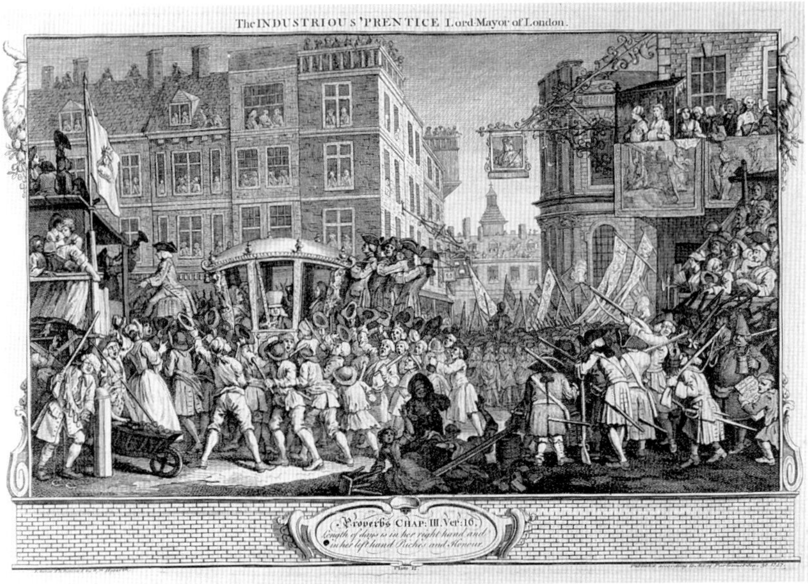

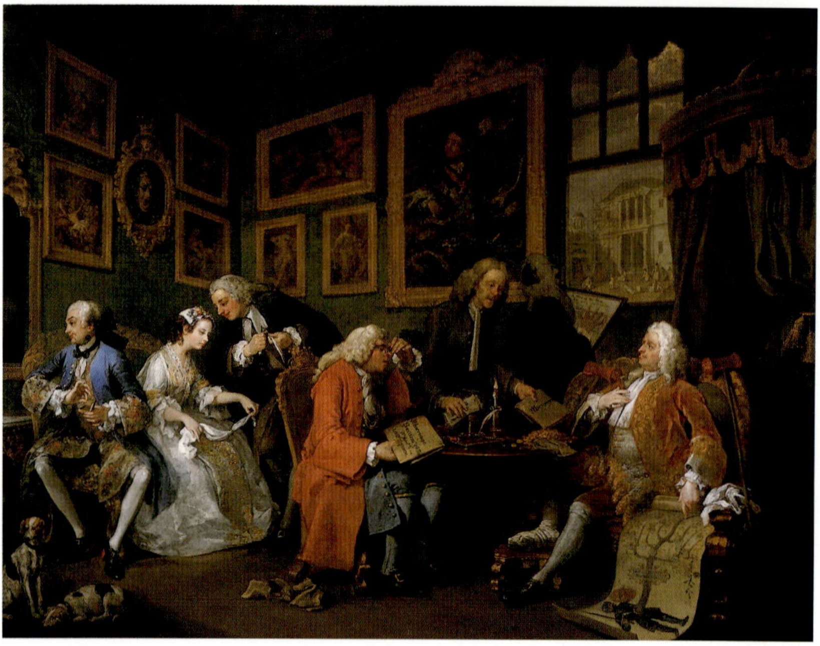

103 Hogarth, *The Marriage Contract*, no. I of the series *Marriage à la Mode*, 1745. Oil on canvas, 70 × 91 cm. National Gallery, London.

104 Hogarth, *Shortly After the Marriage*, no. II of the series *Marriage à la Mode*, 1745. Oil on canvas, 70 × 91 cm. National Gallery, London.

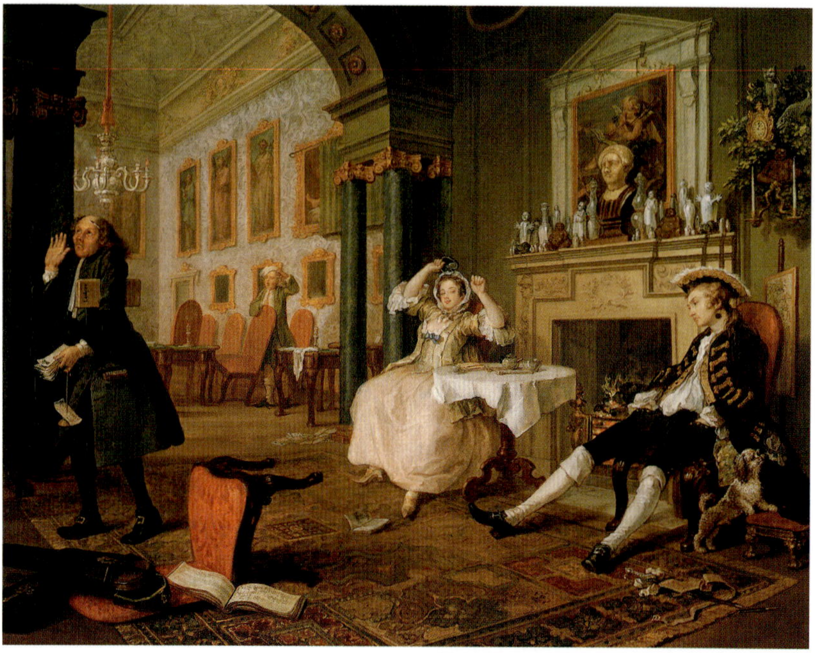

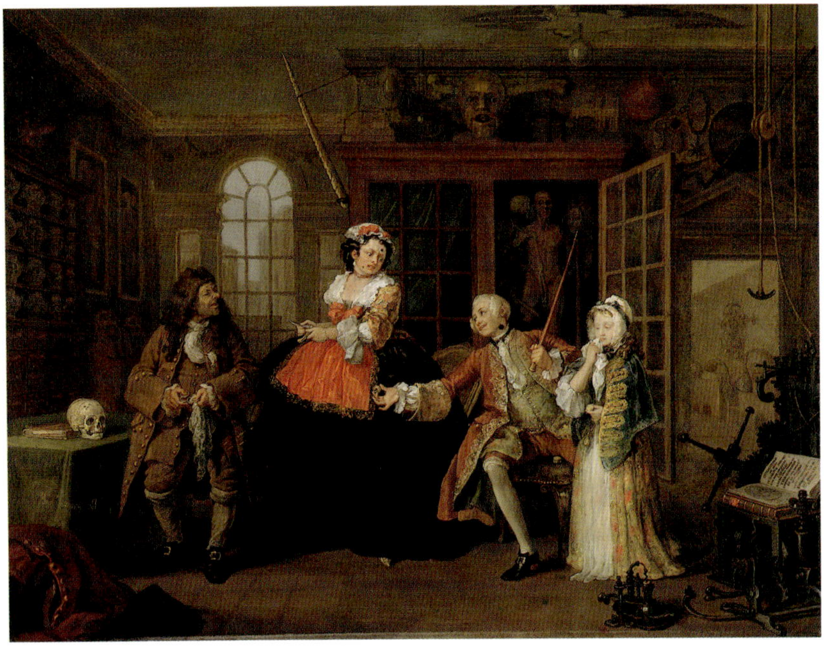

105 Hogarth, *The Visit to the Quack Doctor*, no. III of the series *Marriage à la Mode*, 1745. Oil on canvas, 70 × 91 cm. National Gallery, London.

106 Hogarth, *The Suicide of the Countess*, no. VI of the series *Marriage à la Mode*, 1745. Oil on canvas, 70 × 91 cm. National Gallery, London.

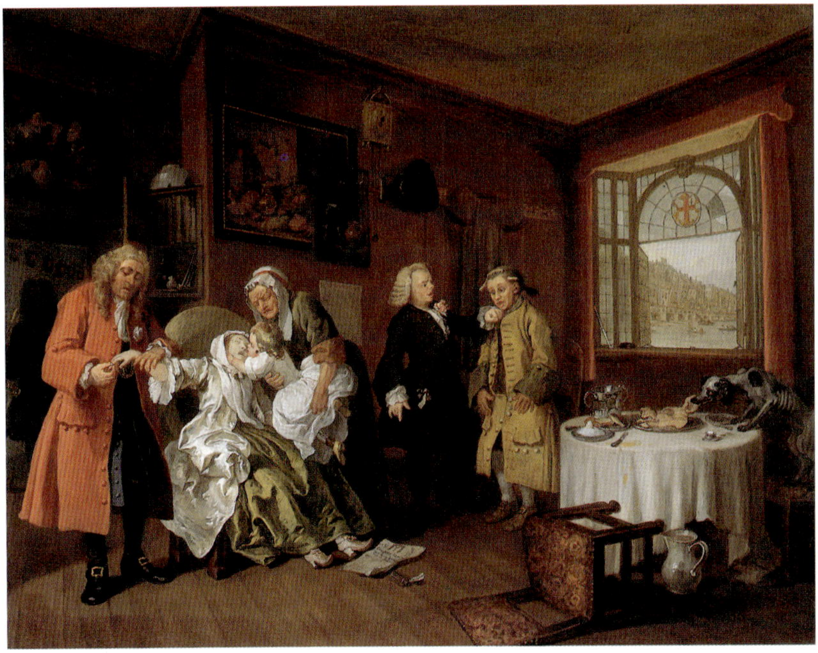

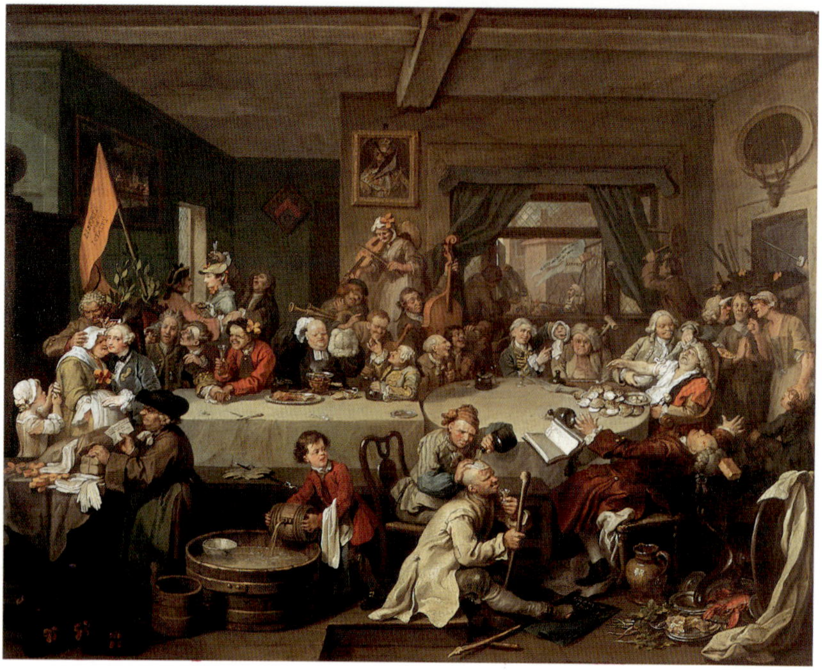

107 Hogarth, *The Election Entertainment*, no. I of the series *The Election*, 1754. Oil on canvas, 102 × 127 cm. Sir John Soane Museum, London.

108 Hogarth, *Canvassing the Voters*, no. II of the series *The Election*, 1754. Oil on canvas, 102 × 127 cm. Sir John Soane Museum, London.

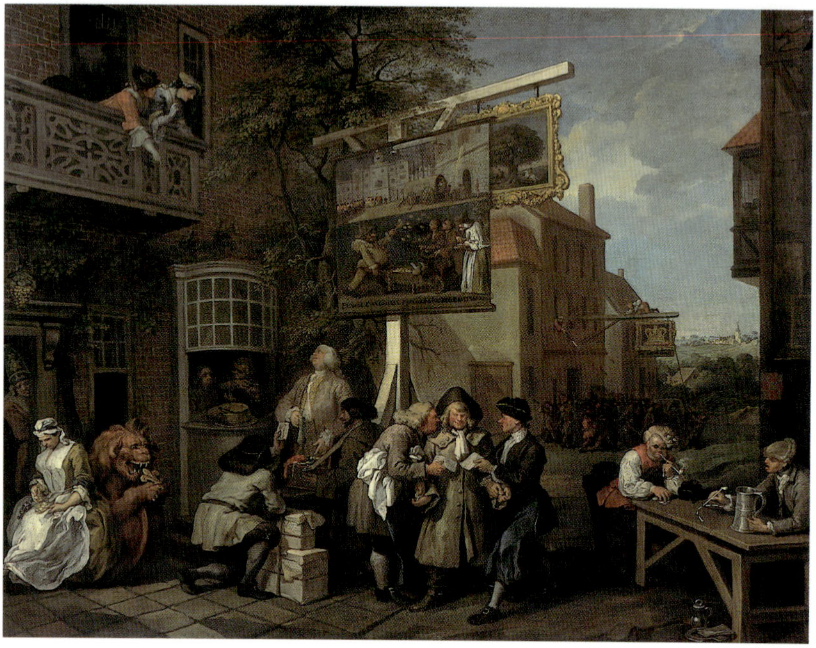

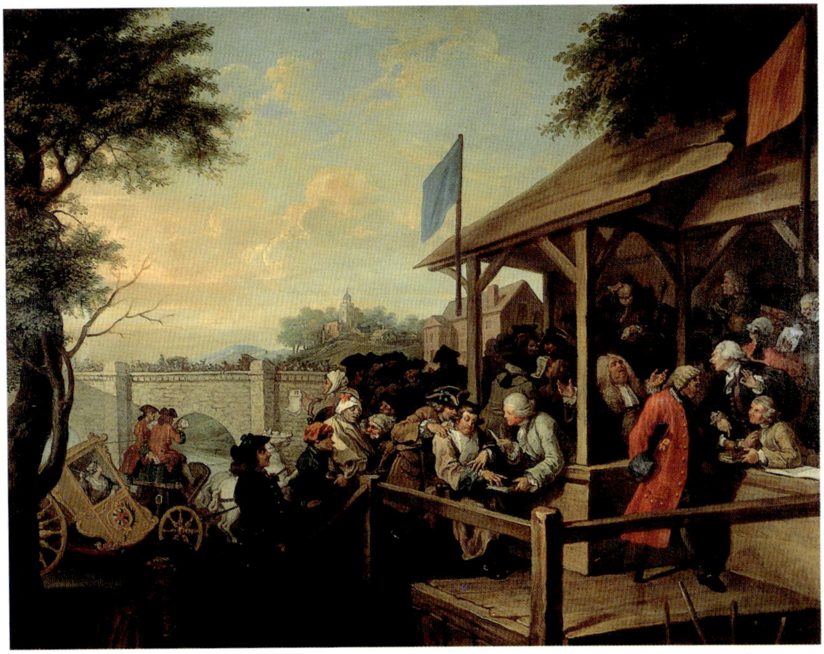

109 Hogarth, *The Polling*, no. III of the series *The Election*, 1754. Oil on canvas, 102 × 127 cm. Sir John Soane Museum, London.

110 Hogarth, *Chairing the Members*, no. IV of the series *The Election*, 1754. Oil on canvas, 102 × 127 cm. Sir John Soane Museum, London.

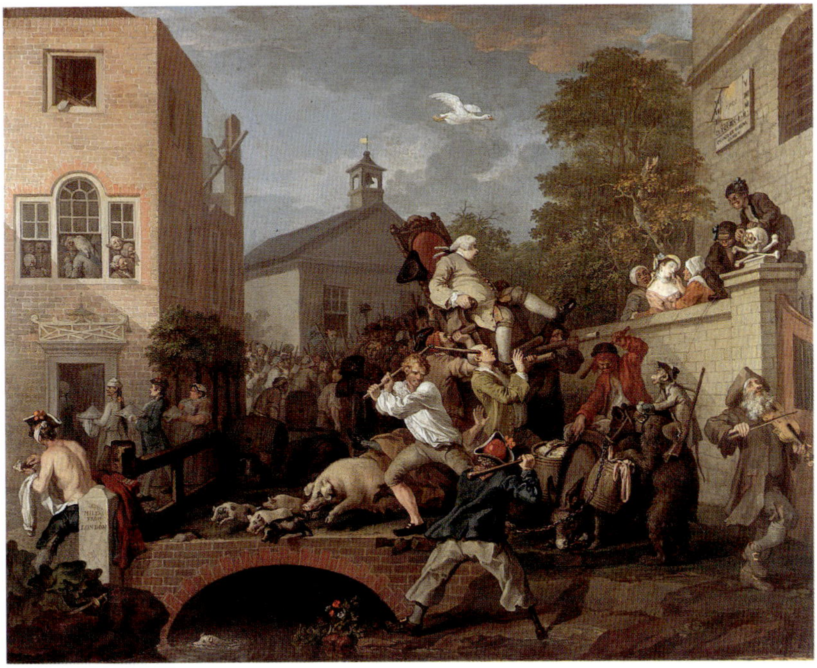

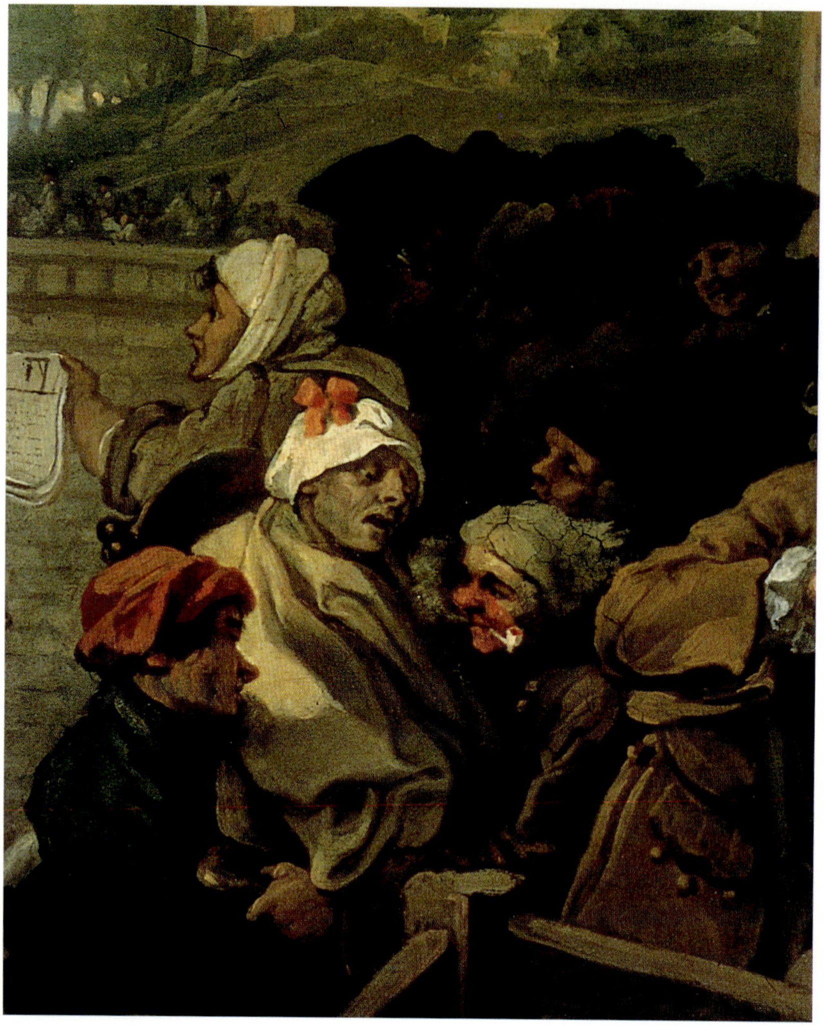

111 Hogarth, *The Polling*. Detail of fig. 22.

integrates and interprets his subject matter; that it analyses the interaction of component factors within painting. This would leave unchallenged the other point of Busch's argument: that the loss of traditional hierarchy and purpose was a loss of cultural centrality. Hogarth did indeed disrupt that hierarchy and its presumed unity, but to call this a loss of centrality is to assume some parameters – religious or neo-Hegelian – that are hardly compelling. If centrality is made an issue, then it must surely be to its own culture, and if that is so then the answer to Busch is that at the core of British eighteenth-century thought were conflicts that Hogarth encompassed, like the tensions between the Anglican inheritance and independence of mind, independence of mind and the uncontrolled Enthusiasm, between the ideal of an aristocracy and the commercial culture, between the ideal of the poet or musician and the practicalities of earning a living; it was part of Hogarth's achievement to encompass these within painting, and of the *Analysis* to show how painting was the kind of activity in which this was possible.

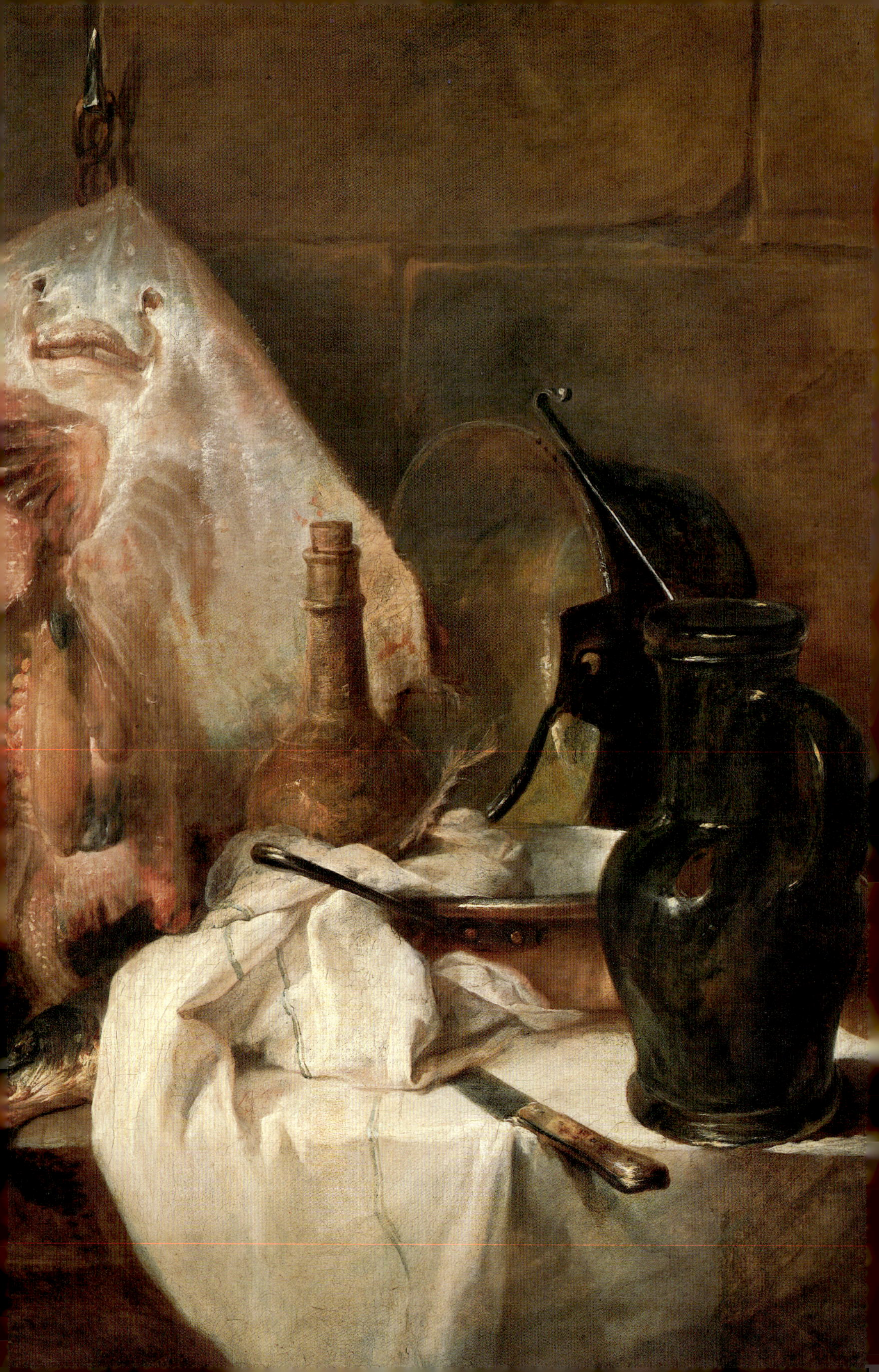

Chapter Six

Apropos Chardin

I

We have observed how subject matter sustains itself in our awareness through the complexity of its representation; but that complexity has a further function – it is inherently expressive. This is not a matter of particular emotional effects or moods that we find in one painting as opposed to another, but of an expressiveness that arises from the very nature of depiction as we have considered it so far.

In order to clarify the sense of expressiveness here, I shall first take up the question of the expressive properties of nature: how, except by reference to personal associations, could scenes of a river valley or an urban street at dawn take on properties like melancholy or cheerfulness – which strictly belong to sentient beings not inanimate objects? The question has been raised again recently by Richard Wollheim and his suggested explanation – once fortuitous associations are put to one side – is in two stages: first, that the features of the external world at some early phase of mental development may have become enmeshed in fantasy: that is, in early infancy our desires, frustrations, tension and remorse – inward states – may have been projected onto and become inextricable from the world around us. Second, that subsequently scenes or objects in the world may be felt as of a piece with such internal states – continuous with them; and this early condition is reactivated in later stages of development so that external situations take on the qualities of internal states[1]. A precondition of the expressiveness of inanimate objects or scenes had, in this account, been laid down in our earliest relations to the world. Although this

112 Chardin, *The Ray*. Detail of fig. 127.

psychological theory was about phenomena in nature or the inanimate environment and not about works of art, it provides a strategy for explaining the expressivity of depiction: the strategy is to trace a condition for a phenomenon of mature experience in the structure of an early phase of psychological development.

In seeking to clarify the sense of urgency that attends depiction – in the elaboration of recognition within a painting – the stage of early experience that is most obviously pertinent is, again, when the infant's internal and the external worlds are incompletely differentiated. The infant – so it is assumed – experiences both a progressive realization of separation from its mother but also a progressive capacity to tolerate it. While there is considerable doubt about the maturation rate, the degree of early integration of awareness, and above all about different respects in which the infant has an integrated sense of the mother, we take it that it starts out with the assumption – however indeterminate – that there is someone to communicate with. In that phase it has been observed how infant and adult respond to each other – not mimicking but varying each other's gestures and movements – matching the excited rising voice with a rising arm gesture, the infant's banging with the adult nodding in time, attunement going both ways. What the infant subject finds in the interchange is both a form for its internal condition – its sense of itself – and a response to it. In D. W. Winnicott's famous account, the infant is initially dependent and then gradually gains independence from its mother. The mother initially responds to infant needs so that it feels as if its own urgencies had brought forth its satisfactions (the first illusion); gradually she adapts less completely and there is a stage of partial disillusion and separation; separation becomes tolerable by means of a second illusion; some feature of the external world (the transitional object) becomes a substitute maternal presence, again eluding the realization of objective separateness.[1] (These two illusions may be less a matter of sequential phases than structures potentially in operation at the same time, dominant in different circumstances.) The transitional object is transitional in two senses: between the mother and the object and between the internal feelings and fantasies of the child and the externality of the object. From this conception of the infant-mother dialogue we gain a sense of 'keeping our inner and outer reality separate yet interrelated'.

How should this early situation be regarded as bearing upon

what we have observed about depiction, its internal correspondences in which one form – one feature or one aspect – rehearses another, where we see one in accordance with another, or one figuring within another? We might map this early dialogue onto the structure of depiction in this way: we find in the internal order of depiction (or any work of art) one motif (say, the recognized subject) taken up into another (the variation provided by the subject as reconstituted within the medium); this may be thought of as corresponding to the gesture and variation of the early interchange. But secondly, and more specifically, it is assumed that for the infant there is no determinate borderline between its own gesture or expression and the response that takes it up – which joins in with it and varies it. The transaction occupies a transitional space in which external and internal pass into each other; correspondingly, depiction occupies a transitional space between literal presence and what is imagined in it. One can elaborate on the correspondence in various ways, but the crucial feature is straightforward: the propensity to pursue similarity through difference – including the extension of recognition in depiction – would seem to rehearse an archaic urgency within us and its corresponding satisfaction.

II

This sense of urgency and satisfaction might be given both wider and narrower application. We may think it present in all depiction, but we might also think of certain kinds of depiction as making thematic the interplay of the viewer and the work, something that it might do in part by the diminution of other kinds of interest – dramatic, literary, religious or didactic – and in part by focusing on the elusive relation between the medium and the subject, both of which are generally accepted as central to the painting of Chardin.

In eighteenth-century France critical writing drew particular attention to the sensuous and optical nuances of painting as distinct from its capacity for dramatic exposition. Diderot had written of the responsiveness to art as setting up internal rapports within the musical instrument of the soul.[3] But if he is the most impressive figure in the wider context of eighteenth-century criticism his aesthetics adjusted to the peculiar 'magic' of painting in a less focused way than narrower writers for whom it was their central concern. For instance the painter and critic Michel-François Dandré-Bardon in his *Traité de Peinture* of 1765 wrote in some detail of the sympathy and antipathy of colours, the transitions between contrasting tones, describing an ideal painterly harmonics: 'there are no colours, however close their affinity, that the maladroit cannot make discordant, and none so antipathetic that the ingenious artist cannot bring into an intimate harmony by the agreement of primary lights, and by the breaks in the half tones, the modification of shadows and the participations of reflections'.[4] Satisfaction in the execution of such harmonies 'adds to the intrinsic value of the work's merit'; it is a value which is additional, that is, to dramatic exposition.[5] The writer whose remarks on painting are most pertinent for our present argument is the Comte de Caylus, archaeologist, printmaker, playwright and amateur of painting.

He had written a book for those painters who had not received a literary education, on how to choose subjects from the Iliad and Odyssey and other epics,[6] but he had also given papers at the official academy on the material procedures of painting and the values attached to it. Caylus wrote

> the lightness of execution [*légèrté d'outil*] seems to me the final part of what is essential to painting: it completes the sense of movement round the volume of objects, so necessary for the expression of bodies; it catches the bloom of fruit, the freshness of flowers, and still more the charm of youth; it is composed of those omissions [*laissés*] that one can compare to things left implicit, to the words left out, which are the charm of conversation.[7]

But this, he says, must never be sought with glazes: 'the lightness of execution should never be confused with the neatness and finish of the Flemings and Dutch. In order to be brilliant they cease to be light'.[8] Earlier he had written: 'Let us paint everything with a loaded brush: one does not care to see a mechanical procedure, above all when it is to produce pleasing illusions'.[9] The painter must show an ease in his execution without the sense of laboured subservience to the appearance of the depicted object; he must seem superior to his task in having the ability to select and leave out, to hold the subject in mind without miming it – the wit to leave things implicit. This independence toward the appearance of the subject in turn allows the viewer to imagine what is left underdetermined. That conception was not original to Caylus; it went back to sixteenth-century discussion in Italy, was current throughout the seventeenth century in the Netherlands, and in France was rehearsed by de Piles who, in his section on landscape in the *Cours de Peinture* of 1708 distinguished an energetic from a polished style of handling (*le style ferme* and *le style poli*). 'The energetic style gives the work life . . . the polished style finishes and polishes everything and leaves nothing to the imagination of the spectator, which takes pleasure in finding and completing things that it attributes to the painter, although really it is drawn out of itself'.[10]

Writers on painting constantly stressed the need for the appearance of a wise negligence, ease and a loaded brush.[11] There are several different values that come together in this conception: first it is a matter of the painter's relation to his subject: it insists on his spontaneity and independence rather than following a prescribed model – a quality of mind; secondly it is a matter of his relation to other viewers of his painting, his tact which does not pre-empt their thoughts, exercizing restraint by leaving things out; in both respects the painting maintains a fluid boundary between the explicit and implicit, what is manifest and what is inward.

There is a continuity between Caylus's remarks on the lightness of handling and his remarks on the delicacy of the feeling:

> I regard [the gentle passions] incontestibly as what constitutes the sublime in painting and the most difficult of all its parts; for, without disregarding the terrible passions [*les passions terribles*], I believe that it is easier to declaim the ragings of Orestes than to render well the character of Bérénice. In anger, rage, indeed in all the transports of passion, nature offers so many inflections, so many pronounced manifestations, that it is enough to seize on one of them for the expression to be established . . . But the gentle movements of the soul hang by a thread [*ne tiennent à rien*]: the slightest alteration of an interior or exterior feature dissolves the expression: a mere nothing alters it in nature, a mere nothing makes it disappear in art.

And he cites – lacking, he says, a classical example – a modern drawing, a head by Raphael, and he describes it as registering multiple sentiments, confidence, submission, hope, resignation. 'The more the eye catches onto this trait, the more other sentiments succeed and supersede each, contesting the occupation of our pleasure and satisfaction.'[12] There is an unavoidable convergence between that suggestive lightness of execution that is the 'final and essential part in painting' and the expression of elusive states of mind 'the sublime in painting and the most difficult of its parts'; each is an extension of sensitivity that will not resolve its object into literal or dramatic determinacy; each involves the inward participation of the painter and viewer to complete the painting from within himself. (The older painter Antoine Coypel for whom Chardin expressed admiration, had also talked of the charms of tranquility that painting affords, in contrast to tumultuous feelings of heroic drama, for those capable of meditation – those who can 'sacrifice to the goddess of tranquility'.[13])

There seems no record of the relations between Chardin and Caylus although they were members of the same academy, one as amateur, the other as professional and had acquaintances in common, including the dealer and collector Mariette and the engraver, writer and friend of Chardin, Charles-Nicolas Cochin. (There are anecdotes that suggest that Chardin would hardly have found this patronizing and manipulative grandee very agreeable.[14]) But it is not their immediate personal relations, nor even the possibility that Caylus might have responded to Chardin in this way that makes his writing peculiarly appropriate to the character of Chardin's art, but rather the form of attention to painting that Caylus recommends.

III

A pervasive characteristic of Chardin's painting is the combination of substantiality and elusiveness: aspects of the subject, the bloom on fruit, the surface of silver, of a joint of meat, of glazed or unglazed pottery, seem to arise in the matière of the paint (figs 113 and 114). The paint provides the depicted objects with a sense of physical presence, making them palpable while at the same time subsuming them within an overall play of illumination and the texture of the painted surface. The shift between the real paint surface and the fictive object is given a peculiar focus in a number of small canvases: in *The Scullery Maid* in Glasgow (fig. 115) the rich paste of the paint emerges to substantiate the apron; this is pressed even further in the two very small paintings on oak panels

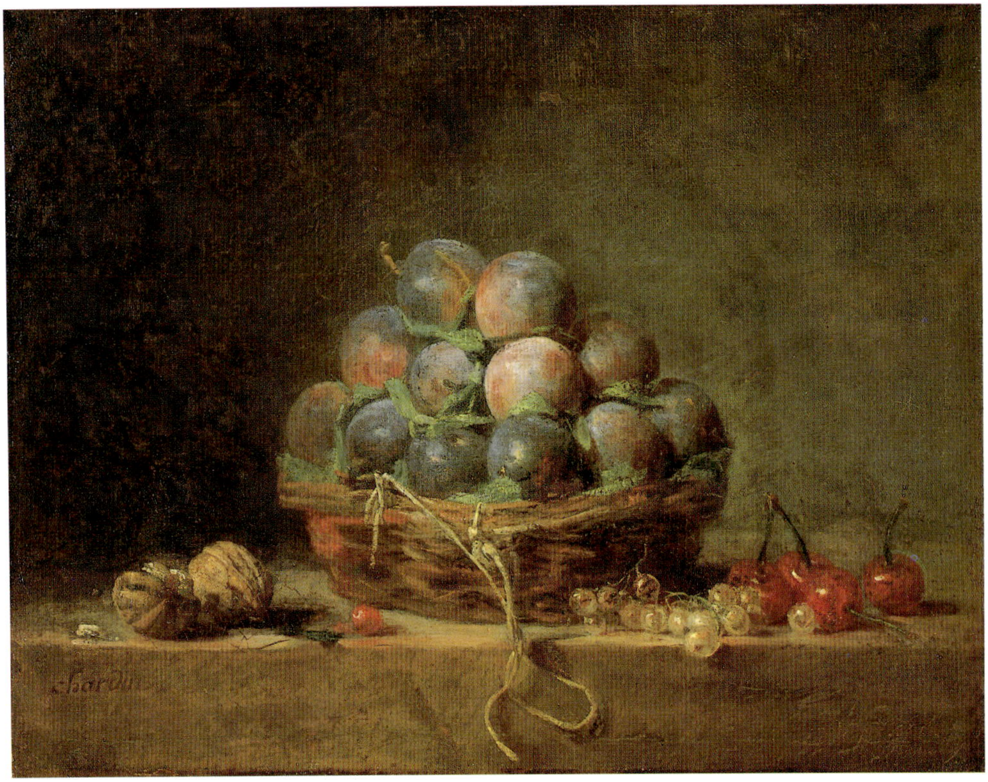

113 Chardin, *Still Life: Basket of Plums*, 1764–5. Oil on canvas, 32 × 42 cm. Gift of Walter P. Chrysler Jr., Chrysler Museum, Norfolk, Virginia.

now in Stockholm, *The Embroiderer* and *The Draughtsman* (figs 116 and 117), in the second the figure is set against the other with the sense of contiguous surfaces, the broad back virtually cosubstantial with the corresponding area of the panel while the shadow cast by the drawing pinned to the wall (which the young man in his turn is copying) seems as much to be cast by the paint as by the drawing; there is a similar ambiguous shadow in the lap of the embroiderer. The inscrutibility of the border between the painting and its subject is made firmly thematic, a moment of the most complete pictorial concentration; this was for Chardin a peculiar value related to elusiveness of other kinds.

In a late still life, *The Sideboard* (fig. 114), as we look at the laden table, the dome of the soup tureen may be conceived as aligned with the plate behind it – its halo; the relation is one that

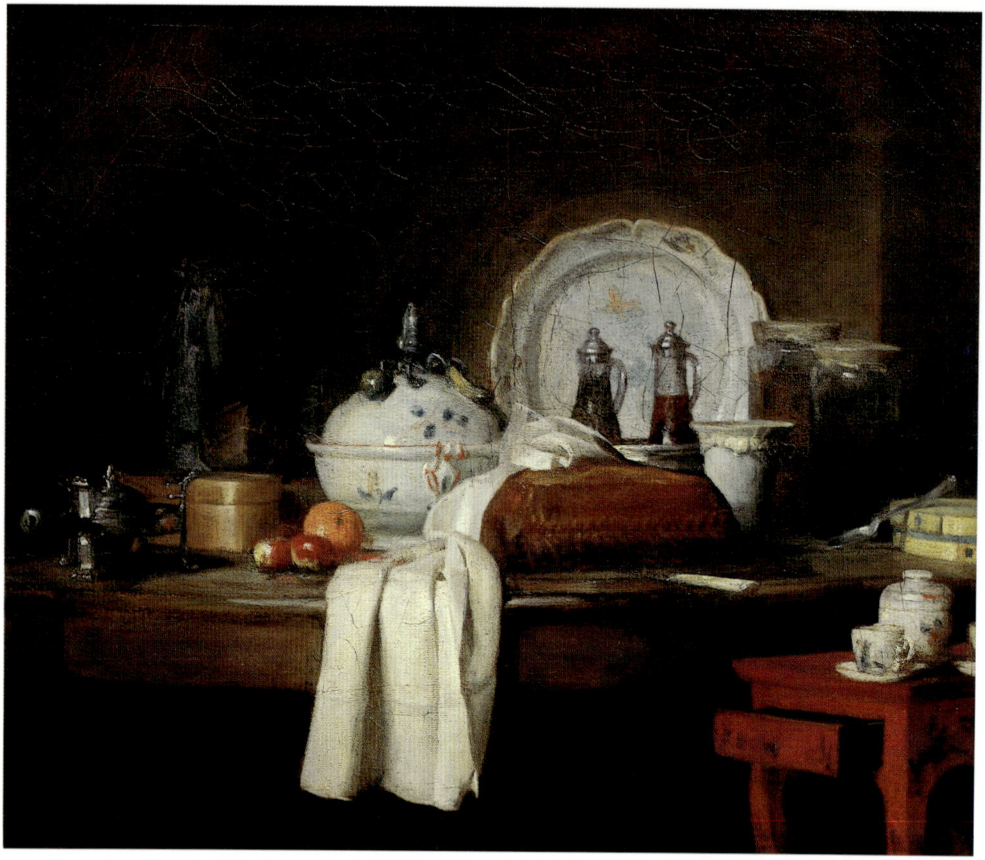

114 Chardin, *The Sideboard*, *c.*1763. Oil on canvas, 38 × 46cm. Musée du Louvre, Paris.

we can neither avoid entertaining nor avoid setting aside, and setting it aside remains part of our global sense of the picture rather than being effaced as a misreading. For seeing the tureen and plate as both lying in the same axis in relation to the viewer and also as not doing so, is enforced by the twin verticals of the decanters which may be aligned symmetrically either with the tureen or with the plate. The uncertainty of orientation is further enhanced by the curving edge of the table that slips out of alignment with the picture plane: more generally, the ambiguous edges and incomplete rhymes coming together with the small scale suggest a landscape distance and alternative vistas. This kind of

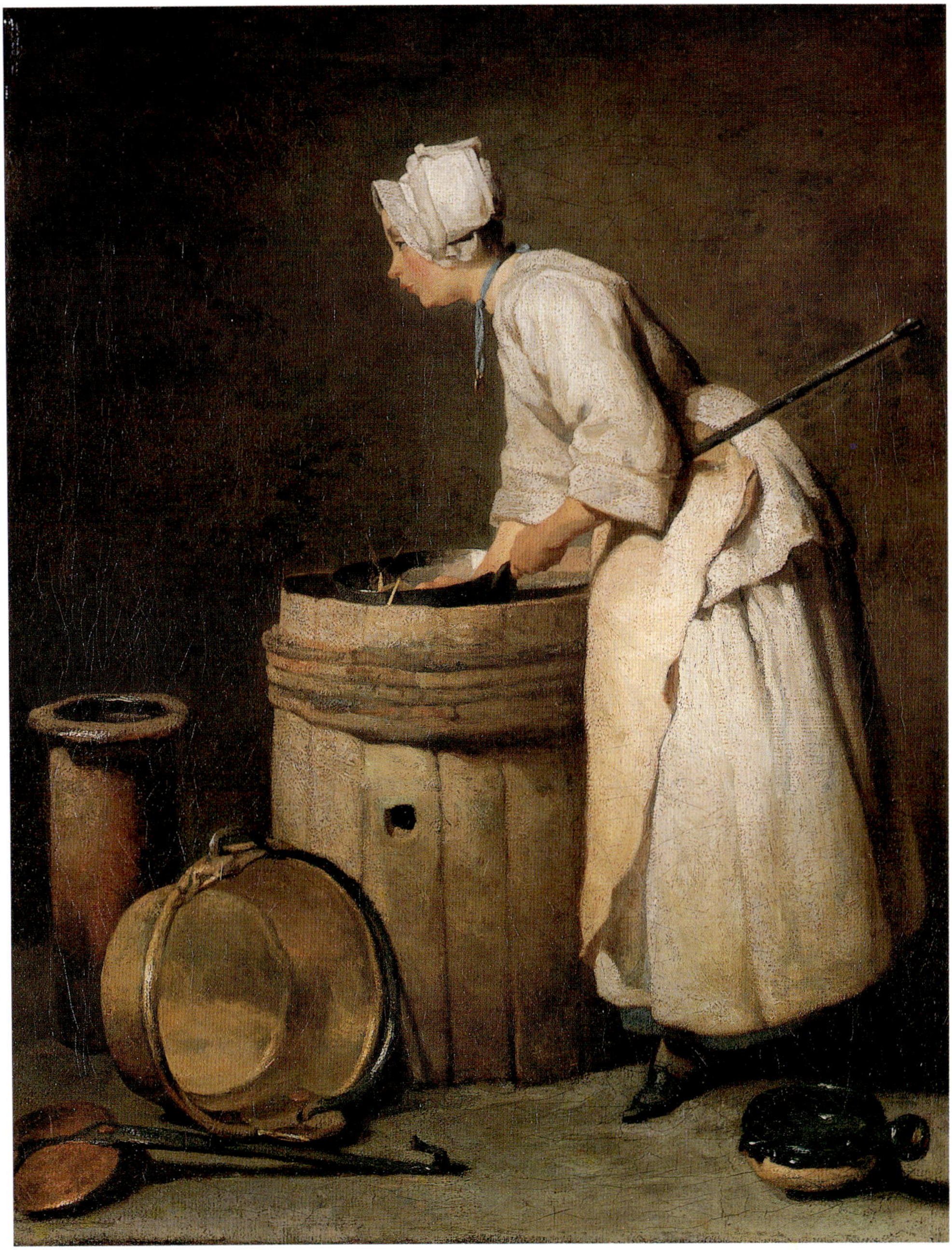

115 Chardin, *The Scullery Maid*, 1738. Oil on canvas, 45.4 × 37 cm. Hunterian Museum and Gallery, Glasgow.

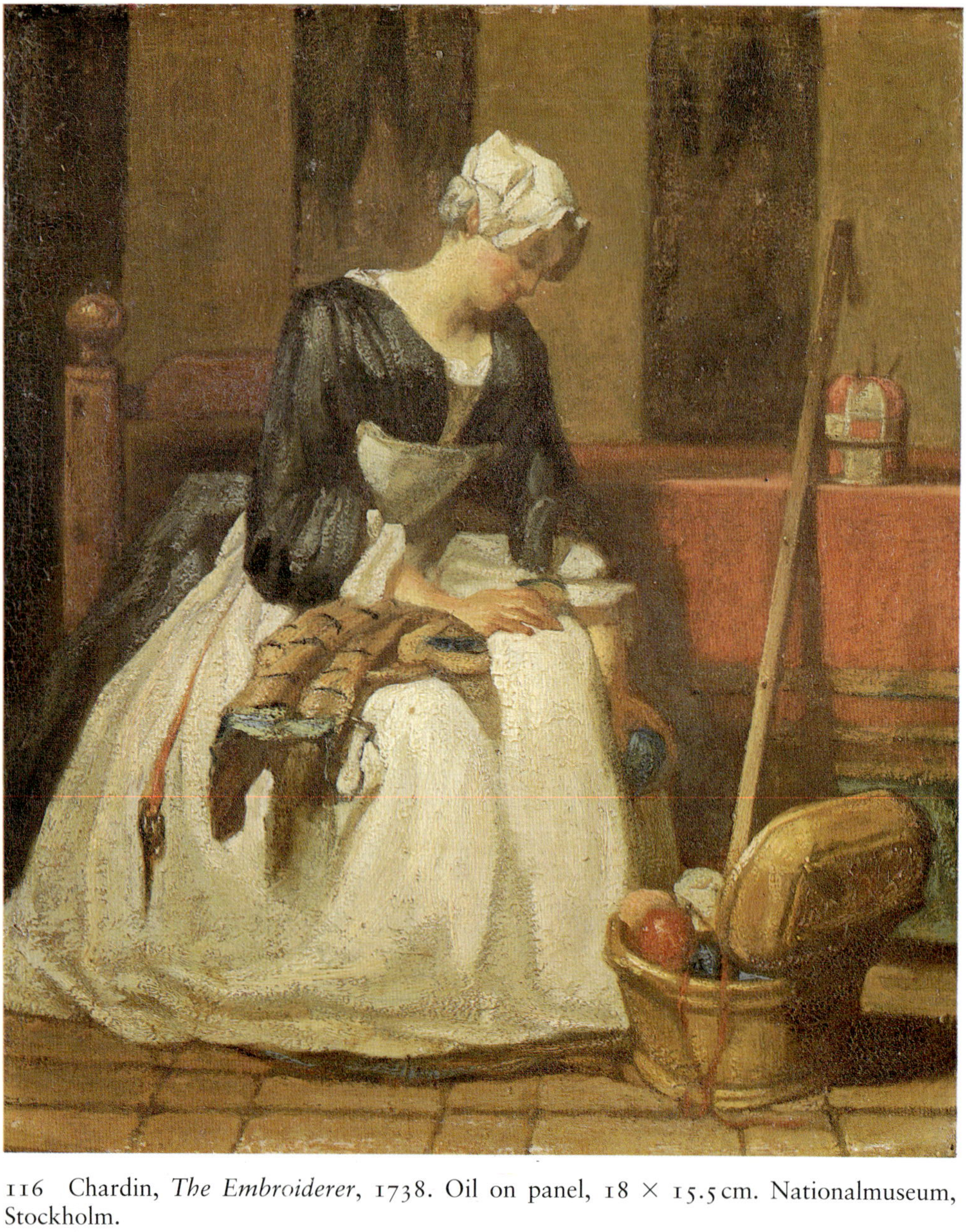

116 Chardin, *The Embroiderer*, 1738. Oil on panel, 18 × 15.5 cm. Nationalmuseum, Stockholm.

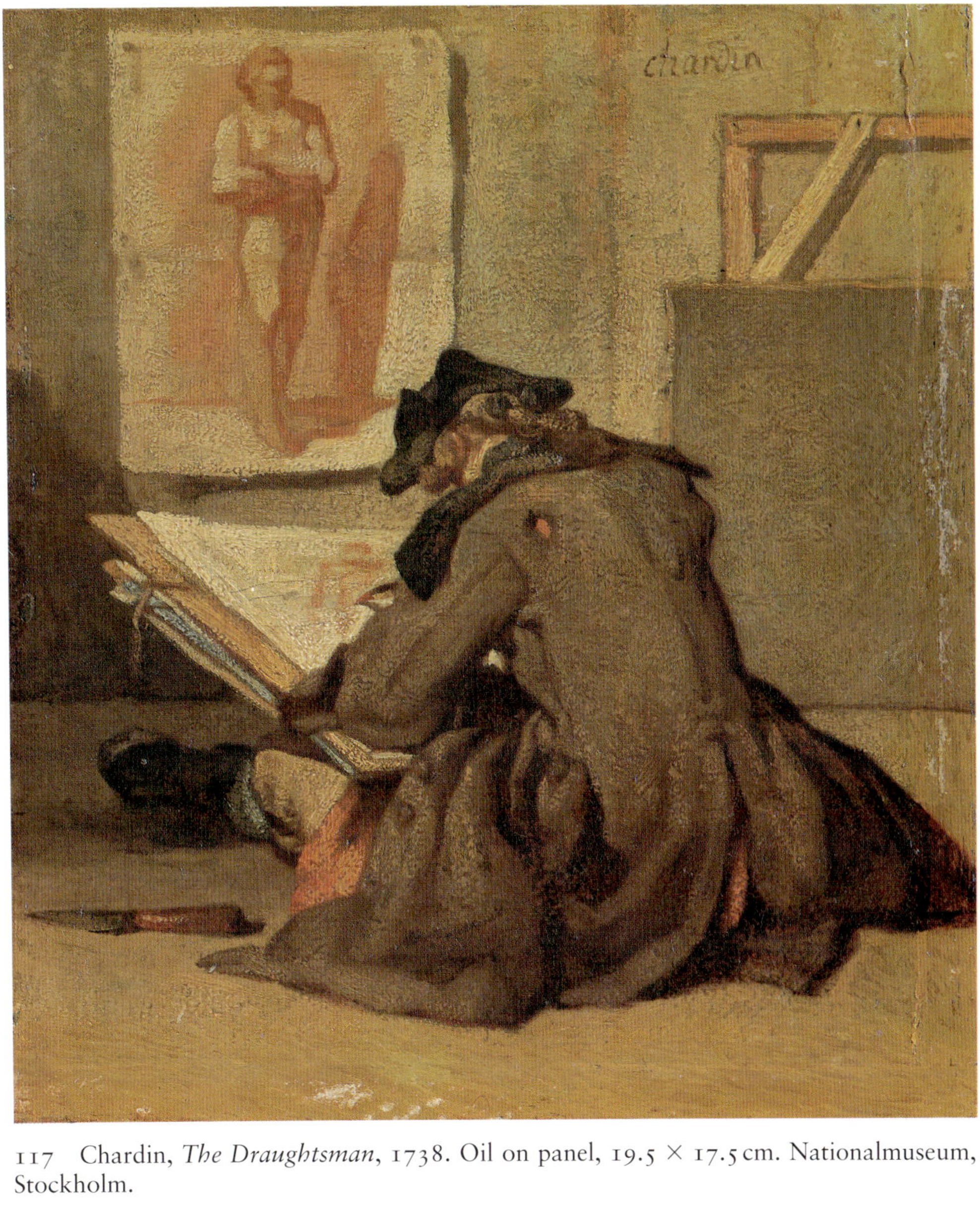

117 Chardin, *The Draughtsman*, 1738. Oil on panel, 19.5 × 17.5 cm. Nationalmuseum, Stockholm.

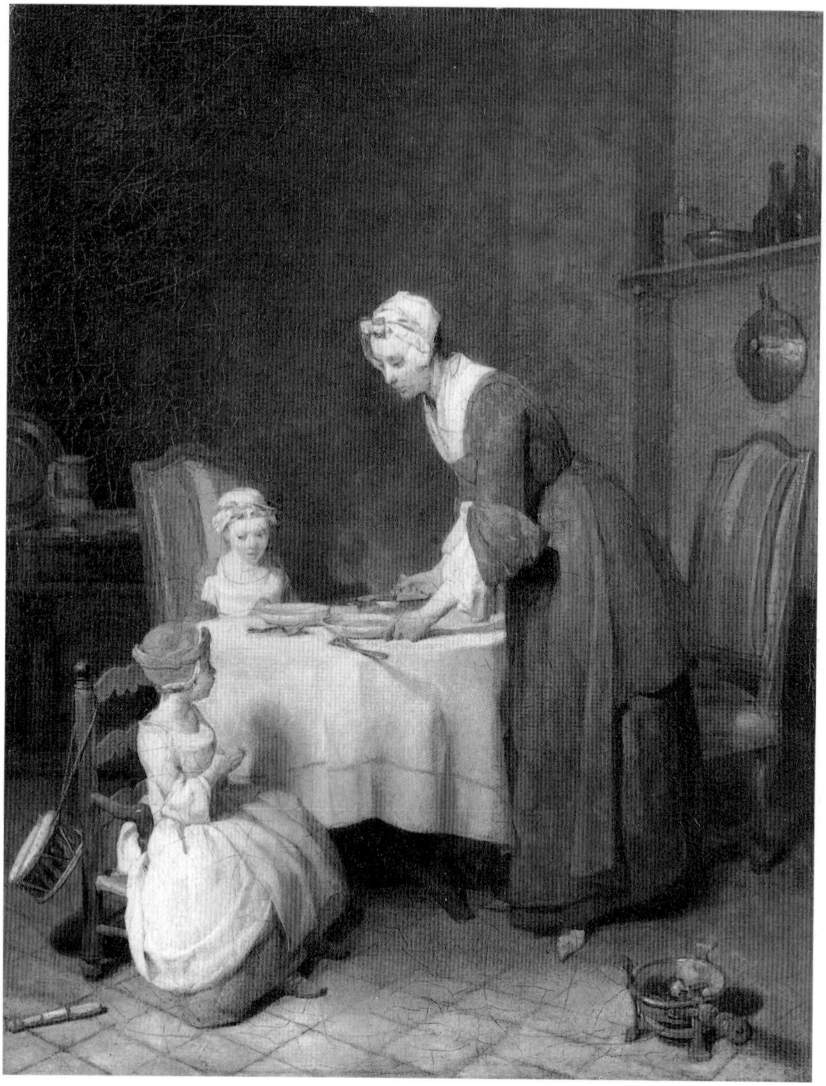

118 Chardin, *Saying Grace*, 1740. Oil on canvas, 49.5 × 39.5 cm. Musée du Louvre, Paris.

uncertainty has an analogue in the paintings that concern the relation of adults and children.

In *Saying Grace* the mother waits for the small boy to say the words: what is in question is his capacity and willingness to bring them out (fig. 118). Similarly the girl in *The Lesson* waits for the

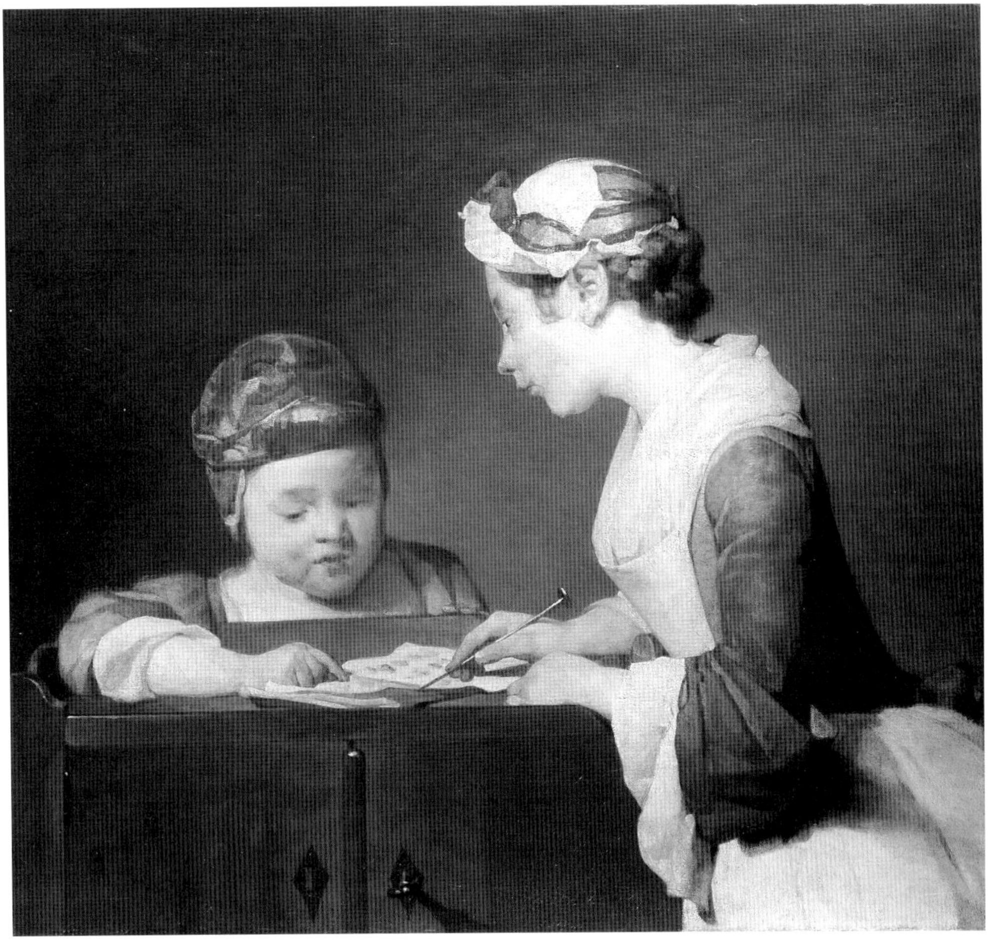

119 Chardin, *The Lesson*, *c.*1736. Oil on canvas, 61.5 × 66.5 cm. National Gallery, London.

child to read (fig. 119). This sense of anticipation is not a matter of imagining what will happen next, but of one person imagining and identifying with another, aware of something inward to them which has not come out and been made manifest. The theme recurs in *The Governess* (fig. 120) as the woman bends forward to the boy about to pass through the door into the adult world, and in the woman looking at the uncertainty of her daughter in *The Industrious Mother* (fig. 121).

Elsewhere the sense of what is psychologically latent converges with what is visually implicit. For example, in the *Morning*

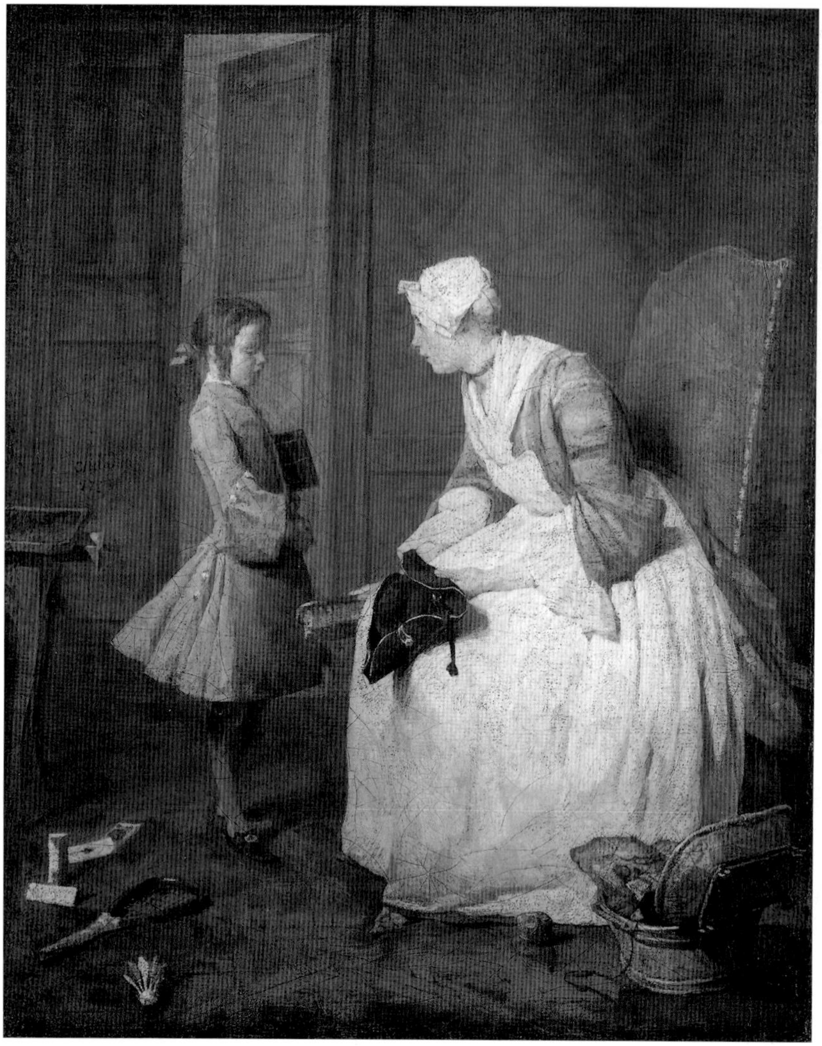

120 Chardin, *The Governess*, 1738. Oil on canvas, 46 × 37.5 cm. The National Gallery of Canada, Ottawa.

Toilette (fig. 122) the mother is depicted in an elaborate dress with striking shapes, but they are not shapes that clarify her posture; it is only when we think how the direction of her head, shoulders and hips must relate to each other that we realize the serpentine pose and imagine rehearsing it. We realize it without being able to trace it either on the surface of the canvas or on the surface of the figure. The form is intimated rather than shown; and what it leads

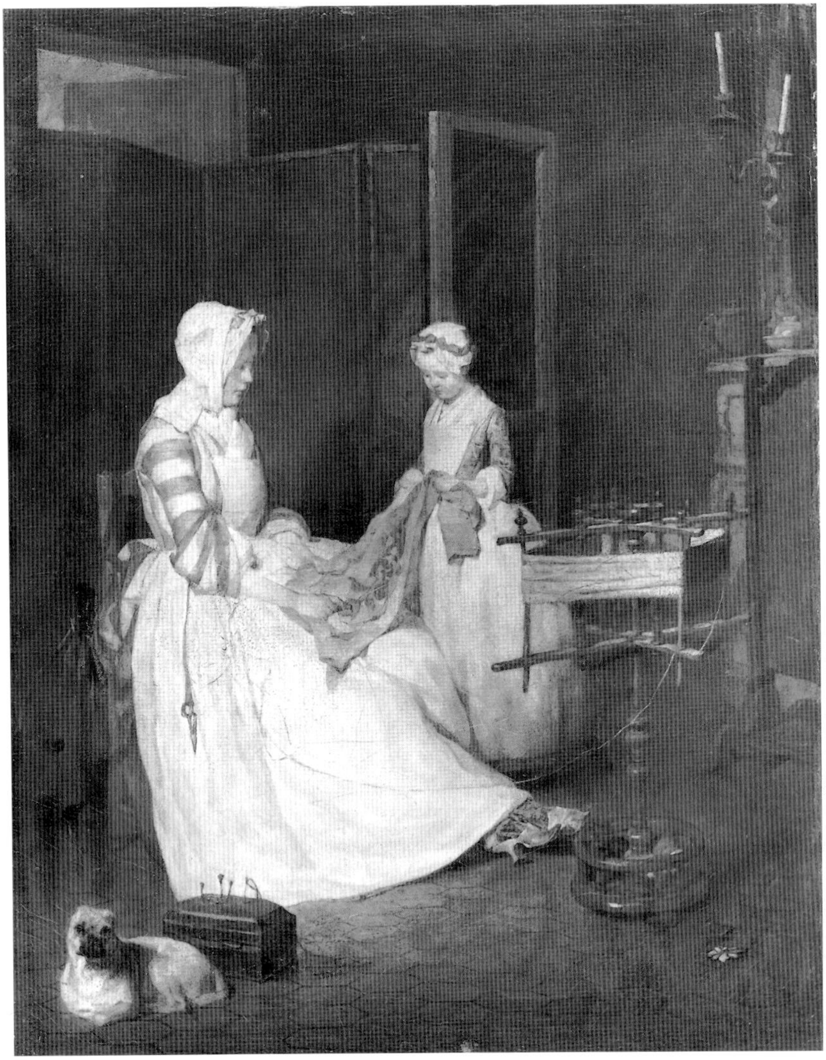

121 Chardin, *The Industrious Mother*, 1740. Oil on canvas, 49 × 39 cm. Musée du Louvre, Paris.

us to imagine is not only the turn of her body but her awareness of herself.

In the *Return from Market* psychological and visual implicitness are pressed into a further conjunction (fig. 123). There are two themes of which the first is provisioning: the woman returning heavily laden, her arm and sleeve pressing against her skirt registered by areas of paint laid into each other, and the sense of fresh

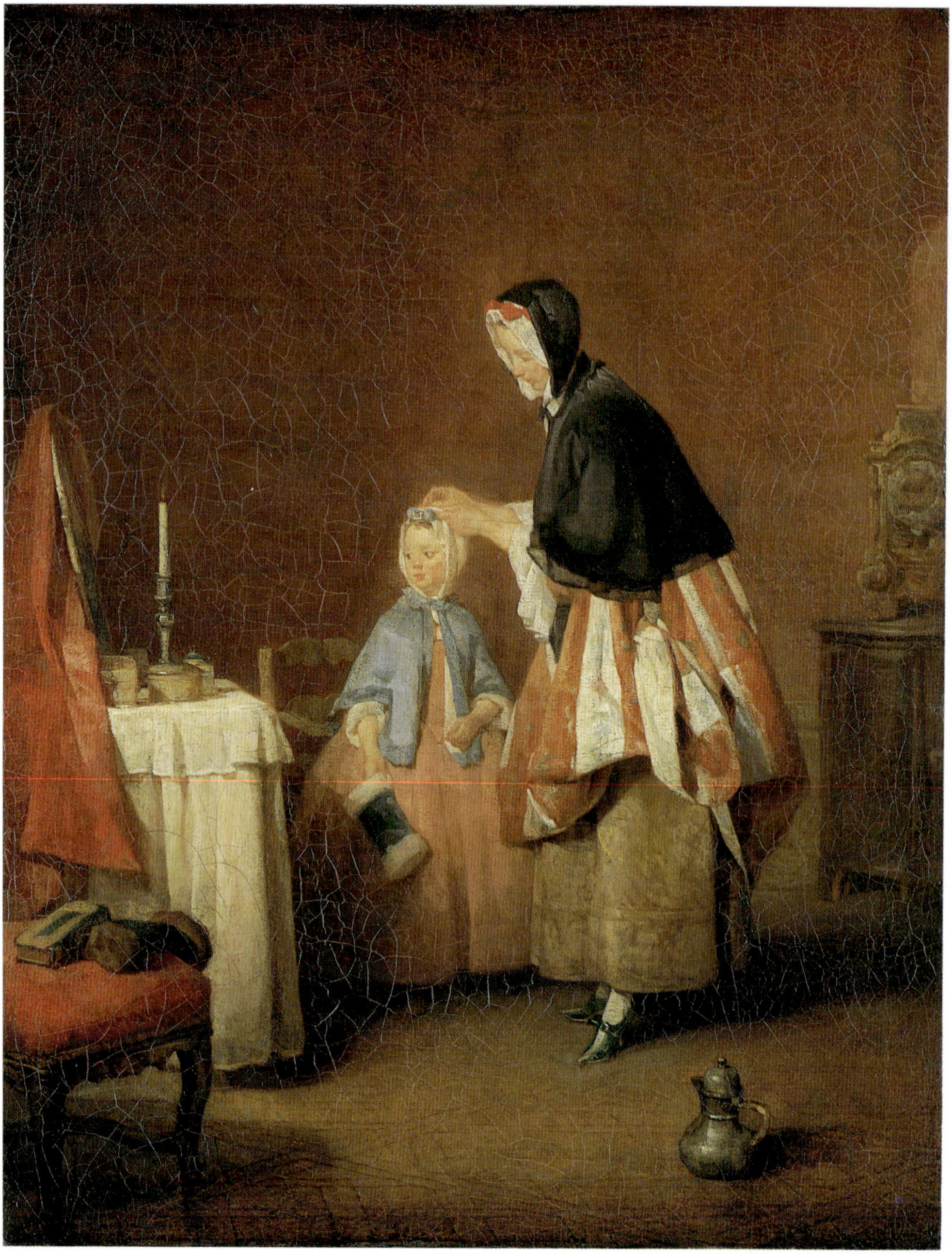

122 Chardin, *Morning Toilette*, 1741. Oil on canvas, 49 × 39 cm. Nationalmuseum, Stockholm.

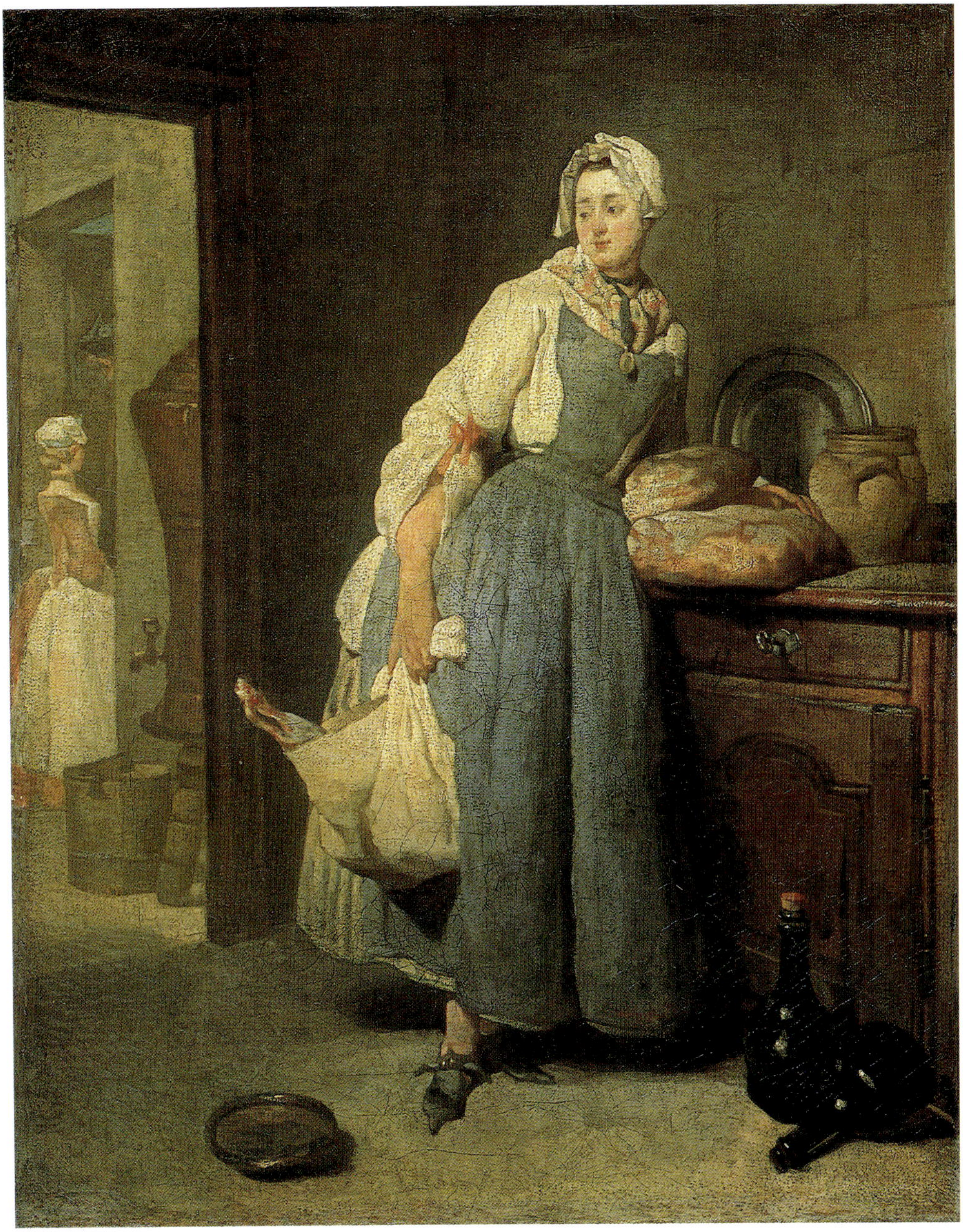

123 Chardin, *Return from Market*, 1739. Oil on canvas, 47 × 38 cm. Musée du Louvre, Paris.

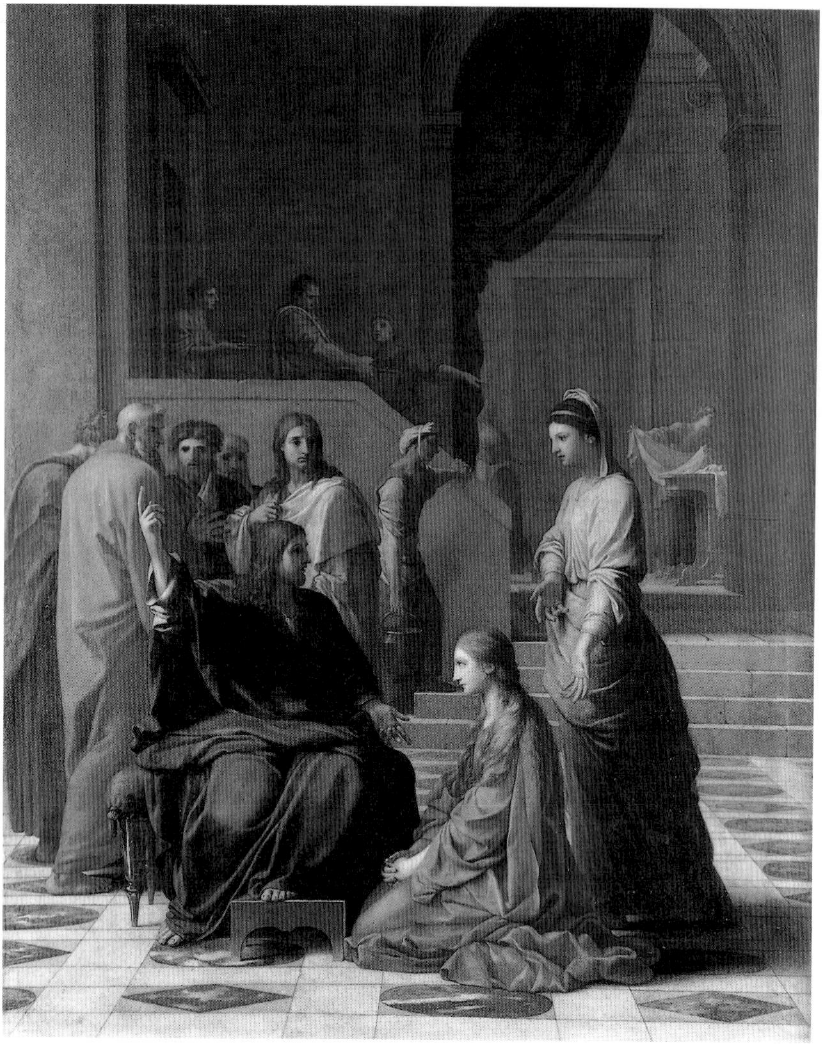

124 Eustache Le Sueur, *Christ in the House of Mary and Martha*, 1650. Oil on canvas, 162 × 130 cm. Alte Pinakothek, Munich.

loaves set in play against the pottery bowl and the polished surfaces of wood and pewter. The second theme is her hearing the encounter the other side of the doorway. We are brought to imagine her attention not just as something to be guessed, a piece of anecdotal filling in or filling out, but as something felt through the forms of the painting. The curved side of the water vat responds to that of the young woman in the foreground, something confirmed by the rhyming of the tap with the protruding gigot; but the vat also mirrors the silhouette of the girl in the background and as these relations gather, it visually mediates between the two. If we compare this with, for instance, Le Sueur's *Christ in the House of Mary and Martha* (fig. 124), which was admired by Caylus for the sensitivity with which the Magdalen's inward life was registered in her face and demeanour,[15] we are led to observe how in the *Return from Market*, the density of the painting strictly limits the psychological or moral speculation about the young woman, for its materiality and its structures become our way of imagining her situation. What is so perceptually realized sets the standard for imagining.

IV

Earlier in this chapter the connection was suggested between the experience of reciprocity within the infant's transitional zone and that of depiction. The argument was not that painting represented that early relation but that it mobilized an underlying mental structure which had been laid down in infancy. This theme of an intimate relation to the material world was proposed a century ago in Proust's essay on Chardin. He contrasted the beauty of the everyday objects of the kitchen in their habitual use with the grand scenes by Veronese or van Dyke to be found in pictures in the Louvre; he invented a young man who disvalued his everyday surroundings in favour of those grand scenes, whom he halted before the paintings of Chardin, saying

> The pleasure you get from the painting of a room where a woman sits sewing, a pantry, a kitchen, a sideboard, is the pleasure – seized on the wing, redeemed from the transient, ascertained, pondered, perpetuated . . . You already experienced it subconsciously, this pleasure one gets from the sight of everyday scenes and inanimate objects, otherwise it would not have risen in your heart when Chardin summoned it . . .[16]

He sees painting retrieving for awareness the resonance of ordinary things and the life lived among them.

Recently the historian Réné Démoris has elaborated on the thought by observing that the paintings concern the domestic and maternal world;[17] men scarcely appear within them, nor do the

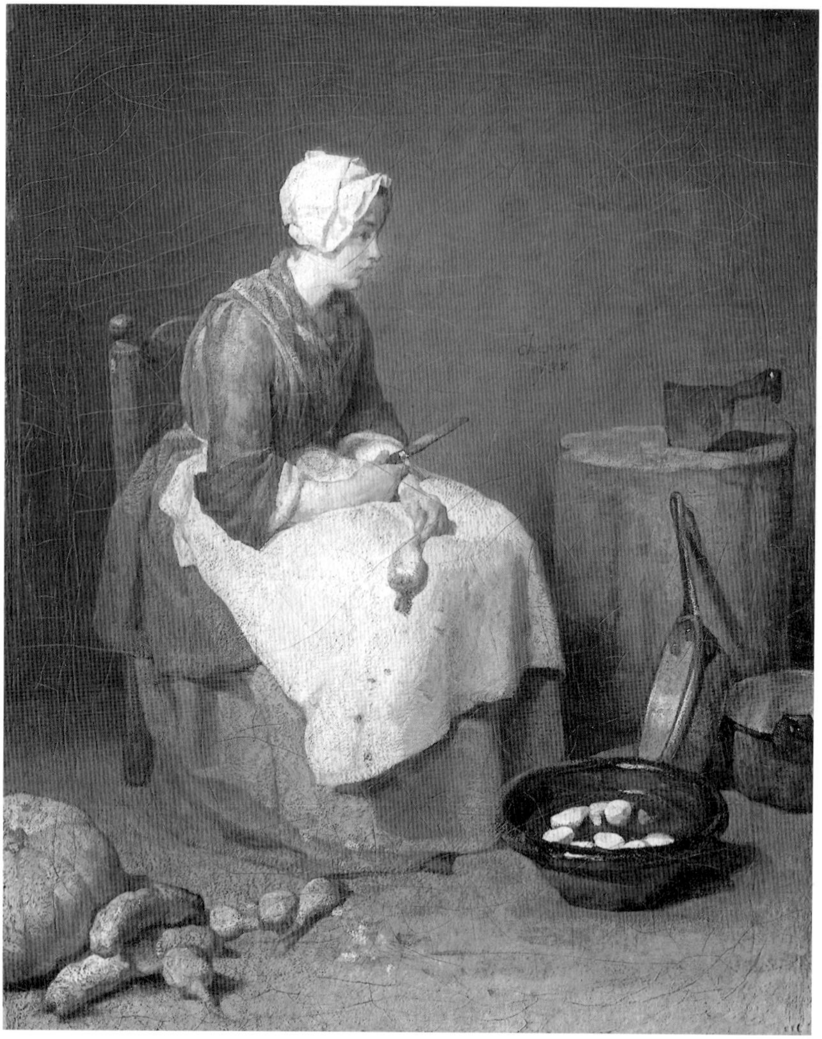

125 Chardin, *Woman Peeling Turnips*, 1738. Oil on canvas, 44.5 × 34.5 cm. Samuel H. Kress Collection, National Gallery of Art, Washington.

formalities of social life; and within that domestic world we are given the young child's sense of the unintelligible juxtaposition of objects, their compelling physiognomy and the sense of menace that can be attached to the preparations of animals for food. For example, the cuts of meat or fish forming strange shapes; or, in the background of the *Woman Peeling Turnips* (fig. 125), the kitchen cleaver on its board with its traces of blood; or the pathos of paintings like the *Dead Hare* (fig. 126) or the bewildering image of the eviscerated fish in the Louvre painting of *The Ray* (fig. 127) in which he sees intimations of an infant's sadistic fantasy; in so doing he indicates a more violent element in the 'intimate relation to things' within the scope of the painting. This is something that

126 Chardin, *Dead Hare with Game Bag and Powder Horn*, *c.*1730. Oil on canvas, 98 × 76 cm. Musée du Louvre, Paris.

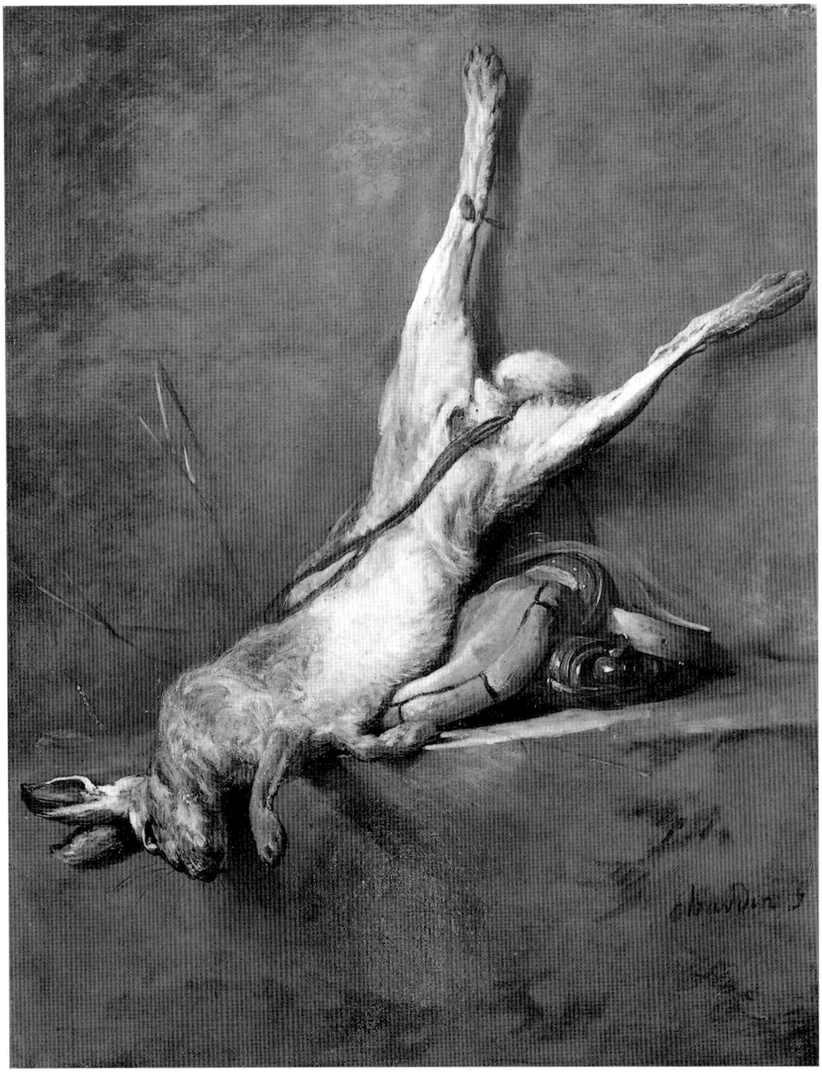

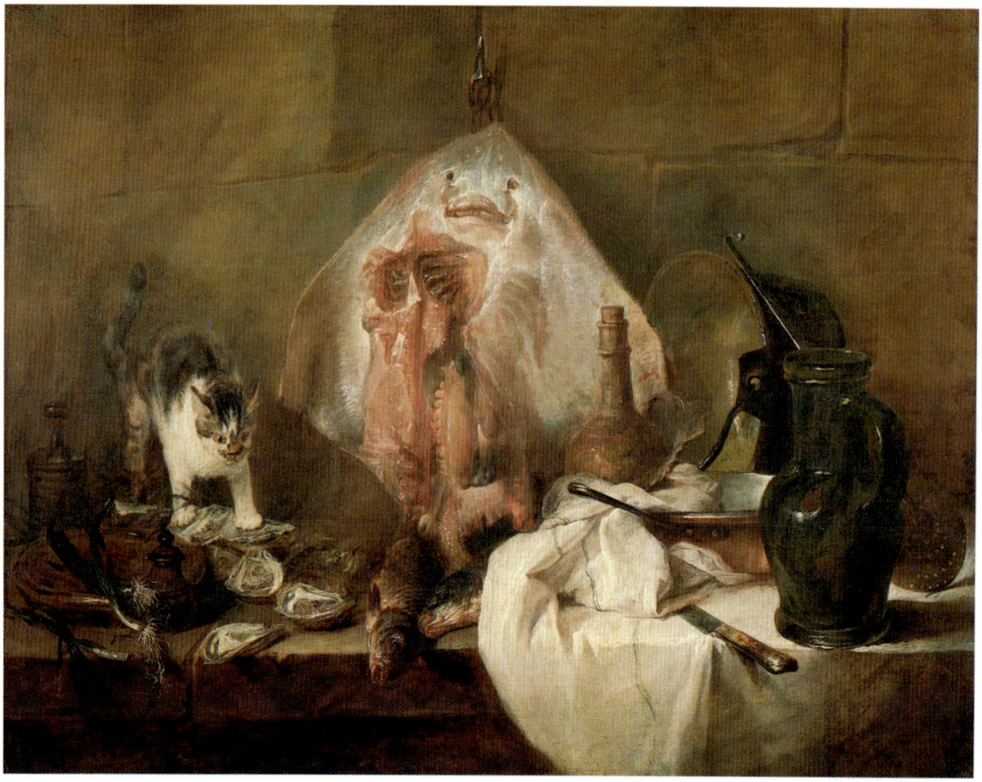

127 Chardin, *The Ray*, 1726. Oil on canvas, 114.5 × 146 cm. Musée du Louvre, Paris.

has yet to be accommodated within our reflection on Chardin and it involves a rather different way of considering how these paintings – and painting in general – may relate back to early childhood.

In psycho-analytic writing – particularly that influenced by Melanie Klein – such infant fantasy has been related to works of art in several overlapping ways: the fantasies of destructive violence and the remorse it engenders have been seen as an underlying theme but also an underlying motivation for making the work of art; the content of the work is conceived as allegorizing them but also as overcoming the repression that excludes them from consciousness. 'Symbols', wrote the Kleinian analyst Hannah Segal,

> are needed not only in communication with the external world, but also in internal communication. Indeed, it could be asked

> what is meant when we speak of people being in touch with their unconscious. It is not that they have consciously primitive phantasies, like those which become evident in their analyses, but merely that they have some awareness of their own impulses and feelings. However, I think that we mean more than this; we mean that they have actual *communication* with their unconscious phantasies. And this, like any other form of communication can be done only with the help of symbols. So that in people who are 'in touch with themselves' there is a constant free symbol formation.[18]

Segal assumes that later symbolic expression relates back to underlying primitive fantasies; as an example she adduces the typical fairy tale: 'It deals basically with the witch and the fairy godmother, Prince Charming, the ogre, etc., and it has in it a great deal of schizophrenic content. It is, however, a highly integrated product, an artistic creation which very fully symbolizes the child's early anxiety and wishes.' The fairy tale is thus thought of as like both the fantasies uncovered in analysis and like the work of art.

The work of art that Segal cites as exemplary is Proust's novel in which the work of the artist is conceived of as recovering earlier experience.[19] She writes of Proust that

> he reveals such an acute awareness of what I believe is present in the unconscious of all artists: namely, that all creation is really a re-creation of a once loved and once whole, but now lost and ruined object, a ruined internal world and self. It is when the world within us is destroyed, when it is dead and loveless, when our loved ones are in fragments, and we ourselves are in helpless despair it is then that we must re-create our world anew.

For Segal the work of art like the process of analysis brings about an acknowledgement of what was otherwise repressed, such acknowledgement is seen above all as renouncing the presumption that all value proceeds from oneself and the acceptance of the good in others. This acknowledgement constitutes an inward reparation to the damaged mother. Proust is seen by Segal as fulfilling this project of redemption, and she cites the thought, expressed through his fictive painter Elstir: 'On ne peut pas recréer ce qu'on aime qu'en le renonceant'. But if we pause on this dictum it would seem to suggest something rather more specifically related to art: to the fact that in order to make a novel or a painting or a poem out of the material of one's life, that material must be given up and put into play within the new imaginative structure that is the work of art. Proust's enterprize of integrating his world, of using his awareness of all those people of his actual life, like the various models for Odette or Charlus, conflating and dividing and reconstructing them to make them into parts of his novel, releases them from the contingencies of his own life so they can reappear within the new structures of the imagination.[20] (Elstir was talking about his relation to past painting, specifically his relation to Chardin. Proust's point in this context is the artist's need to sacrifice adherence to the literal objects of past feelings, whether works of art or people, in order to endow one's use of them with the kind of life that they were originally felt as having.)

This corresponds to the way the painter must give up his dependence upon what is literally before him in order to construct an image that has its own consequentiality and internal informativeness. It may be – following Segal – that our capacity to experience the pity and fear in tragedy depends causally on the fear of earliest anger which we imagine turned against ourselves and the pity for those whom in fantasy we destroyed, but if we see works of art as relating us back to our past – bringing past experience into some intimate relation to the circumstances and objects of the present – it does so in a way quite different to therapy.

One might think of the connection of earlier to later experiences with two different kinds of emphasis: first, as the perpetuation of an earlier experience, in particular an earlier conflict as symbolically rehearsed in the present, or alternatively as the extension of sensitivities and propensities developed in the past investing a new object or situation with interest and feeling. These two emphases correspond to two different purposes: on the one hand the therapeutic purpose of disambiguating the past from the present in order to release the present from the grip of the past; on the other the aesthetic or, more generally, the productive purpose that is not at all concerned with such disambiguation but, on the contrary, with using the sensibilites developed in the past in responding to the present. The difference is between retrospective and prospective orientations.

The distinction between the two orientations was made forty years ago by Marion Milner:

> Certainly for the analyst, in certain stages in analysing an artist, the importance of his work of art may be the lost object that the work recreates; but for the artist as artist, rather than as patient, and for whoever responds to his work, I think that the essential point is the new thing he has created, the new bit of the external world that he has made significant and "real" through endowing it with form.[21]

This involves a sense of symbolism as expansive, as utilizing past experience to engage and endow with value new objects.[22] But if, with Milner, we distinguish the therapeutic from the productive or aesthetic stance, we are still left with the question of how we would accommodate the sense of potential extremity of feeling, including terror and pity, that seems bound to our conception of art. How might our account of the complexity of painting and the viewer's engagement with it be thought of as more than fortuitously related to such extremity?

V

Let us take up the discussion of the *Dead Hare* or *The Ray* (figs 126 and 127) or paintings of, say, the Lamentation, of Lucretia, or of the Flaying of Marsyas, or the shattered body of the woman in Picasso's *Fanny Tellier* (fig. 128) – in each of these cases we would

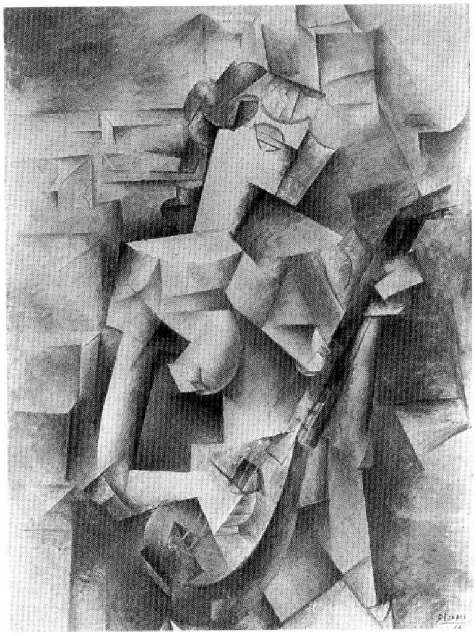

128 Pablo Picasso, *Girl with a Mandolin (Fanny Tellier)*, Paris, late spring 1910. Oil on canvas, 100.3 × 73.6 cm. Nelson A. Rockefeller Bequest, The Museum of Modern Art, New York.

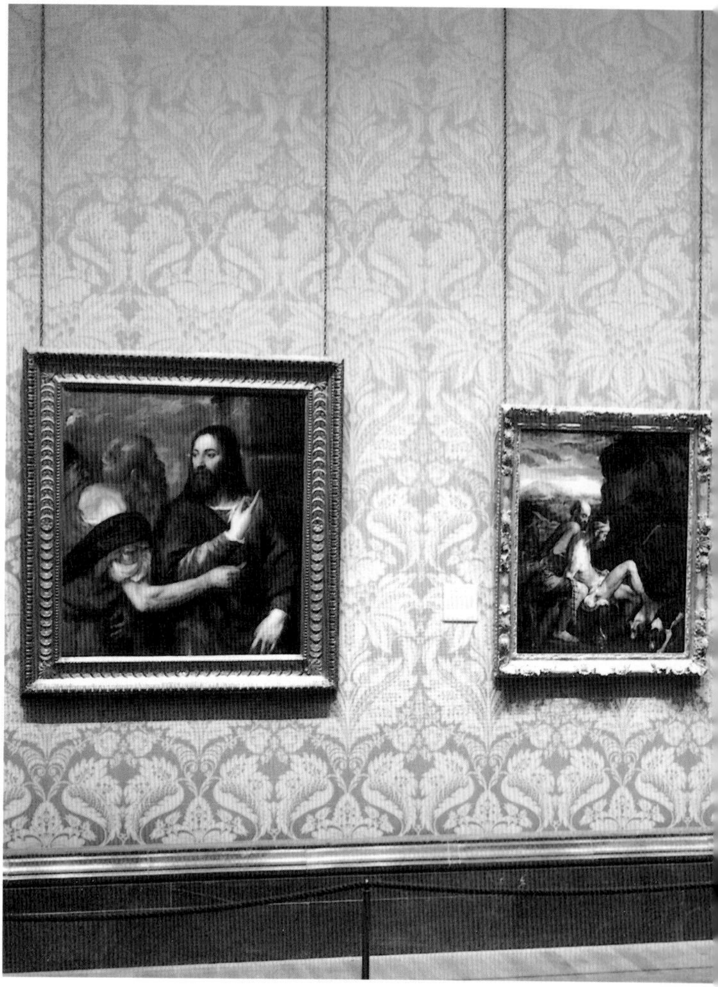

129 View in the National Gallery, London, with Titian's *Tribute Money* and Tintoretto's *Christ Washing the Disciples' Feet.*

say that the painting exhibits or rehearses violence suffered by its protagonist and in each case the violence is more or less implicit, mediated by the complexity of the painting. But what is the relation between violence and the mediating complexity? One ground for the decision of classical playwrights not to present scenes of violence on the stage, but rather prompt anticipations or show the aftermath of tragic events, might have been that it made them more able to engage our feeling. For to exhibit them on stage might have been to rob them of the power to raise interior fears and resonances with which they are entertained in anticipation or description. (Aristotle thought – perhaps from some such intuition

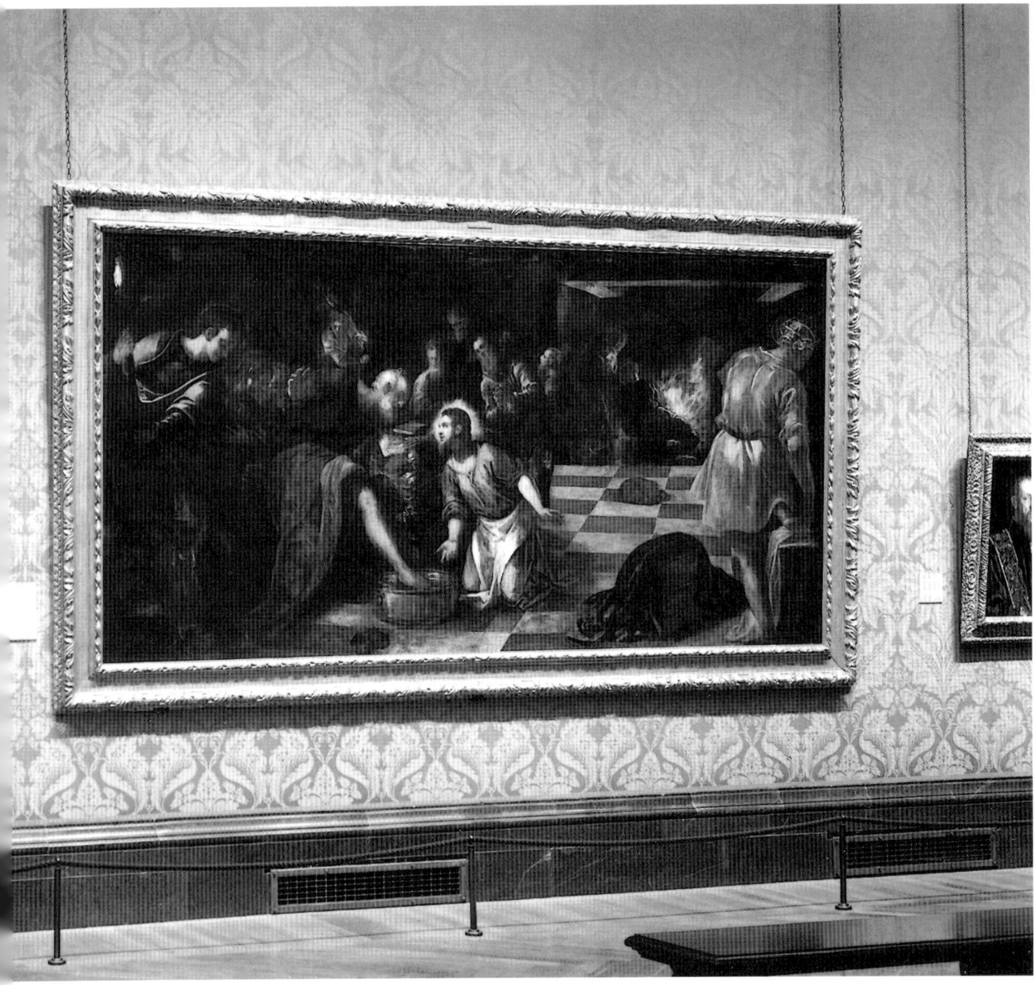

– that the best tragic plot was one in which the catastrophe seemed inevitable but was averted.[23])

Our access to our own responsiveness might require a distribution of attention so that it is not excessively taken up with what is perceptually present, or even with what is actual as opposed to possible. There is a comparable situation with overtly sexual material: the sophistications of painting, the sensuous materiality of the paint, the rhythms and complicated patterns that the depiction makes possible, may not so much mask what would otherwise be an erotic fantasy that threatens to seduce us, but allow an engagement which could be achieved only through the complex use of a

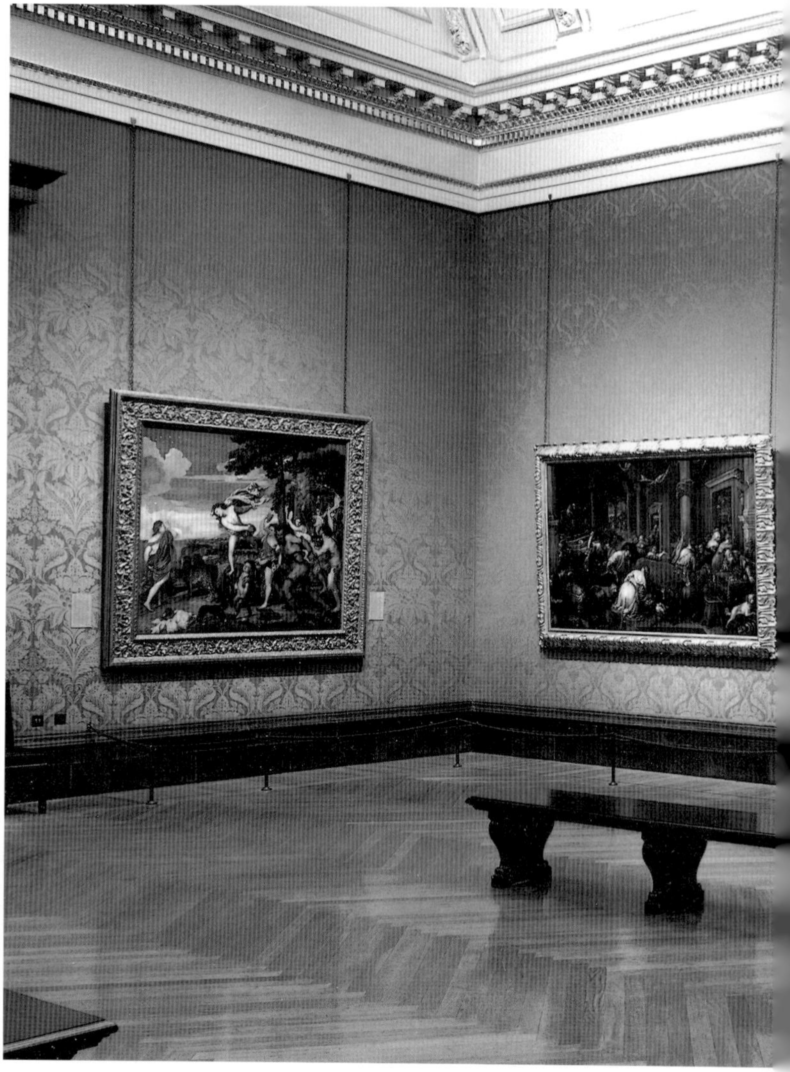

130 View in the National Gallery, London, with Titian's *Venus and Adonis* and *Bacchus and Ariadne* and Veronese's *Adoration*.

medium.[24] On the one hand implicitness leaves room for fantasy while on the other the material presence of the medium enables us to transform and sustain that fantasy in our concrete relation to the world, that is to say, in our perception.

The interaction between what can be scrutinized and what must be imagined can be exemplified in a constantly recurrent motif in painting: that of one figure searching out a response in the eyes of another. It reappears as a nearly continuous theme around the rooms exhibiting sixteenth-century Venetian painting in the

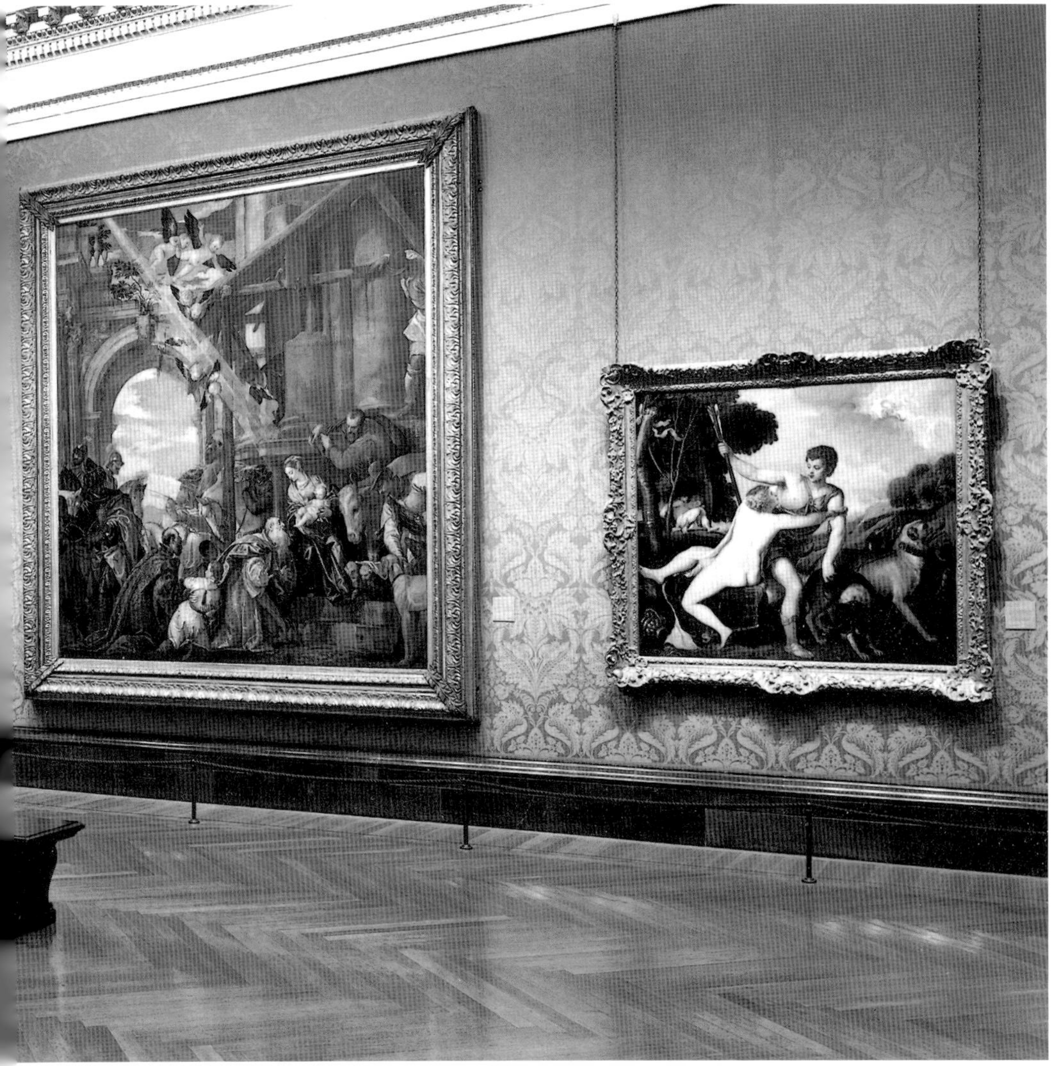

National Gallery, London (figs 129 and 130): St Peter looking at Christ to understand his intention in Titian's *Tribute Money*; Tintoretto's disciples looking at Christ as he washes their feet; Titian's Venus and Adonis and Bacchus and Ariadne; and the figures in Veronese's *Adoration* and *Allegory of Deceit* (fig. 7). For this effect it is not enough that we observe that the figures look at each other – the painting must sustain this reciprocity in the rhythms of their bodies and the whole architecture of the picture. This might serve us as a model for how feelings are lodged within painting; one figure searching out the response of another is something we come to imagine through the painting's complexity. It is a central characteristic of such complexity that we cannot make fully focal what emerges most powerfully. (We might find a fifteenth-century anticipation of this thought in Alberti's conception of the 'istoria', the theme or dramatic story of a painting which is generated out of figures and their gestures as figures are constituted by their limbs and their limbs by the planes that define them.)

It might be asked how there could be equivalent intensity in depicting an undramatic subject. Let us first exclude the line of approach that depends on some form of free association round the literal subject. For instance, in the case of Chardin's *Ray* in the Louvre one way of explaining its psychological force has been to say that it gathers together reciprocally enforcing associations of sexuality and violence, the white flesh of the eviscerated fish, the fur of the cat, the verbal associations of the word 'raie' (slit), the skimmer which gathers up spume off a liquid, the common associations of oysters and so forth.[25] There seems little reason for adducing the associations unless we first assume that the interest of the work lies in some latent or suppressed material; but our grounds for holding this, our evidence for this, would be just such verbal associations. At best these seem marginal to the visual attention that the painting sustains, to the crisply painted course of the cloth which twists over into the copper pan; to the dark grandeur of the pottery jug and of the bottle enfolded at its base in the play of shadows while its neck is given palpable density by a combination of dull translucence and reflected light, and the depiction of the ray-fish itself. The painting catches its unanticipatible shapes, their moist surfaces and differing translucence – now veined, now fatty – and this is done with a remarkable leanness, without insistence or elaboration of the paint. The subtlety of the painting even conceals itself by the effect of the false face – the gills appearing as eyes. This elusiveness of the painting has its analogue in another image of a ray-fish, painted by Chardin at about the same time, that shows it dangling at an oblique angle to the viewer making the overall form and intricate surface patterning hard to grasp (fig. 131). The sense of violence in the subject – which had prompted the search for verbal associations and repressed fantasies – is surely responded to openly in the wit and and delicacy of the painting. The painting is in dialogue with its subject, its suggestiveness the product of tact not repression.

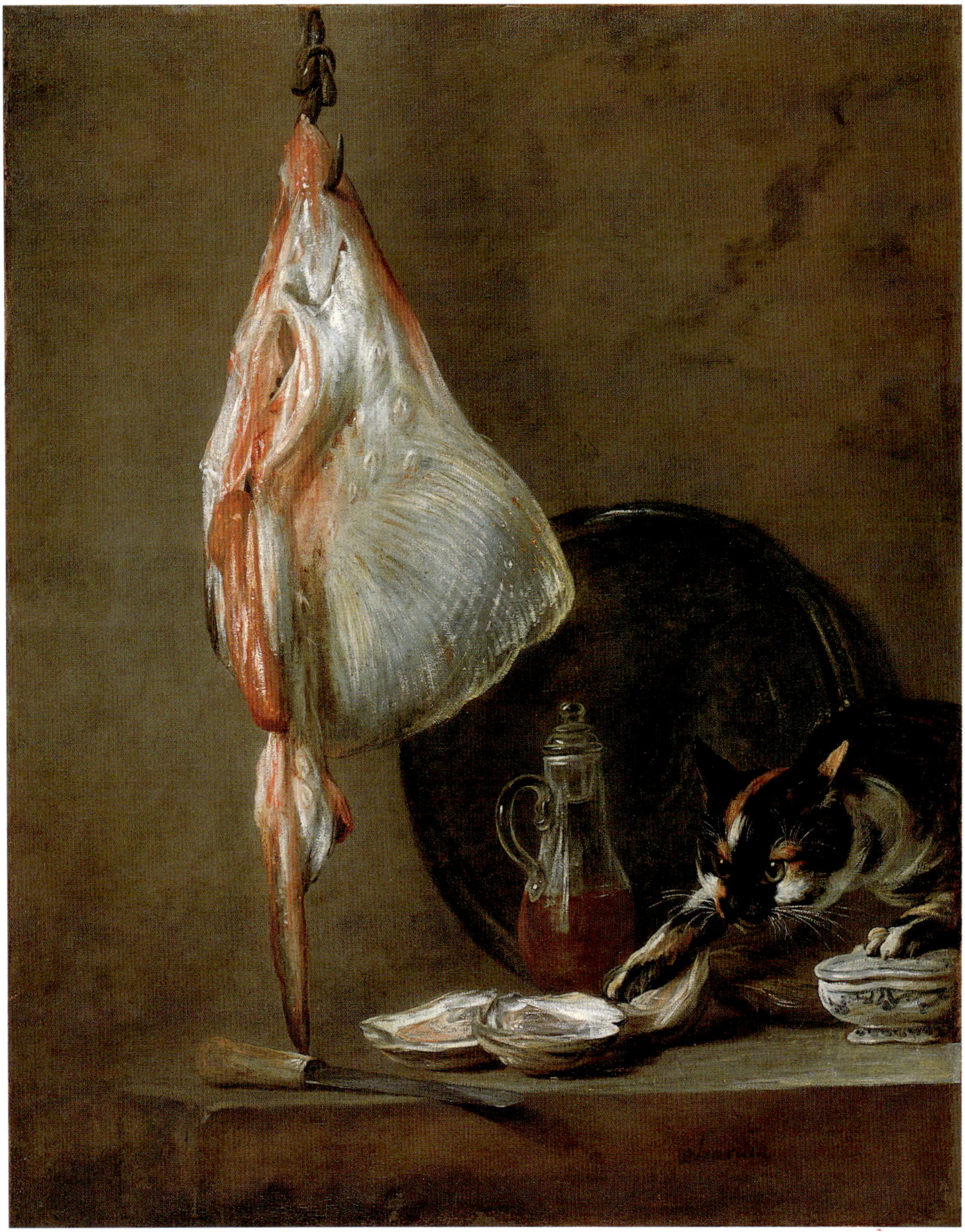

131 Chardin, *Cat with Ray, Oysters and Terrine*, 1728. Oil on canvas, 81 × 64 cm. The Glasgow Museums, Burrell Collection.

The Ray is in an indeterminate position between paintings that have overt dramatic or humanly important subject matter and those that do not. In general the relation between them might be thought of like this: for the dramatic subject to have its imaginative effect the painting would require the kind of structure that we have isolated across the board, even in the still life; on the other hand painting without such humanly compelling subjects would require the painter and viewer to search in themselves for the sense of urgency which – as a matter of cultural history – they could hardly do without having had experience of an overtly dramatic art. This was suggested in a localized way by Démoris with regard to the Louvre *Ray* in which he sought resonances of crucifixions and martyrdoms of history painting. We should surely regard our capacity to invest still life and landscape with such urgency and depth of feeling as dependent on earlier dramatic uses of painting. It was in these subjects that the intellectual and affective potentiality of the medium had been developed; once this had happened that medium could be deployed without such subjects, so that the objects of daily life, of meals or fruit and plants could become, as Cézanne said of landscape, 'essentially dramatic to the real painter'.

The possibility of making this transition depends on the underlying conditions which have been our concern throughout: that paintings are linked to us by sharing our space and materiality, and that we do not merely confront them but occupy them with our thought, adjusting our attention and following the connections they afford us. These two conditions, shared spatial materiality and the structure of adjustment and resolution, are themselves intertwined. For the painter initially proceeds with his work as something to be viewed, and viewed by those who would respond to the implications and relations within it.

* * *

In the first chapter a distinction was drawn between optical effects and the way the imagination was engaged in depiction; the demarcation was between two distinct purposes, between demonstrating some causal mechanism of perception and imaginative seeing; one implication of the difference is that the interest of the figure in the demonstration is completed when it has served as an example or as evidence for the experimenter's argument, whereas in the case of the work of art it is not. But nor is its interest completed or consummated in devising or applying a critical description. Critical description never properly or adequately corresponds to the interest and force of a painting, both because our interest is irreducibly bound to our perceiving, and because what we describe takes on its force for us only in the context of innumerable other recognitions in which it is embedded and which lie beyond the scope of describing. Because of these facts the question arises as to how we should think of criticism as more than a nomadic adjustment to particular works, or ranges of works. The answer that suggests itself in the context of the artists discussed here is twofold; we observe how particular works are mutually informative within the *oeuvre* of one artist or genre and more broadly how those artists or genres themselves are mutually informative, but secondly, we do so not by finding some general concepts under which diverse works can be seen to fall, but by finding how certain crucial concepts like that of depiction, or expression, or the relation of medium and subject take on their distinctive character and value in different circumstances. Regarded in this way the continuity of criticism might be thought of as developing the flexibility of its general concepts by aligning one group of works with another.

Notes

One Sustaining Recognition

1 See Wittgenstein, *Philosophical Investigations* (Blackwell: Oxford), 1954. 'It is easy to have a false picture of the process called "recognizing"; as if recognizing always consisted in comparing two impressions with one another. It is as if I carried a picture of an object with me and used it to perform an identification of an object as the one represented by the picture . . . And it is not so much as if I were comparing the object with the picture beside it, but as if the object *coincided* with the picture. I see only one thing not two.' [Paras 604–5].

The concept of recognition assumes that the viewer brings either an innate capacity or one developed from prior experience and it implies that there are objective grounds, without guarantees of correctness, for that capacity to be exercised. What is crucial about Wittgenstein's point, in our context, is that we recognize through difference and there is no demarcation within our experience that separates what is familiar from what is not, no picking off points on a picture I carry in my head, although we may reflect upon differences.

2 See E. H. Gombrich, *Art and Illusion*, 2nd ed. (Phaidon: London), 1961 for the most comprehensive study of the convergence of pictorial and nonpictorial perception; his further papers regarding this are republished in Gombrich, *The Image and the Eye* (Phaidon: Oxford), 1982. For discussion of this position see Richard Wollheim, 'Reflections on Art and Illusion' in *On Art and the Mind* (Allen Lane: London), 1973, pp. 261–89; Flint Schier, *Deeper into Pictures* (Cambridge University Press: Cambridge), 1986; Michael Podro, 'Fiction and Reality in Painting' repr. in *Explanation and Value in the Arts*, S. Kemal and I. Gaskell (Cambridge University Press: Cambridge), 1993, pp. 43–53; Patrick Maynard, 'Seeing Double', *Journal of Aesthetics and Art Criticism*, vol. 52, no. 2., spring 1994; and Malcolm Budd, *Values of Art Pictures, Poetry and Music* (Penguin: London), 1995, chap. 2.

3 Richard Wollheim, *Art and its Objects*, 2nd ed. (Cambridge University Press: Cambridge), 1980, p. 224; see also Wollheim, *Painting as an Art* (Thames and Hudson: London), 1987, p. 46f. It is the relation between these two apsects of an experience I am seeking to trace out. On Wollheim's position see Flint Schier, *op.cit.* and my review *Burlington Magazine*, vol. CXXIV, Feb. 1982, pp. 100–02, and Patrick Maynard, *op. cit.*

4 The discussion of painterly effects and of forms left implicit runs back to antiquity, see Pliny, *Natural History*, xxxiv–v. For recent studies see Jean-Claude Lebensztejn, *L'Art de Tache* (Edition de Limon: n.p.), 1990; Philip Sohm, *Pittoresco: Marco Boschini, his Critics and their Critiques of Painterly Brushwork in Seventeenth and Eighteenth Century Italy* (Cambridge University Press: Cambridge), 1991, both of which have

substantial bibliographies. See also 'The Beholders Share' in Gombrich, *Art and Illusion*, *ed. cit.*, also below chapter six. Painterly effects are only the most obvious exemplification of the general truth about depiction, caught by Merleau-Ponty when he wrote: 'The accomplished work is thus not the work which exists in itself like a thing, but the work which reaches its viewer and invites him to take up the gesture that created it and leaping over the intermediate steps to rejoin, without any guide other than a movement of the invented line, an almost incorporeal trace; the silent world of the painter, now proffered and accessible'. M. Merleau-Ponty, *Signs*, trans. Richard C. McCleary (Northwestern University Press), 1964, p. 51 (translation altered).

5 Optical demonstrations of illusion and reversal appear in virtually all text books of perceptual psychology between 1880 and 1960. For a selection see R. L. Gregory and E. H. Gombrich (eds), *Illusion in Nature and Art* (Duckworth: London), 1973. For a demonstration of a figure with many potential organizations see, for example, P. Johnson-Laird, *The Computer and the Mind*, 2nd ed. (Fontana Press: London), 1993, pp. 76ff.

6 Maurice Merleau-Ponty, 'Eye and Mind', *Primacy of Perception* (Northwestern University Press), 1964, p. 167.

7 See Merleau-Ponty, *ibid.*, p. 162ff and *Phenomenology of Perception*, trans. Colin Smith (Routledge: London), 1962, p. 160 and *passim*. I am indebted here to Jorella Andrews, 'Merleau-Ponty and the Question of Painting'. Ph.D., University of Essex, 1997.

8 Gombrich, *Norm and Form* (Phaidon: London), 1966, pp. 64–98.

9 For the problem of relating the sense of the harmonics of painting and spatial effects in seventeenth-century theory see Paul Taylor, 'The concept of "*Houding*" in Dutch Art', *Journal of the Warburg and Courtauld Institutes*, vol. LV, 1992, pp. 210–32; Ernst van der Wetering, 'Rembrandt's Manner: Technique in the Service of Illusion' in C. Brown, *et al.*, *Rembrandt: the Master and his Workshop. Paintings* (Yale University Press in association with National Gallery Publications: London), 1991 and Gridley McKim-Smith, Greta Andersen-Bergdoll and Richard Newman, *Examining Velazquez* (Yale University Press New Haven and London), 1988; see also note 4 above, particularly Sohm, *op.cit.*

10 See Benesch, *Drawings of Rembrandt*, 6 vols (Phaidon: London), 1954–7, nos 757–9.

11 On the relation of abstract or non-representational art to its antecedents see Peter Vergo, 'Music and Abstract Painting' in *Toward a New Art* (Tate Gallery: London), 1980. Kandinsky is particularly clear on this in 'Reminiscences' where he writes about seeing Monet's *Haystacks*: Kandinsky, *Complete Writings on Art*, ed. Kenneth C. Lindsay and Peter Vergo (G. K. Hall: Boston, Mass), 1982, p. 263.

12 Kandinsky, *Concerning the Spiritual in Art* (1912), in *Complete Writings on Art*, *ed. cit.*, vol. i, p. 197.

13 Mondrian's own account at least suggests such historical continuity: 'Although composition has always been fundamental to painting all modern painting has been distinguished by a *new way* of being concerned with it . . . While in the art of the past, composition becomes *real* only if we abstract the representation, in abstract-real painting composition is directly visible because it has truly *abstract* plastic means'. 'The New Plastic in Painting', 1917 in Piet Mondrian, *The New Art – The New Life*, ed. and trans. H. Holtzman and M. S. James (Thames and Hudson: London), 1987, p. 39. His notions of 'plastic equivalence', 'laws of harmony', 'equilibrium' and 'aesthetic relationships' that recur through his writing, whatever the wider visionary context, constantly imply a sense of a dynamic equilibriation of elements that are not themselves completely determined or fixed. This becomes a little clearer in his 'Neo-Plasticism: The General Principle of Plastic Equivalence (1920)', *ibid.*, p. 138. See Yve-Alain Bois, 'Iconoclasm', in Bois, Joop Joosten, Angelica Rudenstein and Hans Janssen, *Piet Mondrian* (Leonardo Arte in association with the National Gallery of Art and the Museum of Modern Art: New York) 1994, exh. cat.

14 Dawn Ades, 'Marcel Duchamp and the Paradox of Modernity', *Proceedings of the British Academy*, vol. 90, 1996, pp. 129–45; and Dalia Judovitz, *Unpacking*

Duchamp: Art in Transit (University of California Press: Berkely, Los Angeles and London), 1995.

15 The classic nominalist text is Nelson Goodman, *Languages of Art* (Oxford University Press: London), 1969; see also Goodman, *Ways of Worldmaking* (Harvester Press: Hassocks), 1978. The literature in response is large, but see particuarly Wọllheim, *On Art and the Mind*, *op. cit.*, pp. 290–314; Flint Schier, *op.cit.*, *passim*.

16 Kendall L. Walton, *Mimesis as Make Believe* (Harvard University Press: Cambridge, Mass. and London), 1990. This had been anticipated by a number of papers including 'Pictures and Make Believe', *Philosophical Review*, 82, 1973, pp. 283–319 and 'Categories of Art', *Philosophical Review*, 79, 1971, pp. 334–76. The book is a remarkably sustained realization of the semiotic position. For responses to the earlier papers see Schier, *op.cit.*, and Michael Podro, 'Depiction and the Golden Calf' in *Philosophy and the Visual Arts*, ed. Andrew Harrison (Reidel: Dordrecht), 1985, pp. 3–22 (repr. in *Visual Theory*, ed. Bryson, Holly and Moxey (Polity Press: Cambridge), 1991; on *Mimesis as Make Believe* see the review by Malcolm Budd, *Mind*, vol. 101, 1992, pp. 195–8, and a symposium devoted to the book with papers by Patrick Maynard, Noel Carrol, George Wilson, Richard Wollheim, Nicholas Wolterstorff, *Philosophy and Phenomenological Research*, vol. LI, no. 2, June 1991.

17 Recently John Hyman has remarked that, from Plato onwards, given the assumption that things cannot answer two incompatible descriptions, the imaginary view was identified with a false view. If we see a statue that stands above our eye level as rightly proportioned whereas, in reality, the head has beeen enlarged to make it appear so from the ground, we are subject to delusion. The statue cannot have normal human proportions and also deviate from those proportions. But what the argument really shows, as Hyman makes clear, is that if we were asked to assess the statue from some position *other* than that intended, it would be judged abnormally proportioned or if we subjected it to another kind of interest – like that of physical measurement – it would be found to be abnormally proportioned. What is at issue is the admissibility of different modes of interest in which we may engage with objects. We do not have two incompatible descriptions but two incommensurable ones. Similarly, if we changed our set toward a picture from seeing it as a picture (or picture of a certain kind), taking up some other standpoint toward it that disregarded the fact that it was a picture, it would cease to afford us the same kind of experience or interest. Plato would continue the argument by saying that some kinds of interest are inherently more concerned with truth or capable of more truth than others; the observer who measures the statue is more concerned with truth than the person who observes its proportions without measuring it. Observing the statue as a statue is indeed to be unconcerned with certain specific truths, those yielded by measurement of material, but it is not to prefer a delusion (mistaking the straight stick in water for one that is bent) to truth. To be concerned with the statue is to be concerned with how it looks or how its subject appears. Plato for wider reasons might disvalue such concern but that is a different issue. John Hyman, *The Imitation of Nature* (Blackwell: Oxford), 1989, particularly pp. 84–94.

18 Christopher Peacocke, in his paper 'Depiction', *Philosophical Review*, vol. XCVI, no. 3, July 1987, pp. 383–410 advances an analysis of depiction, broadly, in terms of familiar objects in regions of space having shapes in the visual field that we recognize in pictures. The notion of the visual field here is a term of art and I am unclear whether it is logically presupposed by the notion of a picture or antecedent to it. Either way there is a further issue of how far the subject matter, in its depiction, must retain roughly the shape it would occupy in the visual field. Would it be enough if some features did so, or if we could grasp the mode of their distortion as if the painting had inserted a kind of lense between us and what is depicted? A more liberal version of how we might account for depiction on the basis of resemblance is given as a hypothesis by Malcolm Budd in 'How Pictures Look' in D. Knowles and J. Skorupski, *Virtue and Taste* (Blackwell: Oxford), 1993. Budd writes: 'So when you see what is pictured in the surface you see a relation between it and the objects of the kind

depicted, in a similar sense to that in which you hear a relation between one theme and another when you hear one as a variation of the other . . . For a picture, the perception of the relation is, according to the account I have developed, an experienced isomorphism of relations in the visual field.' (p. 161) This would seem to imply something more than a noticed isomorphism; the musical and pictorial culture are ways of representing and elaborating one thing in another.

Two Donatello and the Planes of Relief

1 The initiating texts are those of Adolf von Hildebrand, *Das Problem der Form in der bildenden Kunst* (1893): 3rd ed. (Heitz: Strassburg), 1901, and Heinrich Wölfflin, *Kunstgeschichtliche Grundbegriffe* (Bruckmann: Munich), 1915, Eng. trans. by M. Hottinger, *Principles of Art History* (Bell and Son: London), 1932, on which see M. Podro, *Manifold in Perception. Theories of Art from Kant to Hildebrand* (Oxford Warburg Series: Oxford), 1972, chap. VI, and *Critical Historians of Art* (Yale University Press: New Haven and London), 1982 pp. 66ff., 71–6 and 118–28.

2 The main monographs on Donatello with *catalogue raisonné* are H. W. Janson, *The Sculpture of Donatello* (Princeton University Press: Princeton), 1963, and Artur Rosenauer, *Donatello* (Electa: Milan), 1993. Other extensive studies include John Pope-Hennessy, *Italian Renaissance Sculpture* (Phaidon: London), 1958; and his *Donatello Sculptor* (Abbeville Press: New York and London), 1993; B. A. Bennett and D. G. Wilkins, *Donatello* (Phaidon: Oxford), 1983.

3 The main writings referred to here are: Guido Hauck, 'Die Grenzen zwischen Malerei und Plastik und die Gesetze des Reliefs', *Preussiche Jahrbücher*, 56, 1885; Frida Schottmüller, *Donatello* (Bruckmann: Munich), 1904; Hans Kauffmann, *Donatello* (G. Grote: Berlin), 1935; John White, *The Birth and Rebirth of Pictorial Space* (Faber: London), 1957, pp. 148–60; and Artur Rosenauer, *Studien zum frühen Donatello* (Holzenhaus: Vienna), 1975, and his *Donatello* (1993).

4 On the technical history and the theory of perspective see J. Elkins, *The Poetics of Perspective* (Cornell University Press: Ithaca and London), 1984; on crucial misunderstandings in the literature of the last fifty years see Patrick Maynard, 'Perspective Places', *Journal of Aesthetics and Art Criticism*, vol. 54, no. 1, winter 1996, pp. 23–40; Martin Kemp, *The Science of Art* (Yale University Press: New Haven and London), 1990, examines the application of the construction in the quattrocento.

5 See note 1 above.

6 M.-F. Dandré-Bardon, 'Essai sur la Sculpture' in *Traité de la Peinture* (Saillant: Paris), 1765 (Repr. Minkoff: Geneva, 1972) 'Les tables d'architecture, qui sont à la fontaine des Saintes Innocens, par Jean Goujon, offrent des bas-reliefs du saillant le plus doux. L'intelligence qui a ménagé les tournans des objets, en laisse apercevoir tout la rondeur. Les figures n'y paroissent nullement appliquées sur un fond: elles ont sur leur milieu une sallie sufficante, qui leur prête la convexité du naturel, et qui les met en harmonie avec l'ensemble dont elles font portion. Cet ouvrage est un de ceux par le stile auquel les Sculpteurs moderns se rapprochent les plus des Sculpteurs anciens', p. 51.

7 Schottmüller, p. 15.

8 Kauffmann, p. 59.

9 *Ibid.*, p. 6.

10 *Ibid.*, p. 62. John White in his *Birth and Rebirth of Pictorial Space*, *op. cit.*, writes in similar terms: 'This new interest in space and movement is accompanied by a new decision in the expression of surface. The frontality of the succeeding architectural planes weaves a network that maintains the surface tension whilst these very forms create the impression of the airy halls beyond the foreground scene . . .', p. 150. White was the first writer in English to make a contribution to this discussion.

11 Rosenauer, 1974, p. 60f.

12 Rosenauer, 1993, p. 138–40.

13 In his extensive work of analysis on Donatello, Rosenauer comes eventually to see two distinct ways in which the reliefs are innovative: on the one hand by dissolving the separation of salient forms and their ground and absorbing the ground in the perspectivally conceived space and on the other by ordering the representation of figures in a plane set against a supporting surface (as he thinks occurs in the *Cantoria*); he sees these modes as separate and the first as dominant. *Ibid.*, pp. 24, 127 and *passim*.

14 See John Pope-Hennessy and Ronald Lightbown, *Catalogue of Italian Sculpture in the Victorian and Albert Museum* (HMSO: London), 1964, pp. 73 f; Pope-Hennessy, 1993, p. 140; and Rosenauer, 1993, no. 27.

15 The originally intended site of the relief is not known. It is first recorded in a Medici inventory of 1492. Pope-Hennessy in *Donatello's Relief of the Ascension* (HMSO London), 1949; repr. *Essays on Italian Sculpture* (Phaidon: London), 1968, suggests that it was originally part of a monument in the Brancacci Chapel in S. Maria del Carmine in Florence on the grounds both that there was a miracle play performed in the church which combined the Ascension and the Donation of the Keys and that it would have fitted with the St Peter fresco cycle. Another proposal, by Kauffmann (1935) was that the relief was originally made for the St Peter niche of Or San Michele. His argument was based on the fact that the St Peter statue was attributed to Donatello by Vasari, which Kauffmann wrongly accepted; however, the association of the niche with Donatello is suggestive: (a) the relief would have been the right size for the base of the niche; (b) it would have been of an appropriate subject; (c) it would have had the right optimal viewing height, a foot or so above one's head; (d) it would have been visible in the same façade as Nanni di Banco's relief of the sculptors' workshop and Donatello's own path-breaking St George relief, the virtuosity of which he here finessed. (A possibility, in the light of Vasari's association of the niche with Donatello, is that he passed on the commission to another sculptor (as he seems to have done in the case of the fourth Evangelist for the Duomo) because he was over-committed in the late 1420s and early '30s, but that he did so only after carving the relief. Did he kept it with him throughout his life before it passed to the Medici, perhaps at his death, because of his sense of its peculiar refinement? This is a tentatively offered hypothesis.)

16 On the perspective of the *Feast of Herod* see Kemp, *The Science of Art*, *op. cit.*, p. 16.

17 On the Old Sacristy of San Lorenzo since its recent cleaning see Pope-Hennessy, 1993, p. 157ff. and I. Balerini *et al.*, *Donatello e la Sagrestia Vecchia di San Lorenzo* (Centro Di: Florence), 1986. On perspectival refinements to 'compensate' for the viewer's position in Donatello's art generally, see Robert Munman, 'Optical Corrections in the Sculpture of Donatello', *Transactions of the American Philosphical Society*, vol. 75, pt. 2, 1985. The valuable observations here are about the adjustments of which we are *not* aware, made to avoid anomalous effects resulting from figures being above eye level rather than those that engage our imagination.

18 On the late pulpits see Volker Herzner, 'Die Kanzeln Donatellos in San Lorenzo', *Münchener Jahrbuch der bildenden Kunst*, 3rd ser., vol. XXIII, 1972, pp. 101–64, and Pope-Hennessy, 1993, pp. 292–312. There are difficulties in reading the Resurrection pulpit; it is remarked by Herzner that the order of scenes is unsatisfactory: the Maries at the Tomb should come after the Resurrection and before the Ascension. He has argued that for that reason the Maries at the Tomb should not be seen as part of the original scheme but part of a cobbled-together arrangement when the project for the tomb was abandoned. Also the sarcophagus types in the two scenes are different (as noted by Pope-Hennessy, 1993). Such objections are unnecessarily literal. If the Maries scene was added later, the effect remains.

Three Orientation in Rembrandt

1 See Thomas Puttfarken, 'Tizians *Pesaro Madonna*: Massstab und Bildwirkung' in Wolfgang Kemp (ed.), *Der Betrachter ist im Bild. Kunstwissenschaft und Rezeption-*

sästhetik (DuMont: Cologne), 1985, and *Masstabsfragen: über die Unterschiede zwischen grossen und kleinen Bildern* (University of Hamburg: Hamburg), 1971. For the compositional difference between small panels, cabinet pictures and drawings on the one hand and large-scale painting in architectural settings on the other see *ibid.* pp. 33 ff.

2 For the analysis of Rembrandt's etching procedure see Christopher White, *Rembrandt as Etcher* (Zwemmer: London), 1969.

3 For the relation between Lastman's and Rembrandt's paintings of Balaam see Astrid Tümpel, *The Pre-Rembrandtians* (E. B. Crocker Gallery: Sacramento, California), 1974.

4 On the *Anastasius* see J. Bruyn *et al.*, *A Corpus of Rembrandt Paintings* (Rembrandt Research Project: The Hague, Boston and London), 1982, vol. I, p. 547 f.

5 On the subject of this painting and the relation of Rembrandt to Lastman see Christian Tümpel, 'Studien zur Ikonographie der Historien Rembrandts', *Nederlands Kunsthistorisch Jaarboek*, XIX, 1969, p. 176 ff. and Astrid Tümpel, *The Pre-Rembrandtists, op. cit.* For recent discussion of the painting see the exhibition catalogue *Rembrandt: the Master and his Workshop. Paintings*, ed. C. Brown, Jan Kelch and Peter van Thiel (Yale University Press in association with National Gallery Publications: London), 1991. For an observation on the sense of being too close for convenient pictorial resolution see Svetlana Alpers, *Rembrandt's Enterprise; the Studio and the Market* (Thames and Hudson: London), 1988, p. 23.

6 The central discussion of the *Syndics* is that of Alois Riegl, *Das Holländische Gruppenporträt* (1902), 2 vols, ed. K. M. Swoboda (Oesterreichische Staatsdrükerei: Vienna), 1931, vol. I, p. 209 ff. For discussion of Riegl see Podro, *Critical Historians of Art*, pp. 81–96; Margaret Olin, *Forms of Representation in Alois Riegl's Theory of Art* (Pennsylvania State University Press: Pennsylvania), 1992, pp. 156–69; and Margaret Iversen, *Alois Riegl: Art History and Theory* (M.I.T. Press: Cambridge, Mass. and London), 1993, pp. 93–122.

7 H. van der Waal, 'The *Syndics* and their Legend' *Steps toward Rembrandt*, trans. P. Wardle and A. Griffiths (New Holland Publishing Co: Amsterdam and London), 1974.

8 For a historical study of the *Night Watch* see E. Haverkamp-Begemann, *Rembrandt; The Nightwatch* (Princeton University Press: Princeton), 1982.

Four Portrayal: Performance, Role and Subject

1 See D. Mahon, *Studies in Seicento Art and Theory* (Warburg Institute: London), 1947, pp. 149 f. and 234, and G. P. Bellori, *Vite* (1672), ed. E. Borea (Einaudi: Turin), 1976. On Domenichino, see particularly p. 347 (original pagination).

2 On Bernini see R. Wittkower, *Gian Lorenzo Bernini* (Phaidon: London), 1955, pp. 176, 183. Citing Domenico Bernini, *Vita del Cav. G. L. Bernini*, Rome 1713.

3 S. Hoogstraaten, *Inleyding tot de Hooge Schoole der Schilder-Konst: Anders de Zichtbaere Werelt* (F. Hoogstraaten: Rotterdam), 1678, pp. 109–10.

4 G. P. Lomazzo, *Trattato dell' Arte della Pittura, Scultura ed Architettura* (1585), 3 vols, (Saviere del-Monte: Rome) 1844; on the analogy with the poet see bk II, chaps I and 2, and on drapery see bk II, chap. 22. English translation: *A Tracte Containing the Arts of Curious Paintinge*, trans. Richard Haydock (1598), repr. (Da Capo Press: Amsterdam and New York), 1969.

5 Georg Simmel, *Rembrandt* (Kurt Wolff: Leipzig), 1916 (reprint with introduction by Beat Wyss (Matthis und Seitz: Munich), 1985, see particularly pp. 22–59.

6 See Anton Springer, 'Das Ende der Renaissance', *Bilder aus der neueren Kunstgeschichte*, 2nd ed., 2 vols (Adolf Marcus: Bonn), 1886, vol. I, p. 367. For the implication of identification and modes of homosocial feeling as well as heterosexual relations see Patricia Simons, 'Homosociality and Erotics in Italian Renaissance Portraiture' in Joanna Woodall (ed.), *Portraiture: Facing the Subject* (Manchester University Press: Manchester), 1997.

7 On Poussin's self-portraits, see particularly Oskar Bätschmann, *Nicolas Poussin. Dialectics of Painting* (Reaktion Books: London), 1990, pp. 45–52, and A. Blunt, *Nicolas Poussin*, 3 vols (Phaidon: London and New York), 1967, vol. I, pp. 263–6.

8 On Rubens's self-portraits, see Michael Jaffé, 'Rubens to Himself: The Portraits sent to Charles I and Piresc', *Rubens e Firenze*, ed. Mina Gregori (La Nuova Italia: Florence), 1983.

9 On Murillo's self-portrait, see *National Gallery Catalogues. The Spanish School*, London, 1970.

10 See H. E. Wethey, *Titian, The Portraits*, 3 vols (Phaidon: London), 1971, vol. II, p. 49.

11 On Velazquez' *Las Meninas*, see Jonathan Brown, *Images and Ideas in Seventeenth Century Spanish Painting* (Princeton University Press: Princeton), 1978, pp. 87–110, which contains much relevant information, and Foucault's *jeu d'esprit* at the beginning of *Les Mots et les Choses* (Gallimard: Paris), 1966, where he gave an account of the painting as an analogy of objective Cartesian epistemology. For Palomino's text see Enriquetta Harris, *Velazquez* (Phaidon: Oxford), 1982.

12 On the tradition of the portrayal of artists, see, with particular reference to van Dyke's *Iconographia*, Hans-Joachim Raupp, *Untersuchungen zu Künstlerbildnis und Künstlerdarstellung in den Nederlanden in 17 Jahrhundert* (Georg Olms: Hildesheim, Zurich and New York), 1984. For the *Iconographia* see Marie Mauquoy-Hendrix, *L'Iconographie d'Anoine van Dyke*, 2nd ed., 2 vols (Bibliothèque Royale Albert I: Brussels), 1991. On the implications of status involved in being portrayed in seventeenth-century Holland see Joanna Woodall, 'Sovereign bodies: the reality of status in seventeenth-century Dutch portraiture' in *Portraiture: Facing the Subject*', *op. cit.*

13 On Rembrandt and Huygens and his gift of a painting see H. Gerson, *Seven Letters by Rembrandt* (Boucher: The Hague), 1961, letters of 1638–9. On Huygens's involvement with van Dyck's *Iconographia*, see Horst Vey, *Die Zeichnungen Anton van Dycks*, 2 vols (Arcade: Brussels), 1962, vol. I, p. 46; on Rembrandt's adoption of the pose of Titian's *Ariosto* see E. de Jong, 'The Spur of Wit: Rembrandt's Response to the Italian Challenge', *Delta*, vol. 12, no. 2, 1969, pp. 49–67.

14 Svetlana Alpers, *Rembrandt's Enterprise; the Studio and the Market* (Chicago University Press: Chicago and London), 1988.

15 John Nash, *Rembrandt* ('The Masters' series), London, 1966, p. 6.

16 Where he does in a very late self-portrait take on a role it has been thought to be Zeuxis who laughs himself to death at the vanity of the old woman who presents herself to be painted as Venus. He addresses her as representative of the world's vanity. Albert Blankert, 'Rembrandt, Zeuxis and Ideal Beauty' in J. Bruyn *et al.* (eds), *Album Amicorum, Jan Gert van Gelder*, The Hague 1973.

Five Hogarth's Analysis *and its Application*

1 Hogarth, *The Analysis of Beauty*, printed by James Reeves for the author: London, 1753 (Repr. Scolar Press: London, 1971). The standard edition is that edited by Joseph Burke (Oxford University Press: Oxford), 1955, which has running numbers marking the page numbers of the first edition. References to Hogarth's text are to the first edition. The major current source of material on Hogarth is Ronald Paulson, *Hogarth's Graphic Works*, 3rd rev. ed. (The Print Room: London), 1989, and *Hogarth, his Life and Times*, 2 vols (Yale University Press: New Haven and London), 1971, and a second, greatly revised edition, *Hogarth*, 3 vols (Rutgers University Press: New Brunswick and London), 1991–3. As an introduction Peter Quennell's *Hogarth's Progress* (Collins: London), 1955 remains unsurpassed, and David Bindman, *William Hogarth* (Thames and Hudson: London), 1980, complements it with a succinct and informative illustrated commentary. The most recent biography with very extensive and vivid social description and documentation is Jenny Uglow, *Hogarth: A Life and a World* (Faber: London), 1997.

2 See Burke, pp. xx–xxii.
3 See Burke, p. xli.
4 Burke, pp. 184f.
5 See David Summers, '*Maniera* and Movement: The Figura Serpentiniana', *Art Quarterly*, 35, 1972, pp. 269–301.
6 F. Hutcheson, *An Inquiry into the Original of our Ideas of Beauty and Virtue*, 4th ed. (D. Midwinter *et al.*: London), 1738 (Repr. Gregg: Farnborough, 1969), p. 44.
7 Burke, p. 171.
8 Roger de Piles, *Cours de Peinture par Principes* (1708) (Editions Haqueline Chambon: Nimes), 1990; within which see the articles on *Coloris*, *Tout ensemble* and *de la Disposition*. For an analysis of these topics see Thomas Puttfarken, *Roger de Piles' Theory of Art* (Yale University Press: New Haven and London), 1985.
9 Jonathan Swift, *A Tale of a Tub and other satires*, ed. K. Williams (Everyman's Library: London), 1975, p. 189.
10 Samuel Butler, *Hudibras*, bk I, iii, lines 1224f.
11 For the relation of the imagery to earlier uses in Hogarth see Charles Mitchell (ed.), *Hogarth's Peregrination* (Oxford University Press: Oxford), 1952, and the entry in Paulson, *Hogarth's Graphic Works*, *op.cit.*, pp. 177f.
12 Speculation on the significance of this symbolism in Hogarth is proposed by Ronald Paulson in *The Beautiful, Novel, and Strange. Aesthetics and Heterodoxy* (Johns Hopkins University Press: Baltimore and London), 1996, pp. xi, 21f.
13 Shaftesbury, *Second Characters or the Language of Forms*, ed. B. Rand (Cambridge University Press: Cambridge), 1914, p. 98.
14 Shaftesbury, *Characteristics*, ed. J. M. Robertson (Grant Richards: London), 1900, treatise III, vol. I, p. 135; repr. with Introduction by S. Grean (Bobbs-Merrill: Indianapolis and New York), 1964. For the tradition of fusing beauty and morality in the eighteenth century, see Robert E. Norton, *The Beautiful Soul. Aesthetic Morality in the Eighteenth Century* (Cornell University Press: Ithaca and London), 1995.
15 Hogarth is defending his art not only against the specific claims of the literary moralist, but against the high level philosophical theories that lose the specific interest of painting in some general sense of morality or universal order. The most comprehensive and accessible theory that connected the beauty of objects in nature, art and morality, and subsumed them all within a sense of divine purpose was that of Bishop Berkeley, in the *Third Dialogue* of his *Alciphron* published in 1732 (together with his *New Theory of Vision).* He traces the beauty of nature and of art to their fitness for function or the appearance of such fitness:

> the beauty . . . or symmetry of a chair cannot be apprehended but by knowing its use, and comparing its figure with that use; which cannot be done by the eye alone but is the effect of judgement . . . Tell me, . . . is there not something truly decent and beautiful in dress? . . . Are any likelier to give us an idea of this beauty in dress than painters and sculptors, whose proper business and study it is to aim at graceful representations? . . . May it not therefore be supposed, on all accounts, most likely, to help us to some rational notion of the *je ne sais quoi* in beauty? And in effect, have we not learned from this digression that, as there is no beauty without proportions, so proportions are to be esteemed just and true only as they are relative to some certain use and end, their aptitude and subordination to that end is, at bottom, that which makes them please and charm.

Berkeley was concerned with the fact that our sense of beauty involved reflection or judgement and not merely an appetite (which, misleadingly, he implies that Shaftesbury denied) and this is transferred to morality:

> let me entreat Alciphron to explain to me wherein consists the beauty of a moral system, with a supreme Intelligence at the head of it, which neither protects the innocent, punishes the wicked, nor rewards the virtuous. To suppose indeed a society of rational agents, acting under the eye of Providence, concurring in one

design to promote the common benefit of the whole, and conforming their actions to the established laws and order of the divine parental wisdom (*Alciphron*, dialogue III, paragraphs 8–10, *The Works of George Berkeley*, ed. A. A. Luce and T. E. Jessop (Thomas Nelson: London), 1948–57, vol. III).

Such views were everyday currency among the deists and the orthodox, for instance George Turnbull in his *Treatise on Ancient Painting* of 1740 – a book consigned for waste paper in *Beer Street* – writes that there could be no effects of beauty without a sense of moral worth, as if they stood as original and copy. 'Our notions of harmony, regularity, and unity in bodies must be transferable to moral objects . . . the same language applies in both fields . . .', *Treatise on Ancient Painting* (1740) (Repr. V. M. Bevilacqua (ed.) (Fink Verlag: Munich), 1971), pp. 138 f.

16 Hutcheson, *Inquiry*, p. xv.
17 *Ibid.*, p. 209.
18 Burke, p. 190.
19 Burke, pp. 170 f.
20 Thomas Morell, *Notes and Annotations on Locke on Human Understanding* (G. Sael: London), 1794, p. 5.
21 Morell, p. 30.
22 *Ibid.*, p. 8.
23 Bernard de Mandeville, *The Fable of the Bees* (1724), ed. Philip Harth (Penguin Books: London), 1970; on Mandeville and Hogarth see Jules Lubbock, *The Tyranny of Taste* (Yale University Press: New Haven and London), 1995, pp. 193–204.
24 See Sean Shesgreen, 'Hogarth's *Industry and Idleness*: a Reading', *Eighteenth Century Studies*, 1975, 6, pp. 569–98.
25 F. Hutcheson, *Thoughts on Laughter and Observations on the Fable of the Bees* (D. Baxter: Glasgow), 1750, p. 18 f.
26 Such readings as Burke p. 170; Paulson (1971), vol. II, p. 167; W. Busch, *Das Sentimentalische Bild; Die Krise im 18 Jahrhundert und die Geburt der Moderne* (Beck: Munich), 1993, pp. 247–9.

Six Apropos Chardin

1 Richard Wollheim, 'Correspondence, Projective Properties, and Expression in the Arts', *The Mind and Its Depths* (Harvard University Press: Cambridge, Mass. and London) 1993.
2 D. W. Winnicott, *Playing and Reality* (Routledge: London), 1971; 'The theory of Parent-Infant Relationship' (1960) and 'The Capacity for Concern' (1963) in *The Maturational Process and the Facilitating Environment*, 1965 (repr. Karnac: London), 1991. On infant-mother interchange see Daniel Stern, *The Interpersonal World of the Infant* (Basic Books: New York), 1985; Colwyn Trevarthen, 'Playing into Reality. Conversations with the Infant Communicator', *Winnicott Studies*, no. 7, spring 1993, pp. 67–84. See also Kenneth Wright, *Vision and Separation: Between Mother and Baby* (Free Association Books: London), 1991, chap. 1 and *passim*.
3 For Diderot's philosophical aesthetics see particularly his essay from the *Encyclopédie*: 'Sur L'Origine et la Nature du Beau', *Oeuvres Esthétique de Diderot*, ed. Paul Vernière (Garnier: Paris), 1965. For an account of the development of Diderot's thought, see Jacques Chouillet, *La Formation des Idées Esthétiques de Diderot* (Armand Colin: Paris), 1973. For an English translation of his art criticism see *Diderot on Art*, trans. John Goodman, 2 vols (Yale University Press: New Haven and London), 1995. The standard works on Chardin are: Pierre Rosenberg, *Tout l'œuvre peint du Chardin* (Flammarion: Paris), 1983; *Chardin 1699–1799*, exh. cat., ed. Pierre Rosenberg (Editions de la Réunion des musées nationaux: Paris), 1979; and Philip Conisbee, *Chardin* (Phaidon: Oxford), 1986.

4 On discussion of perceptual refinement in the ambience of Chardin, see Michael Baxandall, *Patterns of Intention* (Yale University Press: New Haven and London), 1985, chap. III, and the same author's *Shadows and Enlightenment* (Yale University Press: New Haven and London), 1995.

5 M.-F. Dandré-Bardon, *Traité de Peinture* (Saillant: Paris), 1765, pp. 203–5.

6 Caylus, *Tableau tiré d'Iliad et de l'Odyssée d'Homere et de l' Eneide de Virgile* (Tilliard: Paris), 1757. For an account of Caylus see S. Rocheblave, *Essai sur le Comte de Caylus* (Hachette: Paris), 1889.

7 'De la Légèrté d'Outil' in Comte de Caylus, *Vie des Peintres de XVIII Siècle*, ed. A. Fontaine (Librairie Renouard: Paris), 1910, pp. 152f.

8 *Ibid.*, p. 155.

9 'Sur l'Harmonie et sur la Couleur', *ibid.*, p. 140.

10 R. de Piles, *Cours de Peinture par Principes* (1708) (J. Chambon: Nimes), 1990, pp. 123f.

11 For example, Chardin's friend, the engraver Cochin wrote of Veronese's *Rape of Europa*: 'The brush is admirable, fluent and rich, unforced, with an appearance of negligence which forms perfectly all the details, whether of flesh or fabrics . . .', C.-N. Cochin, *Voyage d'Italie*, 3 vols (Heubach: Lausanne), 1773, vol. III, p. 5.

12 Caylus, *op.cit.*, pp. 178f.

13 A. Coypel, *Discours Prononcez dans la Conférance de l'Academie Royale de Peinture et Sculpture* (Collombat: Paris), 1721, pp. 6f.

14 See Charles-Nicholas Cochin, *Mémoires inédit de CNC sur le Comte de Caylus*, ed. C. Henry (Baur: Paris), 1880: 'Gens de condition . . . il est rare que leur protection ne dégénère en queslque peu de tirannie'. (p. 25). See also Conisbee, *Chardin*, pp. 218–19 on Chardin's relation to the director of the Académie Pierre defending Cochin.

15 Caylus, *Vie de Peintres de XVIII Siècle, ed. cit.*, p. 180.

16 M. Proust, *Essais et Articles*, ed. T. Laget (Gallimard: Paris), 1991, p. 68f. English translation appears in: Proust, *By Way of Saint Beuve*, trans. Sylvia Townsend Warner (Chatto and Windus: London), 1958. This passage of Proust's essay is discussed in Richard Wollheim, *Painting as Art* (Thames and Hudson, London), 1987, pp. 98f.

17 Démoris's papers on Chardin include: 'La Nature Morte chez Chardin,' *Revue d'Ésthétique*, vol. XXII, 1969, pp. 363–85; 'Original absent et création de valeur: Du Bos et quelques autres,' *Revue des sciences humaines*, vol. 40, no. 157, 1975, 1, pp. 65–81; and 'Chardin et la Cuisine en peinture,' *Dixhuitième Siècle*, XV, 1983, and his book *Chardin, la Chair et l'Objet* (Adam Biro: Paris), 1991.

18 Hannah Segal, 'Notes on Symbol Formation' (1957) in *The Work of Hannah Segal* (Free Association Books: London), 1986 (1981), pp. 57f.

19 'A Psychoanalytic Approach to Aesthetics' (1947) in Segal, *op. cit.* (1981), pp. 189f. The sentence quoted comes from *A la Recherche du Temps Perdu*, 4 vols, ed. Jean-Yves Tadié *et al.* (Gallimard: Paris), 1989, vol. IV, p. 620 (*Remembrance of Things Past*, 3 vols, trans. C.K. Scott Moncrieff, T. Kilmartin and A. Mayor (Penguin Books: London), vol. III, p. 1102.

20 See George D. Painter, *Marcel Proust. A Biography*, rev. ed. (Penguin: London), 1996.

21 'The Ordering of Chaos' (1957) in Milner, *The Supressed Madness of Sane Men* (Tavistock Publications: London), 1987, pp. 216–33. This was published as an appendix to the second edition (1957) of *On Not Being Able to Paint.* See also Milner's 'Role of Illusion in Symbol Formation' in the same volume for the transition from symbols representing the past to symbolization used to establish relations in the present.

22 For the expansive sense of the unconscious see C. Bolas, *Cracking Up* (Routledge: London), 1955, chaps 1–3.

23 *Poetics*, XIV, 1453b–1454a.

24 I am here responding to E. H. Gombrich, 'Psycho-analysis and the History of Art' (1953) repr. in his *Meditations on a Hobby-Horse and other Essays on the Theory of Art* (Phaidon: London), 1963.

25 Réné Démoris, *Chardin, la Chair et l'Objet*, *op. cit.* (1991), p. 37 and *passim.*

Index

Photograph Credits

Alinari: 1, 18, 19, 20, 21, 22, 31, 32, 33, 34, 40, 41, 42, 44, 45, 47; Scala: 2, 23, 24, 35, 36, 37; RMN: 4, 74, 77, 114, 118, 121, 123, 126, 127; Antonio Quattrone, Florence: 13, 48; © V-G Bildkunst, Bonn and DACS, London 1998: 15; © 1998 ABC/Mondrian Estate/Holtzman Trust. Licensed by ILP: 16; Bridgeman Art Library: 38; © Photothèque des Musées de la Ville de Paris: 58; National Gallery, London: 60, 129, 130; BPK: 66; © 1997 Board of Trustees, National Gallery of Art, Washington: 72, 125 English Heritage: 87; © 1997 The Museum of Modern Art, New York & © Succession Picasso/DACS 1998: 128

DATE DUE
